IT PROFITS A MAN . . .

He knew all about gaining the world. He learned it fast. You hold out your hand, and someone puts money in it. You smile, and a beautiful woman smiles back. You hop a plane to Paris or Rome or Hongkong —wherever the jet set goes—and head-waiters bow to you, friends embrace you, all the world's excitement lies ahead of you. But to save his soul—that he had to learn the world's hardest way. . . .

PLAYBOY
TO
PRIEST

Rev. Kenneth Roberts

OUR SUNDAY VISITOR, INC., Publisher

HUNTINGTON

DEDICATION

This book is dedicated to a lady whose eyes glowed with an inner peace and watched over me all my years prior to the priesthood, turning those same eyes to her Creator in constant petition for my welfare, a lady I called MOTHER.

To the many whose eyes I have loved because they were the eyes of someone I called FRIEND.

To a lady whose beauty has never been painted with justice and whose eyes have watched over me always; a lady whom Christ called MOTHER.

Published by Our Sunday Visitor, Inc.
200 Noll Plaza, Huntington, Indiana 46750

Copyright © 1973 by Rev. Kenneth J. Roberts
ALL RIGHTS RESERVED
ISBN 0-87973-782-4
Library of Congress Catalog Card No. 73-169145

PRINTED IN U.S.A.   782

CONTENTS

PREFACE

This book is a real thriller. It is the colorful story of a long and adventurous road to the priesthood. At the age of nineteen, Kenneth Roberts applied for acceptance, but received a rebuff. The examining priest judged that there was insufficient evidence of maturity and stability to stand up to the long and arduous training required; but the next ten years showed that this judgment had been too hasty. What an odyssey those ten years were! Travelling to New York, South Africa, Singapore, Hong Kong, Germany, Portugal . . . steward in the B.O.A.C., interpreter on the ocean liner *Queen Elizabeth,* soldier in the British Army Intelligence Corps, engaged to be married, entangled with gold smugglers . . . he mixed with men and women, some good, and some not so good, shared their pleasures and disappointments, helped them and was helped by them, and at the end of ten years still felt that his ideals and quest for happiness could be fully achieved only in the priesthood. When he was finally accepted at Osterley, I revised my previous judgment and began to admire his zest for life, his powers of leadership, and his perseverance. He was bringing to the priesthood not only enthusiasm, but a certain maturity, and a rich experience of human nature, its fine possibilities, and its spiritual hunger. His persistence in clinging to an ideal, through many vicissitudes, should be an inspiring example to many young men, who may be only dimly aware that there is something more satisfying in life than just making money and having a good time. The ultimate measure of human happiness is the love of God, and, for those with the requisite qualities, it finds its noblest expression in the priesthood.

CLEMENT TIGAR, S.J.

INTRODUCTION

"*Whose Sins You Shall Forgive...*"

Several of my close friends, lay and religious, have made the suggestion from time to time that I write a book about my life preceding the priesthood. They would usually end their statement with something like, "... but who would believe it?" I never took it too seriously.

It wasn't until I began reading story after story about ex-priests and nuns, disgruntled Catholics, conservative and liberal, that I started to toy with the idea a bit. It seems one can't pick up a periodical without finding an article written by or about an ex-cleric who finally "found himself" outside the "grip" of the church. Most of these accounts I found most distressing. I was getting sick to death of reading about the "in" life and "new freedom" found by these former religious. They all seemed to me that they wanted Christ to join their church rather than they join His.

I must admit there are many men and women who have left the religious life in what they have felt was "good conscience," and are leading very rewarding lives in other fields. I will not be their judge. Unfortunately, the press exposes the public to the negative side. It's a better seller to picture a hippie-like group sitting around the floor discussing their new rewarding life, while in the background, you can almost hear the strains of some current protest song; caption reading: "From left

1

to right, the former Father . . ., Brother . . ., Sister
. . . ." I felt it might be a welcome change to hear from
someone who "in good conscience gave it up when he
had it 'all.'"

It was the youth with whom I meet every day, that
helped to sway me more. I hear things like, "Ya Father,
religion is fine for you; that's your bag, but not mine."
Well it wasn't always my "bag." This kind of talk and
reaction persuaded me to share my past experiences
with others to show how someone who has really
"lived" finally found out about living. I wasn't always a
priest, in fact, I was many things before entering the
seminary. Mine is what is sometimes referred to as a
"late vocation."

In the following pages, I'm inviting you to go back
with me to England and share the experiences of a
lonely child living in uncertainty and fear of the bombs,
not knowing for three years if his family was alive or
dead. Amid the misery, I shall show you the humor as
we laugh and cry together in war-torn England. We will
experience the conflict of a teen-ager seeking to find
himself in the confusion of post-war Europe: France,
Switzerland, Italy, Spain, Portugal; always searching—
you will get a glimpse of what it's like to be trained as a
soldier in the British Army Intelligence Corps. Finally
we will fly together on one of Europe's leading airlines
to all the great cities of the world where I served as a
steward for five years. We will live the fast life and look
for kicks in all the great cities of the world from London to the Far and Middle East and all the points in between. I'll share with you my wildest years from the
beauty of Rome to the intrigue of Hong Kong. You
shall even see what it's like to be involved in an international smuggling ring. We will live a more "sober" life
as we sail the high seas aboard the elegance of an ocean

2

liner, *The Queen Elizabeth,* where I served as a ship's interpreter.

Throughout all of this, you will meet all kinds of people, people that touched my life: the rich and the poor, the honest and the dishonest, the holy and the unholy, the famous and the infamous; all the people, places and things that led me away from my affairs to the ultimate love affair, with Christ.

My reason for sharing all this with you is quite simple. Today, when the "pursuit of happiness" includes such things as free love, pot, speed, alcohol, riots and demonstrations, I hope to show you where the action really is and how I found it.

When we read signs saying, "Is God Dead?" I want to testify that He is not. He is alive! He's here! He's with it! He loves. He waits. He forgives. Perhaps He is waiting for you? How long He waited for me! And how glad I am He once said, "WHOSE SINS YOU SHALL FORGIVE . . . ."

CHAPTER ONE

"Suffer little children"
Mk 10:14

"Ego te absolvo peccatis tuis in Nomine Patris et
Filii et Spiritus Sancti. Amen." The sound was
coming from my mouth. My lips were forming
the words. My hand was tracing the sign of the
cross. I had just heard my first confession! Christ
had used me to forgive sins!
I closed the sliding door over the grill to my
left. A whispered voice came from the darkness
on the other side of the grill.
"Bless me, Father, for I have sinned." It was a
child. The litany of little sins filled my ears,
what innocence. If only this was all the evil in
the world, the sins of a child. It was a
litany of imperfections that seemed somehow
to be a hymn of praise and love. My memory
went back to my own childhood and my own
first confession.

JUNE, 1939

"Now children, pay attention. No Kenneth, not your
left hand, your right . . .," screamed my teacher as she
pulled my left hand down and pointed the fingers of my
right hand to my forehead. "Bless me, Father, for I
have sinned. This is my first confession. In the Name of
the Father, and of the Son, and of the Holy . . ., No

4

Kenneth, your left shoulder!" She redirected my right palm toward my left shoulder as we completed the sign of the cross.

My class had been preparing for several months now. We recited imaginary sins, repeated acts of contrition and traced the sign of the cross almost daily to our second-grade teacher who substituted for the priest in mock confessions.

The day we waited for so long was finally here. We marched in single file out of the classroom, across the yard, and into the church, our hands joined as if in prayer. We moved into the pews, each one genuflecting in turn before the tabernacle. The teacher placed her forefinger over her lips as a warning to us to be silent.

"Kneel and let us examine our conscience."

Eight years of sins to think about. Boy, how will I ever be able to remember so much life? I guess I have to think real hard. Was I disobedient? Did I lie? Was I selfish? Did I fight? I do all those things almost every day.

Just about every afternoon I climbed over our garden fence and down the embankment to the railway track that carried those fast trains to London. It was great fun to put a penny on the rail and watch the wheels speed over it, leaving the coin wide and flat. The only bad thing about it, was that my three-year-old brother, Jackie, had a bad habit of finding my flat pennies and putting them in his mouth. This made Mother angry as she yanked them away scolding, "Kenny, you've been down to that track again: haven't I told you time and again how dangerous it is? And Jackie is going to choke on one of these pennies some day!" Not only would I get into trouble because of that, but my older brother, Roy, would always accuse me of stealing his pennies to use on the track; and that wasn't always true 'cause sometimes they were mine. This always finished up in a fight over ownership and the pennies usually ended up in Roy's pocket 'cause he was bigger. Why should I give up something so precious when I had to work so hard to get them? Let me see, was the sin in the fighting or the not sharing? I know I lied and was disobedient 'cause Mum would ask, "Kenny, have you been down to the track today?" I always answered, "No, Mum." Gosh, I guess it was all a sin. I didn't mind Mum, I fought with my brother, I was selfish 'cause I didn't want to share. . . . I hope I won't be in there too long. Everyone will know I got a lot to confess.

The line of waiting children grew smaller and now I was standing in the aisle. My hands were cold and wet. Soon it would be my turn to go in the confessional. Have I forgotten anything? I suppose I should tell the priest that I don't always finish my night prayers, especially if it's the rosary, cause I fall asleep, and sometimes I don't pay attention to the Mass, no, most times.

The door opened and another child walked out. It's my turn! I'm going to tell my sins to Jesus and He is going to wash me clean, and I'm going to promise not to ever sin again. Already I felt homesick for the track. As the door closed behind me I knelt in front of the crucifix and waited for the little door to open. It's sure dark in here, I thought. SWISH . . . . It slid open! "Bless me, Father, for I have sinned, this is my first confession. . . ."

At supper that night, we all talked about the big day, my First Communion. "Are you excited about tomorrow, Kenny? You should be, it's a great day when you receive Jesus for the first time. Best you get to bed early tonight," Mum said as she nodded to me to start eating.

"I am excited, Mum. And I'm glad I went to confession today. It's really not too bad, you know?"

"Nothing is ever too hard when you do it for the love of God, Kenny."

"Yes, Mum, I guess so."

Later that evening as I was getting ready for bed, I walked toward the window where I could see the railroad track from my room. As I sat there gazing, a train sped along. I wish I was on one of those trains, I thought, but if I were, where would I be going? No matter where it was, it could never be as good as home. I loved our house, and all the people in it.

We lived in an old English house with cellars, attics, halls and creepy staircases, one in the front hall and one in the rear of the house; the latter would have served as a part of the servants' quarters when the house had known better days. There were fourteen rooms in all with two baths and a large entrance hall; the stables in the back were converted into a washroom. There was a large garden which contained several flower beds, an orchard and a greenhouse. You could see our parish church from the yard; it was only one block away: an old church, cruciform in shape with a white wooden cross over the porch which jutted out from the green painted, corrugated iron building. A signboard near the road read, "St. Patrick's Roman Catholic Church." On it was printed the schedule of the masses and confessions.

Besides the two lady boarders Mum and Dad took in to help in the upkeep of such a big house, there were Kathleen and Grandad. Kathleen was an Irish girl who assisted Mum as a nursemaid for us kids. There was a lot of excitement in our house, but then there was so much peace too, thanks to Mother.

Mother was a fantastic person. She had six children of her own; they were all grown up and married now. The only one left at home was Roy, he was just five years my senior and still attended grade school with

7

me: we were very close. I was orphaned at the age of six months when Mum and Dad adopted me: I was the first and eldest of six foster children, five boys and one girl. I remember very little about the other foster children since their stay with us was temporary with the exception of Jackie. Mother was a very devout Catholic and it was from her that I learned a deep appreciation of my religious faith. My foster father, John Robert Seagrave, was a retired army man, the son of a Protestant minister, but Dad rarely went to church. When he did, he attended ours, confining his visits to the feasts of Christmas, Easter, and Corpus Christi. And then there was Grandad, a real character. He resembled a typical old sea-farer with his white beard and captain's hat. His rosy cheeks always bulged with a wad of chewing tobacco which he carelessly spat out in our fireplace to Mother's disapproval. We loved him, in spite of his, sometimes, distasteful habits. He liked to surprise us kids with candy sticks which we held tight in our teeth, mimicking him with his pipe. One of his favorite pastimes was to entertain us kids with his old exaggerated stories of the sea, and we loved them.

I began to grow sleepy. As I climbed in bed, I remembered the track, and how in confession that very afternoon I promised not to go down there again. Boy, I would miss it but Mum said, "Nothing is too hard if you do it for the love of God."

The next morning, June 29th, was the feast of Sts. Peter and Paul. This is to be a great day! Mother, Father, Grandad, Kathleen, my brothers, in fact, the whole school watched me as I walked down the aisle. I was wearing a white suit and black tie. The teacher had tied a white bow on my arm which I prayed to God wouldn't come undone. I couldn't bear the humiliation

8

of having to stoop down and pick it up. All the girls wore white dresses and veils. We walked very, very slowly as the organ played softly.

I felt happy, but still a little nervous. Why shouldn't I? Hadn't the teacher told us this would be the happiest day of our lives; but if that was so, why is everybody crying? She told us too that we must keep our eyes forward, but the temptation was too great for me: I peeped at Mum and Dad. They seemed to be crying too, or at least there were tears in their eyes. Funny how grown-ups smile and wipe their tears at the same time, I thought. I looked at my brothers. They weren't crying. Wonder if they have any of my flat pennies in their pockets?

Finally I knelt in front of the altar. My teacher said that what was about to happen would be the greatest experience we ever had, and whatever we asked Jesus for, would be granted if we really believed. I wonder what I should ask Him? Suddenly the priest was in front of me and was holding that little white host over me. He made the Sign of the Cross with It and said, "Corpus Domini Nostri Jesu Christi." I opened my mouth as he placed the Host on my tongue. Jesus was inside me!

I don't remember all the things I asked or said to Him; but I do remember one: "Dear Jesus, when I grow up, I want to be a priest too. I want to give children their Holy Communion and forgive their sins; that is, if You let me. I guess You will let me know."

The summer months flew quickly. I spent a great deal of time helping Mum in the garden. This was her favorite pastime and her only recreation. She dearly loved her flowers. Every Saturday, she took a bouquet to our parish church to adorn the altar. Sometimes I would accompany her since I had to go to confession;

those railroad tracks again. I often thought I would have less to confess if Mum just wouldn't ask me if I had been down there, because when she did, I not only had to confess disobedience but I had to tell about the lying too. I didn't always go down to the track though, sometimes, I climbed trees in the garden or had fun on the swing but for real excitement, I would get Roy to push me down the coal chute that led from the yard into one of the cellars. It made a really good slide if you sat on a sack, but you got real black as you fell in the coal dust. I couldn't lie about this: I came up looking like a chimney sweep boy out of a Charles Dickens novel. I was usually scolded, bathed and sent to bed— but the thrill of that fast slide was worth it.

Soon it was time to return to school. There seemed to be a lot of excitement going on. They started to have what they called, "air-raid drills." That was when we had to put on those funny masks we carried in a little box hanging from our shoulders. We only had to put them on though, when the sirens sounded.

The grown-ups all talked about England getting ready for war. They weren't happy about it, but we kids thought it was great fun. On September 1st, all the school was going on a vacation together, or at least, that's what we were told. The adults had another name for it: they called it, "Evacuation." That morning the parents and students attended Mass.

After Mass, all our baggage was loaded onto buses; we seemed to have an awful lot of baggage for a short vacation. The adults tied labels on us. Mine read, "Kenneth Roberts, St. Patrick's School." It seemed we weren't the only school going on vacation 'cause the terminal was jam packed with kids: they all had labels on them too. The small children, including myself, were quite happy about the whole thing. My brothers were jealous because they couldn't go; they weren't in school yet. The bigger kids didn't seem to think it was such great fun and the adults, well, they were all crying. I asked Mum when we would be coming back but she wasn't too sure or perhaps I was too excited to hear her answer. All I was concerned about was that we were going to the country and I had never been there before.

My hometown was quite large, it was a seaport and most people had heard of it. It was called, "Southampton." The place where we were going, was a small village and I couldn't even find it on the map, "Old Basing."

We all boarded the trains, the teachers, the kids and just a handful of parents; most of them were staying home. As the train pulled out, I waved to Mum. I don't think she saw me, 'cause she was wiping her eyes with a handkerchief. I remember the parish priest there too. He was making the sign of the cross wide in the air as he gave us his blessing. I didn't know then, as we pulled away, that it would be three years before I was to see Southampton again.

After about an hour of travel, the train pulled into a station where a sign read, "Basingstoke." We left the train and boarded the buses that were to take us to the country village. It was very exciting as we wound along those country roads. I saw my first real cows. The roads were so funny; they were narrow and winding. The houses were even funnier; they were so different from any I ever saw. I thought the people must be real poor because the houses had dead grass and sticks for a roof. The teacher later explained that it was, "Thatch."

Soon we arrived in the village square. There were a lot of grown-ups waiting for us. They divided us up according to age; that meant my brother Roy and I had to be separated. I remember I didn't like that part of it at all. A lady took him and another eighth grader; a different lady picked me and a second grader. She was a

11

harsh woman. She didn't smile and her eyes were cold, almost cruel, I thought.

The village had a main street; at one end, there stood an old Anglican church that dated back to the Middle Ages and at the other end, was a big old house which belonged to a general. In the middle of the street was the village hall. In between the church and the hall, on the side of the road, was a line of modern-built houses. My companion, Eddie, and I accompanied the lady toward the largest and most modern of these.

As soon as we entered the house, she made certain the rules established must be obeyed or we would be severely punished. We were not allowed in the house except for meals or if it was raining, in which case, we were to stay in our room. The only parts allowed to us in the home, were the kitchen and our bedroom. All meals were to be taken promptly and always in the kitchen. We were to be in bed by 6 p.m. without fail. I remember her being quite angry when she found out we were Catholics. She said we were the first Catholics in their village and she warned us right then and there that we had better not bring our evil ways into her home or community. I wondered what she meant by that?

That night she showed Eddie and me to our room and our bed; that truly was "our" bed since we had to share it. Neither of us could get to sleep that night. It wasn't because we were excited about our "vacation" either. Eddie turned to me and said, "Ken, do you like this place?"

"No, and I don't like this vacation either. I want to go home, Eddie."

"So do I."

And we cried ourselves to sleep.

I especially hated mealtimes here. They were so different from meals at home. Mum always hummed or whistled happily some hymn to the Blessed Mother as she prepared our food. When we all sat down to eat, the food was set before us and we helped ourselves to as much as we wanted. As we ate, we exchanged conversation about our day. Here our plates were handed to us already rationed out, and seconds were scarce. Silence was maintained throughout the meal. I felt we were in a small institution.

September 3rd, 1939 was the beginning of our third day in the country and already it seemed like a year. It was Sunday and we were permitted to go to Mass even though our temporary guardian hated the idea. There was no Catholic church in the village so a priest came from the nearest town, Basingstoke. We were allowed the use of a barn for Mass. What a change from the warm simple parish church I was so used to. We knelt on the earth floor of the barn; there was hay and cow manure all over. The chickens ran around cackling and the cows chewed their cud indifferently while Mass began.

The priest began the prayers and soon it was time for the gospel. Just as he started his sermon, a farmer came rushing in and whispered something to the priest. He looked shocked, and turned to the people: "England has just declared war on Germany. Let us pray." The sobbing could be heard coming from the adults (some of the parents who were able, came along as helpers to the teachers). The priest continued the Mass and soon it was time for the consecration. The priest took the bread in his hands and said, "Hoc Est Enim Corpus Meum," he raised the Host for adoration; the altar boy forgot to ring the bell: but in the distance a cock crowed.

This was the last week for us to have Mass in the barn. The next day, the retired army general gave us his stately country home at the end of the street to

13

serve as a school. The principal, the Honorable Miss Enright, was from a titled family and her brother was an admiral in the navy. It was no doubt his influence that had gained us this beautiful house and garden for a school. Miss Enright took a particular interest in me since I was her god-child. Under her direction, the house was soon converted into a suitable learning place and its largest room became a Catholic chapel.

Food was rationed and so was love in most homes where we were temporary guests. It seemed that the local inhabitants really suspected us of a gigantic plot to take over the village for the pope. One would have thought that the pope, not Hitler, was the enemy of this little village; and the local children made that quite obvious to us as we passed through the streets. From what they shouted at us, I felt they were quite sure the pope would not make heaven; at least they expressed a strong desire to see him go to the "other place." Perhaps this is the reason why we became so clannish and made few friends with the local children. Miss Enright became more than a principal, she was our protector and guide.

The next few months passed slowly and I grew more homesick with each passing day. It was Christmas now and some of the older children were allowed to visit home for the holidays. Roy was able to leave but I had to remain. Now I felt completely alone. At least, the first few months I would see Roy occasionally. He lived next door with Eddie's fourteen-year-old brother, Tony. We were not allowed to visit each other in the homes as the landladies (our temporary guardians, who were paid by the government) would not allow us in the house unless to eat or sleep. I didn't play too much with Roy because he was too big, but at least I could talk with him from time to time about home.

While the children were away for the holidays, the

bombs began to fall on Southampton. So many of the children didn't return; Roy was one of them. Most of the roads leading from the major cities were cut off from all travelers except the military.

How I hated that first Christmas there. Not only were there no treats or toys, but I was separated from everything and everyone I held dear. What a difference from my last Christmas at home.

Christmas always centered around Midnight Mass. All the family would attend, all those over eight, that is. Children who still believed in Father Christmas (Santa) went to bed and had to be sleeping before the adults returned from church or he wouldn't fill those large pillow cases we laid at the foot of our beds.

Last year, I was still awake when the family returned from church. Dad crept into my room and told me Father Christmas was just down the road so I better get to sleep fast. In the darkness, I could hear him putting something in the closet. That night I couldn't get to sleep and the kind old gentleman with the white beard and red suit didn't come. I know for I was awake until daylight. I looked at the foot of my bed; there was nothing there! I started to cry, but Dad told me not to worry. Father Christmas left it in the closet. Now I knew the truth! My disappointment didn't last long as I soon lost myself unwrapping presents from the well-stuffed pillowcase. Downstairs, under the tree, was a new bicycle.

I can recall almost fifty of us around the tree: all of mother's children and grand-children were there. Each year, they would grow in number and sleeping so many became more difficult, but we seemed to manage. It was our family custom to spend the entire two-day holiday together (Christmas followed by Boxing Day). There was food galore, turkey or goose, ham, roast beef, roast pork with crackling, stuffing, and all kinds of vegetables and fruits, but the most traditional was the plum pudding that Mum prepared weeks in advance. There was quite a ritual in serving the plum puddings: it commenced in the kitchen, brandy was poured over them and ignited. The blue flames lighted the darkened dining room as they were carried in to the accompaniment of our singing, "Silent Night." We smaller children all searched our slice for a six-penny piece and made a wish: This was a tradition in England, and we all looked forward to it. Mum bustled about from one to the other making sure all were having a good time. Her excitement was contagious; we bubbled just to watch her. How excited she was as she watched our reaction when we opened our gifts around the tree. Eventually the family coaxed her to sing a duet with Dad; their favorite was, "The Old Rustic Bridge," which they both sang every year without fail. Grandad always regaled us with old sea chanteys. Each one of us, from the youngest to the eldest took a turn entertaining around the piano. My specialty was a tap dance in soccer boots followed by a poem recitation.

When the celebrating calmed down, Mum sat back, a little worn out, but glad to know she caused so much happiness: her peaceful eyes wandered over all of us and we got lost in their contentment. After we had our turn at performing, we were sent to bed as the adults continued their festivities throughout the night. Mother tucked us in, listened to our prayers, kissed us, and said, "Good night and God bless." As I lay in bed listening to the singing downstairs, Mother's words echoed in my ears: "I wonder if we will all be together next Christmas."

Now one year later, on Christmas Eve, Eddie and I went to bed at the usual hour, 6 p.m. Nobody was going to Midnight Mass and we weren't waiting for Father Christmas. When we awoke Christmas morning, we found a sock, with an apple and a candy bar in it, left there by our landlady. Later in the day, after a simple dinner of sausage and potatoes, we were given a present to share! a clockwork train with two carriages. The Christmases during the next three years seemed even worse as the food and love became an ever rarer commodity.

1940 saw the great blitz of England and the beginning of the Battle of Britain. France had fallen and the invasion of England was expected any day. Each night the bombs and the destruction they brought increased. There was little of Southampton left standing. My Southampton home too was gone; that big house with the creepy stairs, the cellars with my favorite slide, the beautiful garden and greenhouse that Mother loved so much, were all destroyed. My family, however, escaped unharmed in the air-raid shelter. Now they were homeless. Later Mum and Dad were fortunate in procuring another house in the suburbs of Southampton. It was small, not nearly as stately, but at least, it was a home and they were safe inside it.

After three years of my "vacation" had passed, I received word where my family was. I was still not permitted to return to the "dangerous area," but I felt it had to be a better place than this "miserable safety" provided for me. I could stand it no longer. I would rather live in danger with my loved ones than spend another day of uncertainty in this God-forsaken place.

I was eleven now and a little more confident. I took off for school one morning with my pockets loaded full of apples that I had stolen from an orchard. I made my way to the highway that said, "Southampton - 35 miles," and I walked. After several hours and two sore feet, a truck came along the road. The driver asked me where I was headed.

"Southampton, sir."

"Climb in. I'll drive you there. That's where I'm going too."

Finally, after three years and many, many, bombs later, I was going home to Southampton, but not really the place I once called home. I would never see Southampton again as it once was: all the beautiful buildings, shops, churches, and tree-lined streets were gone. In their place were temporary one-floor shanties surrounded by destruction and ruin. It wasn't the town I knew and loved as a small child, but it was home to me; my family was here and soon I would see them again. A city that had suffered so much could surely suffer one more child to come home.

CHAPTER TWO

"Peace be to you...."
Jn 20:26

The truck driver dropped me off in what was once the treelined main street of elegant shops. Southampton now had the appearance of a pioneer town at the time of the gold rush, after an earthquake. There were piles of rubble, where once stood a twelfth-century church; gaping holes where once shoppers crammed food in their baskets; and amid the debris, little one-story buildings, built since the blitz, broke the landscape of destruction and despair. They called these little shacks "shops," but they had little to display; everything was rationed and in short supply. Food, clothes, furniture, everything was snatched up by lines of hungry people, anxious to buy anything. A line formed without anyone realizing or even caring what was left them at the end of a two-hour wait. It could be a pack of cookies, a can of dried egg powder, a pound of sausages or a bag of potatoes: whatever the commodity, one thing was certain; it was always needed. Once a line started, it grew and formed its snake-like shape out of the store and down the street, attracting in minutes hundreds of hopeful shoppers until the supply was sold. Many such lines formed this wonderful morning, wonderful, because I was home. I whistled a happy tune as I skipped by the lines of joking women who passed the time complaining cheerfully to themselves as only the English can do.

A policeman was directing traffic at the intersection; his helmet shielded the sun from his eyes and the white armband he wore over his sleeve contrasted with the dark blue of his uniform.

"Please sir, can you tell me how to get to this place?" I showed him the paper with the address. He looked at it for a moment, then stared in front of him: he seemed to be concentrating.

"Let me see . . . Pound St., Bitterne . . . Well, Bitterne is about three miles from here. Keep going straight down this road till you leave the city, then you will come to a big steep hill. When you get to the top, that's Bitterne. Better ask more directions once you get there." He returned the paper to me smiling. "Why don't you take the bus? It leaves from that stop over there, No. 1, 3, or 5 will pass it."

19

"I don't have any money," I replied as I took the paper, carefully folding it back in my pocket.

The kindly bobby reached in his pocket and drew out a sixpence and gave it to me. "Here sonny, it's too far to walk. Ask the conductor to put you off at the top of Lancers' Hill."

"Thank you very much, sir."

I ran across the street and jumped on the back platform of the bus just as it was about to pull away. My thoughts raced as quickly as the wheels sped along the pavement. Finally the conductor shouted, "Top of Lancers' Hill." His voice broke into my thoughts, increasing my excitement. This is it! This is Bitterne, the place my family now calls home!

I jumped off the bus and asked a passing lady directions. "Please Madam, can you tell me where Pound St. is?"

"Yes dearie, it's the first turning on the left. There's a bank on one corner and a Methodist church on the other . . . Can you see it there?" She reached down and ran her fingers through my brown curly hair.

"Yes Mam, thank you." I returned her smile. Everyone seems so much happier here, I thought, and I knew I just loved them. Southampton people are great and I am home!

Pound St. was a quaint street: the houses were small and close together, yet each one had a garden around it. I began to count the numbers on the gates, "4, 6, 8, 10." Soon I would see my house for the first time!

On the left side of the road was a recreation park where some children were playing. I thought for a moment that one of them could be Jackie. He had fair blond hair, light blue eyes and well cut features: he was bigger than I remembered, but as I watched more

20

closely, I realized this definitely had to be Jackie. I ran across the street toward him.

"Are you Jackie?" I asked anxiously.

"Yes," he answered, a little puzzled.

"Don't you remember me? I'm Ken."

He studied me for a second then his expression changed completely, "Ken, I remember now. You're in all Mum's pictures. When did you come home?"

"I haven't been home yet. I haven't seen Mum yet either."

"Come on then. I'll take you there." He grasped my hand and led me along.

"Where are the others?" I asked.

"There is only Roy. The other kids don't live with us any more, Ken. Mum will tell you all about it," he said as he pointed to the gate.

"34 Pound St." The house was even smaller than I imagined it, but the garden was beautiful. Knowing Mother's talent with flowers, I could have picked out this house as ours without the number. The garden was laid out in a pattern with a precision of a drill sergeant. There were rose beds, lily beds, and dozens of other flowers in all colors. The pathway was made of crazy pavement, flagstone, in pink, green, blue and yellow, and at periodic intervals were trellises covered with roses. Mother always said she could find Christ in her garden; she certainly created a paradise here.

Halfway down the path, Jackie broke away and ran excitedly toward the door, shouting, "Mum, Mum, Ken's home!"

I can see her face still: her deep blue eyes which shone with nun-like serenity, showing an inner peace that was perpetually hers; her light brown hair curled loosely about her head. "Kenny!" Her eyes filled with tears. "How are you? How did you get here?" The questions poured from her lips as we threw our arms around each other. The words wouldn't come. I was home! The questions and answers had to come later: this moment was too good to spoil with words.

The months rolled by and it seemed like the three years at Old Basing were just a bad dream now. It didn't take long to settle back to a routine. Before leaving for school, I served the 6:30 Mass at the convent in Bitterne. Every morning, Mum and I walked up Pound St. in the early morning dark to the convent chapel, just two streets away. After a quick breakfast, I'd catch the 8 a.m. bus to my old parish school, St. Patrick's. It had just re-opened to accommodate the children who were returning from evacuation.

We didn't have a parish church yet, although we did have a pastor, Fr. Denis Walshe. He had been appointed by the bishop only a year before to form a new parish. We had to use the convent chapel as our church and the nuns, Sisters of Our Lady of Charity, taught us our religion in class on Sundays. We soon became great friends of the Sisters: whenever Mum had a problem or needed prayer, you could find her in the nuns' parlor at Redcote Convent asking Mother Agnes to get the Sisters praying for a special intention.

The home in which we now lived was much smaller than the one we were used to, a tiny kitchen, dining room, and front parlor downstairs, and three bedrooms upstairs. The house, being old, didn't even have a bathroom so Dad built an extra room for the bath and washing machine at the rear of the house. Our family was smaller now too; just Mum, Dad, Roy, Jackie and me. Kathleen was married and Grandad had passed away. The other foster children were all gone: their parents had reclaimed them since none of us were legally adopted. The fear of our real parents turning up one day and snatching us away was always present to

22

Jackie and myself. Perhaps this insecurity was the cause of my behavior at this stage of my life.

I was approaching my twelfth year and my deportment at school left much to be desired. I was constantly in hot water for showing off and insolence. It seemed a week couldn't go by without my being reprimanded for my boisterous behavior: oftentimes at the expense of some humiliating experiences suffered by the principal of the school, Miss Archdeacon, whom I cruelly referred to as, "The Giraffe." She had an extremely skinny broomstick-like body and extraordinary long neck that supported a wrinkled giraffe-like face framed in a mop of white hair. She was a hopeless disciplinarian and had a neurotic obsession for cleanliness.

One afternoon as she was rushing around wiping up the tables after lunch, I began to aggravate her by stamping my feet and mocking her. The children began to laugh at my performance; I was thrilled by the audience and my antics became bolder as Miss Archdeacon's tolerance became weaker. She wheeled around the table in a frenzy, not realizing she was still carting the pail of soapy water and began to chase me in and out of the maze of tables. The laughter grew even louder and I couldn't resist a finale: I stopped abruptly and SWOOSH. A stream of soapy foam drenched the "Giraffe" from the top of her white head to the bottom of her match-stick legs. The children's roars formed a musical background for the comic figure who stood motionless, screaming, mouth open wide like an opera star. She was singing my "Swan Song," for this was my last performance!

Miss Archdeacon took me to the pastor of St. Patrick's, Father Martin. He asked to see my parents as I "seemed to be a discipline problem." He recommended that I be sent to a boarding school under the supervision of the Irish Christian Brothers. If anyone could straighten me out, they could, and so it was arranged for me to enroll at St. Charles, a Catholic boarding school near London. Once again I was to leave home.

It was a warm September morning when we arrived at Waterloo station where I was to be met by a brother from St. Charles. Mum and Roy accompanied me on the train from Southampton. I remember Mum sitting opposite me on the train, her eyes sad, but peaceful. Roy tried the whole trip to convince me how fortunate I was to be getting the opportunity to study under the Brothers, but to me the whole journey just meant a prologue to another "good-bye"! I tried hard not to let the brother see me cry as he led me to the bus that was to take us to St. Charles. Mum gave me all the last-minute instructions. "Be a good boy, Kenny, and mind the Brothers. Promise you won't forget to write and let me know how you're getting on." I kissed her good-bye once again and I felt the lump in my throat grow tighter as I boarded the bus and took my seat.

St. Charles looked like an English stately home: it could have been the house of some English duke, judging by the regal entrance and park-like grounds with its tall trees and rolling lawns. The building was ancient, but elegant.

I was taken to the principal's office upon arrival.

"What do you want to be when you grow up?" asked the principal.

"A priest!" I answered.

The brother looked a little surprised. I guess he must have been, if he read the reports forwarded to him by my former teacher. I certainly lacked the image of the pious, intent scholar. I wonder now if he really thought I was sincere or trying to be sarcastic.

I shared a dormitory with fifty other students. I shouldn't be lonely with fifty kids around, I thought. Unlike my evacuation days, here I could feel free to worship whenever I wanted. I should say however, that wasn't my primary concern at this particular time, still it was a comfort to know the people around me shared the same beliefs.

One week later, it was my birthday, September 14th. I was twelve years old. When the package arrived from Mum with my present in it, I took it to my bed and read the note alone. I was so homesick and I didn't want the other guys to see me cry. After all, I was twelve years old!

"Happy Birthday, Kenny. I love you. Mother."

Some boys were beginning to file into the dorm. I ran to the chapel where I was sure to be alone. I took a place in front of the statue of the Blessed Mother. How I wished I could see my own mother Elizabeth, now.

"Please Blessed Lady, help me to get straightened out so I can be with my family soon. I miss them so much . . . and how am I ever going to get to be a priest when I get in so much trouble all the time? If I could only get this business of growing up over with, maybe things would be different . . . But I have so long to wait. . . ."

When Father Martin assured my mother that the Irish Christian Brothers could surely straighten me out, he was certainly correct. By December, when I returned home for the holidays, the change was so obvious that it was decided I needn't return to St. Charles, but instead, they enrolled me in Southampton's most elite school run by the French Christian Brothers of Instruction, St. Mary's. It was a school for "sons of gentlemen, English gentlemen" (that's the best kind). It was situated just a mile from my home; you could see it from quite a distance; the landscaping was beautiful.

Situated on a hill, it reigned regally on a pedestal of green.

We wore an elaborate uniform consisting of a brown cap with a gold cross, a brown blazer edged with gold piping emblazoned with a colorful school crest on the pocket, a brown and gold tie covered by yards of a brown and gold striped scarf that wrapped several times around the neck with one end hanging down the back, the other draped in the front. I was gift-wrapped for school!

It was during this time of my life when I really began to know my family. Dad was a strict man with very strong opinions. He had aged prematurely due to four years as a prisoner of the Germans in the First World War. He returned from the prison camp bald, except for white curly hair at the sides and back. After thirty years as a military man, he retired from the army, but he still kept his military bearing and was known to the locals as, "The Major." Now he was working for the local government as the City Hygiene Inspector. We didn't have the best possible relationship, he felt I spent too much time over books and too little time in the playing field. Jackie was the athlete in the family and that made him Dad's favorite. With each additional trophy won, Dad and he became closer. It was Mother who became prouder of me with each scholastic award I achieved. I really missed Roy not being around as my "big brother," but he was away serving as a sailor aboard a British destroyer in the Royal Navy on Russian convoy duty.

John, the eldest son, who we referred to as "Big Jack," and Susie, the eldest daughter, were both married and living in the United States. Although I had never met either of them I came to know them quite well through their letters to Mum. The second eldest son, Nat, was serving in the army in North Africa and we had little to do with his family due to Dad's dislike of his choice of wives. George, Mother's second youngest natural son, was in his thirties and a carbon copy of his father except for his complete head of fair curly hair. He, his wife Marian, and their three children visited us from time to time. And then there was Lorraine, the youngest daughter: she was in her late twenties. She was married to a timid and rather nervous man, also named George. Often she took me to her home for weekends, for at this time, she had no children of her own.

In my early teen years, I came to know Father Walshe, our parish priest, very well. I served his Mass daily at 6:30 a.m. and once a month he would call for me at 5:45 to go to the local hospital for the aged and nervous patients to celebrate Mass for the shut-ins. I served Mass at all the special times too, Easter liturgies, Christmas solemnities and the clothing ceremonies for the novices and Sisters at Redcote Convent. One Sister I remember especially well because she was later to become such a good friend, was Sr. Claire. I assisted the bishop as an altar boy at her clothing as a novice.

The Brothers at St. Mary's were really great men; one in particular was Brother Gregory, an extraordinary man. He had short cropped hair combed down on his forehead in a Buster Brown fashion. Being bashful, he blushed easily, especially in the company of women. He was exceptional in that he had a most fantastic memory: he remembered every student by the date of his birthday. Before he asked your name, he always said, "When is your birthday?"

A year earlier, I had met him at Redcote Convent during the funeral services for one of the Sisters. The Brothers' choir sang the Requiem Mass at which I served. At the breakfast served later in the convent parlor, he asked his usual question of all the altar boys present, "When is your birthday?" I answered, "September 14th." Imagine my surprise one year later when he came to my class as my Latin teacher and greeted me with, "Hello September 14th!"

Brother Alphonsus taught us English. He was a tall, dark serious man with a deep sonorous voice that vibrated as he read large chunks of *Lorna Doone*. Our foremaster, Brother John, whom we affectionately referred to as "Bonkers" gave the appearance of being an extremely strict disciplinarian, but as we grew to know him, we learned his bark was worse than his bite.

The most outstanding Brother in my memory was Brother Michael, the Superior and Head Master. I remember him mostly for his kindness and saintly face: he smiled more with his eyes than with his lips. And it was he who taught me my first lesson in Christian forgiveness, one that I shall always remember.

I was sent to his office to be reprimanded for an incident that could have been sufficient to expel me. When I entered his office, he was seated behind his desk and his smiling eyes were not smiling: they seemed to be suffering.

"Well Kenneth, what do you have to say for yourself?"

"I don't know what exactly to say, Brother. I was angry and I just couldn't stand it any longer," I answered hesitantly.

"Why don't you tell me the whole story from the very start," he said patiently, then motioned for me to sit down.

I told him of how that very morning when I walked into my class, I had, by mistake, said "Good morning, Brother," to my lay teacher, Mr. Murray. It seemed he took great exception to this and screamed back, "I'm

28

not your brother." Then later, when called upon to recite a vocabulary assignment, he seemed unnecessarily stern with me. I was becoming more and more perturbed until I talked back to him, a transgression that never went by without punishment. He came at me and began to hit me in real anger. The blows continued to rain upon my head until I could stand it no more. I gave him a straight right with my fist to the pit of his stomach winding him momentarily. I finished my account with simply, "So here I am."

"Kenneth, is this any way for a Christian to behave?" Brother Michael asked.

"No Brother, but he did strike the first blow and . . . ."

"Kenneth, I want you to go in this minute and apologize to Mr. Murray," he said rising from his chair.

"But why, Brother? He was wrong too, and besides he hasn't been completely fair to us and I don't see why I have to. . . ."

"Apologize, not because you are completely wrong, but you are a Christian in a Catholic school where non-Catholics look to us for example. Now go ahead and do it, son." Brother Michael's eyes were saying more than his words.

"It'll be hard, Brother."

"I know Kenneth, but no harder than it will be for me to forgive you." His eyes began to smile again, this time with understanding.

"Alright Brother, I'll do it."

His kindly compassion and refusal to punish me was my greatest punishment and this incident had a tremendous impact on me. After I apologized to Brother Michael and made friends again with Mr. Murray, I wrote this apology to the Blessed Mother which I still remember today:

Hail Mary, full of grace,

Pray for me, who of this race
Art weak in strength and with blushing face
Do ask of thee, make not a hypocrite of me.
Holy Mary, for me pray,
To score a goal this very day
In the game of Christian living not yet won,
Let me be chosen by your Son.

"Make not a hypocrite of me!" In spite of Mum's prayers and my religious training, that was just what I was to become.

The months went by and soon another year passed. The Germans were in full retreat. British and American soldiers were fighting on German soil. The Russians were about to enter Berlin. At last it came: Germany capitulated in May of 1945. For all practical purposes, England could begin to feel peace, for Japan was a long way from our shores and the effects of that war were not felt in the British Isles. If peace meant freedom from destruction, no more bombs, no more sleeping in air-raid shelters, then we already knew peace. We still had severe rationing, but in six years of war, we became used to the lack of luxuries in food; in fact, I couldn't even remember them.

August 15th, 1945 was really the great day. It was the feast of the Assumption of the Blessed Virgin Mary, a first class feast in the Church. It was also the day Japan accepted the Allies' peace terms and a first class feast for the world. The treaty was signed on September 2nd: this was "V.J. Day." Now there was peace at last.

In twelve days, I would be fifteen!

CHAPTER THREE

"And getting into one of the boats . . . ."
Lk 5:3

In spite of the fact that I was doing well in school, Fr. Walshe talked Mum into taking me out and permitting me to take advantage of a "golden opportunity" to go to work in a steel construction company as a junior clerk. The manager lived in our parish and he guaranteed that soon I would be a man of position. The fact that I left St. Mary's before graduation was not important: what was important was that I had attended a good school and that was status symbol enough. Furthermore I was entitled to wear the school tie and that's all that mattered in a country where the emphasis was placed on the right school, the right family and the right accent. If you wanted to attain real "class," you must really work on that accent: a sinus condition always enhanced it and if you could manage a slight expression of boredom and a rigid jaw, well then—"By Jove, I think you've got it!"

It was a typical Friday night; I was decked out in my charcoal grey suit and maroon tie. Just a little Brylcreem on the hair and I'm ready to go.

"Your cultured friends are waiting for you downstairs," Dad said sarcastically as he entered the room. "Why do you put all that stuff on your hair . . you'll be bald by the time you're twenty-one."

"Yes, Pop," I answered, not resisting the temptation to stare at his shiny bald head.

"Did that fancy school teach you to talk like that? Some manners you learned there," he shouted.

"Sorry, Father," I answered in mock politeness as I ran down the steps.

"No later than eleven . . . Understand?" he called after me.

"Yes, Father, I understand."

John and Max were in the parlor making small talk with Mum. I bent down to kiss her forehead and started for the door with the boys when she took my arm. "Be a good boy, Kenny. Remember our Blessed Lord can see you even if I can't," she said with a knowing eye.

"Yes, Mum," I answered, but smiled to myself. How could I ever forget when she reminded me each time I left the house for an evening with the boys.

"And don't forget, eleven o'clock, even if you are sixteen!"

John, Max and I had been friends for about two years. They both worked as telegraph messengers at the Post Office: they too, left school early. We had good times together and by the people who knew us, we were called, "The Three Musketeers." Most of our nights together were spent the same: a visit to the Bitterne Brewery Pub for a quick beer and a fast game of darts, then off to St. Theresa's Hostel for Girls for a few dances.

A pub is more than just a drinking place, it's a community living room. Most pubs are divided into three sections: the public bar, where men could go in their working clothes and just relax over a few drinks; the lounge, where a gentlemen could take his ladyfriend and sit in a more elaborate decor; and the bottle and jug, this bar was mostly for carry outs.

Percy, the bartender for the public bar, always greeted us with, "Here come the three musketeers!" Our welcome at St. Theresa's was much warmer; this was a boarding home for hard to handle girls under the supervision of the Sisters. Friday and Saturday nights, fellows were allowed to visit and dance, but they had to leave by 10 p.m. Whenever we entered the recreation room, the girls swarmed about us like bees; and we were the flowers!

This particular evening, after a few dances, one of the girls invited me out for a stroll in the garden. The grounds were filled with beautiful trees, and if one wanted, it would be quite simple to get "lost," or at least, out of view. We walked till we came to one of the benches. Now is the time!

"Would you like to sit a while?" I asked, trying to be quite casual.

"If you want to," was her shy reply.

We were both grown up and felt we were ready for grown up friendships, so after a little small talk, I reached for her hand, but it took half an hour to do that.

"Do you mind if I kiss you?" I asked awkwardly.

"If you want to." Again, the same reply.

I leaned over and barely brushed her lips. "Perhaps we should go in." I guess I wasn't so grown up, after all.

John and Max were sitting in the recreation room when we entered. I received a nudge and a wink from them, but I caught the "eye" from Sister Martha. I was glad it was 10 o'clock and time to leave.

Once outside, John began with the inevitable question, "Did you?" To avoid answering with a direct lie, I just grinned and replied, "What do you think?" By the look he gave me, I realized I hadn't fooled anyone, but myself.

33

It was a twenty minute walk home from the hostel, which meant we always had time for one more game of darts at the pub, and if Percy permitted, one more short beer.

I didn't work Saturdays so this was the day, besides several evenings, that I devoted to study and completing my assignments for the correspondence course I had enrolled in at Bennett College, Sheffield. Already, I had finished a great deal of work on my major subject, French. My two minor subjects were English and Latin. Each week, I studiously applied myself to the given material. By the time of my seventeenth birthday, I was in possession of several college certificates in these subjects.

Evenings not spent in study were similar to the one already described. Our favorite haunt was St. Theresa's and we usually started and ended our evenings the same way. The only thing that changed was our choice of girlfriends. Occasionally, we would depart from our routine and take in a movie, sometimes we would take a date with us, but that was rare. We preferred to be free agents when it came to being involved with girls.

Then it happened: I met Eileen, very English, with her fair hair and light complexion and blue eyes. Eileen was sixteen too. Our first date was a simple visit to a movie and a good-night kiss at her front door, but soon we became quite friendly as the dates became more frequent and I became a regular caller at her home. As the weeks went by, I saw less of John and Max. My routine changed as did my ideas and aims in life due to the influence of her father, who was a chief steward for the Union Castle Line. This was a very good job on one of the big liners that sailed regularly to South Africa, and I was very impressed when he took me aboard his ship and gave me the grand tour. I knew that day I would never be fulfilled in any office, no matter how important the job may be in the future, status-wise. I felt the call of the sea! I had to answer it.

After much persuasion and convincing Mum that this was the real "vocation" for me, and with the help of Eileen's father, I enrolled in a Merchant Navy School for a two month course. Again, I was to board the fast train to London.

At Gravesend Sea School, I attained honors which entitled me to wear a huge star on the sleeve of my uniform. Because of the honors, I was the proud possessor of the title, "Captain's Tiger and Commodore," a title bestowed to one achieving the highest merit.

After graduation, I walked down the platform of the Southampton terminal sporting my naval uniform with the huge star on the sleeve. I really thought the whole world was looking at me and realized the importance of my position. Imagine my disgust as I was hailed by an old lady who cried, "Porter, take these bags, will you?"

This was not to be the last of my humiliations as slowly I was to learn the real worth of the title, "Captain's Tiger and Commodore" in the real world of sailors.

As I stood in line at the office of the Shipping Federation, I realized I was the only one in uniform except for the staff behind the counters. I was sure if they saw that enormous star on my sleeve they would recognize immediately that I did well at training school and my first position would be of great importance. An official took my graduation papers and school report, looked me up and down and when his eyes rested on my enormous star, he said sarcastically, "Proud of that patch, aren't you, son?" He smiled almost sadistically, handed several stamped documents to me and told me to report to the union office.

The waiting room was full of seamen, many were

35

very rough and dirty looking, but all of them seemed to share the same trait, their language. I had heard vulgar language before, but never in such profusion and by so many. I felt the color come to my cheeks as I tried to affect a nonchalant attitude to their filthy and blasphemous choice of adjectives. Suddenly I realized I was the object of their attention; I knew immediately that I made a bad choice in wearing my uniform here. I would have welcomed the humiliation of the kindly old lady who mistook me for a porter: it was certainly a position of greater dignity than the one these, not so gentle, gentlemen were suggesting.

Many hours later, after being photographed, interviewed and mocked I was given a slip assigning me to a ship and my first real job at sea. The ship was a freighter, *The Rochester Castle,* destined for New York where it would load cargo to South Africa. I was so excited as I read the name and destination of my ship, until I took a good look at the top of the slip that read, "Kenneth John Roberts, PANTRY BOY!" I looked down at my enormous white star on my sleeve . . . a lot of good that did me.

My last two nights before I sailed were spent quietly, one evening with John and Max, the last with Eileen.

While John, Max and I were walking home and I was telling them of all the fabulous adventures that awaited me, I could sense something was wrong. Finally Max spoke up, "You know Ken, we're both really happy for you. Everything sounds great, but you know since you have been seeing Eileen so much, we've missed a lot of good times together. I hope your new job will get her out of your system."

"One other thing, Ken," said John hesitantly.

"What? For God's sake, come out with it." I was becoming impatient.

"I just hope this whole new life doesn't change you . . . You know what I mean . . . with all that travel, seeing new places and all that."

"Don't be stupid, I just have a new job, that's all. When I'm home things won't be any different," I assured them.

Later that night, as I lay in bed and recalled the conversation, I couldn't help but feel better knowing I had such great friends, but I was still a little confused by their concern. I won't ever change when it comes to my home ties . . . I don't think?

I came home early that last night from Eileen's: I wanted to be rested for my departure and new job the next morning. As I was creeping up the stairs, I didn't want to disturb Mum since she hadn't been feeling well for a few days, I overheard her praying. She often prayed aloud when she thought no one was around. "Holy Mother, I do worry about that boy. Dear Blessed Lady, throw your mantle around Kenny and protect him . . . ."

I wondered why she worried, but I was glad to know she did.

Roy was back at home now and Jackie was a student at St. Mary's and already an outstanding athlete. Dad was retired and had nothing to do but sit at home and criticize or visit the pub recalling days in the army when he was a "leader of men." And Mum, well she was just there to watch over all of us, always bustling about trying to make everything pleasant for "her men."

At breakfast, I felt a little uneasy. There's so much to say because I'll be leaving and gone for three whole months—Why can't I think of anything to say? Dad broke the silence:

"Jackie, turn that damn jungle music off. Are you deaf? How can you call that 'music'!" he shouted.

"Gosh, Mum, it's not too loud," Jackie protested.

"Be a good boy and turn it off, Jackie. You know how it annoys your father," Mum said kindly.

"I have to run off to school anyway." Jack picked up his books, turned off the radio, gave Mum a quick squeeze, then slammed the door behind him. Just two seconds later, he opened the door and shouted "Ken, good luck on your ship. See you—" and slammed the door again. For the second time he opened the door and yelled, "Hey Ken, don't forget to bring me a souvenir from New York!" Again the door slammed.

"Noise, noise, and more noise! Doesn't anyone know how to shut a door in this house?" Dad was becoming more irritable. Roy and I looked at each other in silence, grinning. "And you!" Dad shouted again. I looked up and realized he was directing his conversation to me.

"What did I do?" I questioned, a little stunned.

"Why don't you join the army if you want a man's career? The whole idea is stupid to me. You quit a job with a future to be a pantry boy on some freighter. If you ask me. . . ."

"Nobody's asking you," I interrupted rudely.

Mother was right there again to move in quickly with the newspaper: she handed it to Dad and said calmly, "You haven't read the paper this morning yet dear. Would you like some more tea?" and gave him an affectionate squeeze. Then turning her eyes to me she motioned for me to keep my mouth shut. I obeyed.

Roy gave me his best wishes and some last minute big brother advice. He was the one person I always looked to for advice: to know that he was not opposed to my plans was comforting to me. He jabbed my arm and with a smile said, "You'll do alright," then left for work.

Dad took the newspaper into the parlor while Mum was clearing off the table.

"Mum, I guess I really ought to be getting ready to leave," I said awkwardly. I waited for a reply, but she didn't answer right away. She walked to the sink with a stack of dishes, wiped her hands on her apron, which seemed to take her an unusually long time. Finally, she looked up, her eyes a little watery.

"Son, are you sure this is what you want?"

"Yes, Mum, I'm sure."

"You know I'll miss you, Kenny—But if this is what you really want to do, I won't interfere. I want whatever is best for you," she said walking toward me.

"Just think, Mum, in a few days I'll be in New York. I'll pick something up real nice for you—you'd like that, wouldn't you?"

"All I want is for you to return home safe. That's all I care about." She put her arms around me and kissed me.

"Don't worry so, Mum. I'll be fine." I hugged her one more time. God, how I hate "good-byes"!

I stood on the waterfront looking at "my" ship, *The Rochester Castle*. It was a pretty ship with a light purple hull, white superstructure and a red funnel. I boarded her and asked directions from some men working on the deck as to where I was to report. "Pantry Boy." Well, we all have to start our careers somewhere, besides how many guys my age have the opportunity to travel where I'm about to go: New York, Capetown, then on to Durban and Port Elizabeth. I can't wait to see all these places. My thoughts were broken by a deep voice: "You the new pantry boy—Here are your duties."

After giving me all my instructions, he told me I could go on deck to watch us cast off if I wished—and I certainly wished: this was my first voyage and I wanted to enjoy every minute of it.

"Cast off aft," shouted the first officer. A sailor unhooked the looped rope from the side of the ship and let it fall, snake-like to the dockside below. The ship moaned her farewell to the men on the waterfront as the tugs pulled the freighter away, up the river to the open seas. I stayed on deck watching the shore as Southampton became a skyline in the distance. In front of me was the sea, and more sea.

It was my job to carry the large cooking trays over the open deck to the pantry where the second steward and waiter transferred it to silver serving dishes and served it to the officers. I was responsible for keeping the food supplied, making coffee and tea or whatever other drinks they desired, and washing all the eating and cooking tools. I was so slow and inexperienced, that I would just about finish the mess from the previous meal when it was time to start on the next. It was an exhausted pantry boy that climbed in the bunk about mid-night, only to rise again at 5:30 to begin another day.

The days passed slowly. The romance of the sea had lost some of its charm. It seemed months had passed since I saw land. We passed through a storm about four days out in mid-Atlantic: the sea grew very rough. The ship rolled slowly and steeply to the left and just as slowly and steeply to the right. The bow leaped out of the water like a giant whale only to return as the waves swept over the bow and sides of the ship. The sea was angry and green, but not as green as I felt as I tried to carry the trays of hot food to the pantry. WHOOSH! . . . A wave soared over the side of the ship and rushed madly back to the sea, almost taking me and the tray with it. I was drenched from head to foot from the ocean spray, but I managed to save the food that was protected by a foil covering. I was quite sure that one of the waves would sooner or later get me, and it would be "Goodbye, Ken Roberts," as I sank to my watery grave. By now I knew that if I had survived this sailing in one of the worse Atlantic storms, without getting sick once (although I came close several times), I was a real sailor!

At last the day came. I could really appreciate now those words of the crew that sailed with Christopher Columbus: "Land ahead! Thank God!" Slowly we steamed up the Hudson, passing the Statue of Liberty and the tall skyscrapers of the "New World."

"Who are you going to shore with?" asked the chief steward.

"Nobody, sir," I answered.

"Want to come along with me?"

"Yes sir." I was glad to have someone to show me around.

"Fine then, meet me here at 6:30 this evening and I'll take you to Times Square and Broadway, then we'll take in a show. It's dangerous for a young boy wandering around New York alone—never know what you'll run into," he said with a knowing wink.

Later that evening, I was standing on Broadway, awestruck, watching the lights, intrigued by the hustle and bustle, and fascinated by the American accent. It was the same language but it sure sounded different here. It was like a dream, everything so new: hot-dogs, hamburgers, Coca Cola, 7-Up, delicatessens, street-cars, diners, movies, all were new words and most were new things. It certainly was a "New World." Everyone rushed somewhere, which I thought so strange since everything stayed open so late, all night movies, all night bars, all night stores. Why all the rush? They had "all night."

Two days later we were off to the high seas again,

41

bound for Capetown in South Africa. It was to be more of the same routine, except this time we had much better weather and I was becoming a little more organized now thanks to the galley boy and the dining room waiter. They volunteered to help me wash the dishes so we could sunbathe on the deck in the afternoons. In the evenings we played cards or just watched the sea that spread out like an endless mirror broken here and there by an occasional ripple made by the wash of the ship. The most exciting evening was the night we crossed the Equator when almost the whole crew stripped and danced like African tribesmen, spraying each other with fire hoses as we ran along the open deck.

Although we had acquired quite a tan, we were pale standing beside the natives at Capetown. The only great surprise for me was that this was the first time I had ever seen so many blacks, thousands and thousands of them: I thought we were the only whites there, but later I discovered we never visited the white section of the town. Most of the crew went to the nearest bar and got stoned: I went with them, but drank only Cokes. I had not acquired a manly appetite for liquor like these sailors—yet.

In Durban and Port Elizabeth, I was appalled by the complete segregation: the blacks were considered inferior and treated as such. Their only task was to supply cheap labor for the whites. During our three-day stay in each port, three different blacks did all my work for a quarter a day. We would have been lynched by the whites had we given them any more. I was ashamed when they kept calling me, "master," and embarrassed when they became euphoric over a small tip. I was glad to leave South Africa: it was depressing to see human beings treated so unjustly.

Three months had passed since we sailed from Southampton. As the ship steamed slowly up the water to pull into port, I thought how wonderful to be home again. Bet Mum will be glad to see me—I'll sure be glad to see her—Think of all the stories I can tell Roy, Jackie, Johnny and Max—Wonder if Dad will think I've become more of a man now that I'm a full fledged sailor—I'm going to call Eileen when I get home—wait till she sees this tan—I have to spend a couple of nights up at St. Theresa's—Really miss those evenings with Johnny and Max—Eileen shouldn't get mad at that—I only wrote her one letter since I left—I wonder if she still wants me to be her boyfriend?—I've grown up a lot on this trip though and I'm glad I sailed in the *Rochester Castle,* but I don't want to sail in her again. I don't want to go back to Africa and I'm certain I don't want to become the world champion dishwasher—Life on the big ships is far different and they go to ports "where the action is." It's time to look for something better— AN OCEAN LINER!

CHAPTER FOUR

"To the chief steward . . . ."
Jn 2:8

"Mum, I'm home!" I shouted as I entered the front hall.

"Kenny, thank God. You're home safe," she cried running from the kitchen. She hugged me then stood back. "Let me have a look at you. You've put on

43

weight and look at the color of your skin . . . you're so dark."

"Mum. I have so much to tell you. Where are the others?"

"They're all in the parlor. Come along, I have a surprise for you." She took my arm and led me along. "Your big brother, Jack, is here from the United States with Molly. They came for a visit, just arrived a few days ago. I've told them all about you and they're anxious to meet you."

"I don't know what to say to them, Mum. I don't even really know them." I felt a little embarrassed.

"Don't be silly, Kenny. He's your brother. You've read all his letters and don't you remember when Molly came with the two boys to visit before the war?" She hesitated, then almost as an afterthought, added, "No, I don't suppose you would remember them. You were quite young then. Now, come along, they are waiting." She reached over and kissed my cheek and tightened the hold on my arm. "It is good to have you home again, Kenny."

When I entered the parlor Big Jack stood to greet me. No wonder they call him "Big Jack," I thought.

"Hi," I said awkwardly.

"So you're Kenny. Mum's told us all about you," he said as he put his hands on my shoulders at arms' length, giving me the once over.

"Heard a lot about you, too. It's really great to see you."

"Well, little brother, how do you like the sea?"

"I like it, and I really want to go back, but I hope it's not another freighter."

"You know, I went to sea when I was your age, twenty-five years ago, before you were even born," he said in a distinct Philadelphian accent.

"Mum told me you jumped ship in the U.S. and . . ."

"That's partly true," he interrupted. "I jumped ship in Canada, but then I emigrated to the United States. I live in Philadelphia, now." He led me to a chair. "Sit down, we have a lot of getting acquainted to do." I sat down, still feeling a little dumbfounded.

Molly greeted me and all of us sat for a while exchanging stories: there was a lot to talk about. Later Molly and Mum left to start dinner: Mum had planned a special meal for my homecoming, all my favorite food. To please Jack and Molly, she tried her hand at some American cooking too. The whole evening was spent chatting away and laughing at the way Mum would correct Big Jack's exaggerated stories of his childhood: Mum was in her glory just watching everyone enjoy himself. (Guess I'll just have to call Eileen tomorrow night—)

I picked Eileen up early the next evening: she seemed kind of quiet; I knew something was on her mind. Later, at the movies, I reached for her hand, but she pulled it away pretending to scratch her arm. During the whole bus-ride home, she hardly spoke a word: I knew by now she wasn't too happy with me. As we left the bus-stop and walked slowly toward her home, she finally said, "Dad told me your boat got in yesterday—How come you didn't call me last night?"

"Gosh, Eileen! I wanted to, but that was my first night home in three months and Mum was looking forward to seeing me too, besides Jack and Molly are here all the way from Philadelphia. I never even met Jack before. You know when he was about my age, he jumped ship in Canada and . . . ."

"Why didn't you write while you were away?" she interrupted.

"What do you mean? I did write and I mailed it from New York."

We were standing at her gate.

"But you were in other ports too, Ken. My mother said that you obviously don't have any real feeling for me or you would have written more."

"Well, you know what your mother can do!"

"Thank you, very much," she said half crying, then turned and ran toward her house.

"Will I see you tomorrow?" I called after her.

"No!" she cried, and slammed the door.

I stood there for a moment with my hands on my hips staring at the closed door. Well, I'm too young to go steady, anyway, I thought. I put my hands in my pockets and walked slowly toward the bus stop.

I took a seat by a window and began to ponder the whole situation as the bus pulled away. Maybe I ought to call her tomorrow and apologize—No, why should I give in?—I guess I shouldn't have said that about her mother, but who gave her the right to butt in? . . . She must really like me or she wouldn't have been so upset —I know I like her . . . Maybe she doesn't really like me that much and she's just looking for an excuse to break up—No, that's not it: she really was crying. I know, I'll just call her tomorrow and see how she sounds, but I'm not going to beg. There's plenty of other girls, of course they're not all as nice as Eileen, but so what—

I looked at my watch. It's still pretty early: maybe I can catch Johnny and Max at the pub.

The next day, I tried for a reconciliation, but that was it: Eileen and I were through. I guess I'm too young to go steady anyway.

At breakfast that morning, Big Jack questioned me

again about my desire for a career at sea. "Ken, are you really serious about wanting to go back on a ship?"

"You bet—but I'd really like to get on one of the big liners. You know how hard those jobs are to get, though," I answered.

"I may be able to help you. Bert Jones, the catering superintendent of the Cunard Company is a personal friend of mine . . . we sailed on the same ship years ago. I know he could help you . . . I'll give him a call."

Jack had done very well for himself in the United States: he was the vice-president of a chain of diners in Philadelphia. Now he was using his American know-how in little old England. And it worked! I was to see him at eleven o'clock the next morning.

I can't believe it—nobody will believe it, I thought as I ran down the stairs of the Cunard office building. The world's largest liner, 84,000 tons of it I looked at the slip again:

KENNETH ROBERTS—COMMIS WAITER—RMS QUEEN ELIZABETH.

The greatest luxury liner was my new home and I was to report for duty at 8 a.m. the next morning. In two days, I would be sailing for New York again. This time in real style.

I sat in the pub with John and Max that evening telling them the latest happenings.

"Well Ken. It looks as if you are really getting places. Everyone in Southampton knows the Cunard Line has the prime jobs for seamen," said Max sipping his beer.

"You're lucky too, getting the QE, the biggest ship on the sea," John added.

47

"Big Jack said that you can really make some money as a commis waiter: all the commis' work is in the first-class section and the tips really amount to something," I said excitedly.

"Don't let all that 'first class' stuff turn your head now, will you?" Max said wiping the foam from his lips.

"You know me better than that. The money and all that doesn't mean a thing to me. I just want to travel. I can't wait to see New York again. It's like a whole new world over there." I became more excited just recalling the bright lights in Times Square, but I could tell by the look on John's and Max's faces that they didn't share my enthusiasm. "Come on, I'll play you a quick game of darts."

The next two days were spent learning my duties as a commis waiter and getting the *Queen* ready for her next voyage by polishing silver and making certain all the eating utensils were in tip-top shape. Two other commis waiters, Peter Jelly and Eric Cooper, showed me my way around, but even after two days on board, I still wasn't sure just where I was going. There were first-class sections to learn, the cabin and tourist classes, alleyways, gangways, several bars, sun deck, promenade deck, sitting rooms, ballrooms, a beauty shop, gift shops, restaurants, several dancing areas, kitchens, working alleys, officers' quarters, clerks' quarters, the crew's cabins—it was like a floating village! Men were working everywhere, cooks, barmen, guards, waiters, clerks, bellboys, engineers in their officers' uniforms, greasers in their blue jeans and dirty, oily shirts, stewards and maids. How do they have room for all the passengers? I thought.

Pete and Eric prepared me for my meeting with my new boss.

"Wait till you meet 'Moon Mullins,'" Eric said laughing.

"Moon Mullins . . . who's he?"

"The restaurant manager, he has one of the biggest jobs on the ship. The chief steward is the most important man, but 'Moon' is probably the richest," Eric quoted me a sum.

"How does he make all that?" I asked surprised.

"Tips!" was Pete's simple reply.

Mr. Mullins was a big, stout man with a very Irish face: not the kind of man you would picture as the restaurant manager of such a large and famous dining room. It seated 800 passengers in its palatial setting. He had a bit of a brogue mixed with just a suggestion of an American twang.

"Now stand up straight! Let me get a good look at you all," he said through his teeth. "Make sure you clean those shoes by tomorrow's inspection, Cooper." He walked down the line of commis waiters. "Put out your hands and let me see your nails!" he barked as he returned along the line. He stopped abruptly at the boy next to me. "Do you bite your nails, Kelly?" His face was red and he was shouting. Then he turned his squinted eyes toward me. My insides began to thump: I felt like I was vibrating all over.

"Get those curls cut, Roberts, we want our boys to look good, not PRETTY, and you look too damn pretty!" he screamed.

That's a bad start, I thought, as he passed. He remembers my name already and he isn't too impressed with what he has seen. How could he be so insulting the first day?—As for "looking pretty," I resent the inference—The girls thought I was handsome, I mused, conceitedly, trying to pick up the pieces of my ego which he had just shattered.

After we were dismissed, Peter ran over to me excitedly. "He likes you."

"Likes me?" I questioned confused.

"Yes, he only insults his pets and usually he picks on your best asset. Kelly has the best nails you ever saw on a boy.'" Pete grabbed Kelly's hands to show me. "Get the message, Ken? You're in!"

That evening, the last before I sailed, was just like the old days at Christmas: we had such a houseful. Mum set a big feast before us and after dinner, we all retired to the parlor. Later we all harmonized in a sing-along climaxed by the featured presentation of "The Old Rustic Bridge." During the festivities, Roy winked at me and motioned for me to come outside.

Roy was a man of few words: and I valued his sound opinions and judgments. He was slightly built with fair hair and deep blue eyes: his voice was always soft, never bad-tempered. He always thought a lot before he spoke.

"How did things go today on the ship?" he asked.

"Great." I began to give him a quick rundown on all the happenings but no matter how hard I tried I couldn't even begin to describe the vastness and elegance: I kept rattling on and on until Roy finally stopped me.

"I may not get a chance to see you tomorrow before you leave, so here's some money toward your expenses, uniforms and all that." He pushed a bundle of notes in my hand and gave me an affectionate hug. As we walked back inside, he said, "I'm glad to see you so happy. I don't know when I've seen you so excited."

"Excited" wasn't the word for it. I couldn't sleep that night no matter how hard I tried. Every time I shut my eyes, I could see only that beautiful giant ship, a thousand feet long: her length was almost as long as the Empire State Building was high. I remembered how that very morning, I felt as though a thousand eyes, her portholes, were peering at me from her black hull; I was dwarfed by her upperdecks that towered above the sheds like a twenty story building. She was majestic, with her two giant red funnels that stood like a fortress: she was truly the "Queen of the Sea," and I was one of her subjects.

My thoughts returned to New York: all the tall buildings, the smell of hot-dogs and that tangy taste of a Coke or Pepsi. I couldn't wait to sample the busy scene of Times Square, the bright lights of Broadway, and all the rush and bustle of the New World was waiting for me—But I must get some sleep! I turned and grabbed the pillow around my head as if to lock out more thoughts so sleep would come. Suddenly an uneasiness came over me: my emotions were mixed—Suppose I'm granted this chance in a lifetime and find it's not the life for me? I'll never get this opportunity again—What if I'm not good on my job or the rest of the crew won't like me?—No, I'm not going to think about that—Then my thoughts returned to Eileen, and with them an aching feeling came to my stomach. Did I really like that girl or was I in love with the idea of having a girlfriend just to boost my ego?—Was I upset because I lost her or because she told me to "get lost." I tightened my grip around my pillow: I was reminded of the Christmas Eve when I discovered the truth about Father Christmas. The *Queen Elizabeth* was far more exciting than any filled pillowcases—What things had fate wrapped for me in this luxurious gift?—I may have lost my belief in girlfriends, just as years ago, I lost belief in Santa, but now I was getting lost in unwrapping all the mysterious possibilities in store for me—

It wasn't as difficult to say good-bye to Mum the next morning as it was the last time, since I would be gone

51

for only twelve days, then have two full days at home. Every ten weeks, I had two weeks off. Mum didn't seem to mind these arrangements, though I knew she was always apprehensive about my being so far from home.

Sailing day was thrilling: I was dressed in my new Cunard Navy uniform. One of my duties was to deliver the many flowers to the cabins of the departing passengers. We lined up on the promenade deck and waited our turn to collect a box of flowers: each box had a tab attached to it with the passenger's name and cabin number. Each trip, I received a tip as I presented the flowers. After two hours, I was twenty-five dollars richer, and we hadn't even sailed yet! We had a full complement of passengers, 2500 of them and 800 travelled first class.

"All visitors ashore!" the voice blared from the ship's loudspeakers. The passengers' alley-ways were crowded with excited people as they made their tearful farewells: on the dockside, a band played British and American songs as the visitors and friends of the passengers crowded the rails of the open observation deck on top of the Cunard berth. Paper streamers were thrown by the excited travellers as the band grew louder, the hour for departure approached. Soon seamen were busy throwing ropes down toward the dock. "The Great Ship" gave several deafening blasts from her funnels as she slowly moved away aided by the many tugs alongside. The band played and the people sang, "Should auld acquaintance be forgot and . . . ." The ship slipped away as the crowds on the dockside disappeared in the distance.

We all reported to Mr. Mullins for our assignments, except for Pete. Pete had one of the two plum jobs for a commis waiter, Captain's commis. His only chore was to assist the Captain's valet, tidy the Captain's quarters and assist the waiter at the Captain's table. The other plum job was Chief Steward's commis: his duties were the same. One by one the commis were assigned to different sections of the vast dining room where their duties would be to assist the waiters by handing the elaborate menus to the guests, pouring the water, and bringing in trays of food served in silver dishes to the dining room hot plates then returning the empties to the gigantic kitchen where a vast army of men was busy operating the many washing devices. Wonder where I'll be working, I thought as Mr. Mullins assigned each boy. The line grew smaller and at last, I was the only one left.

"Roberts, you have been appointed commis to the Chief Steward. Report to the Chief Steward's quarters, now!"

"Thank you, sir," I said in amazement.

"Don't thank me, thank the Chief Steward, PRETTY BOY!"

I was so excited, I overlooked the insult.

It was 5 a.m. when I climbed out of the bunk, groped in the darkness for my uniform and crept out of the cabin as quietly as possible: I didn't want to disturb the nine other commis with whom I shared the cabin. When I finished my shower, I began to dress hurriedly: but I took extra time with my hair, trying to get it to "stay down": I didn't want to be referred to as "pretty boy" again. I stood in front of the mirror for a quick self-inspection: I wanted to be in tip-top shape for my first morning at sea. Let's see—"Hair, hands, and shoes. When they're good, you're good. Inspection's a snap." Those were the profound words of advice Pete gave me at supper the night before. Outside, I heard the rattling cups in the alley. As I opened the door, the "Glory Hole" steward was standing there with a cart filled with

53

cups and pots of tea. This was the name given to the steward assigned to make our beds and clean our cabin; for a tip, he would wake you at a given time with tea.

"Do you want tea?" he asked.

"No, thanks, I'm going to Mass."

The night before, as I lay in my bunk, I promised to make the 6:30 Mass as an act of thanksgiving for this wonderful job. I was sure God granted me this favor to show me my vocation in life. I was determined to do my job well and learn as much as I could about catering aboard ship. My ambition was to become the restaurant manager or chief steward, and I was positive with my education, background, zeal and good luck, I'd make it. Although it may take years, I would be patient; my time would come. Yes, this was definitely my vocation, a career at sea, specializing in service to others.

When I approached the chapel, several passengers were kneeling waiting for Mass to begin. There was always a number of priests travelling so there was sure to be a Mass every morning. The priest was vesting at the altar.

"Good morning, Father. Would you like me to serve Mass?" I asked.

"Good morning, yes, thank you," he answered as he tied the cincture and reached for the stole to put over his shoulders.

At communion I was surprised to see Mr. Mullins kneeling there. After Mass, as I was walking out from the chapel, he nodded to me, then resting his eyes on my hair, he gave me a look that seemed to say, "That's better."

John, the Chief Steward's valet, handed me the menu the Chief had already marked off. "Better hurry, he's just finishing his shower and he always demands his breakfast be ready as soon as he's dressed."

When I returned with the tray, John took it from me and said, "What kept you? He's been waiting and 'Dizzy' doesn't like to be kept waiting."

"Dizzy?" I asked confused.

"That's his nickname," he explained as he opened the door that led to the Chief Steward's private quarters.

"Come here boy, let me have a look at you," screeched a high-pitched voice from behind the door. Now I know why they call him "Dizzy" I thought, as I entered. "Come closer, young man."

I entered a little nervously. "Good morning, sir."

"So you're my new commis. Is this your first ship?" he asked giving me a thorough inspection.

"No sir, it's my second, but it's my first passenger ship," I answered awkwardly.

"This is not just a passenger ship. It is THE passenger ship, the Queen of the sea, and don't you forget it!" he said turning his nose in the air. "You may take my tray when I'm finished with it."

That afternoon, John gave me a run-down on what to expect in my new job. "It's very important to look attractive and give the best possible impression to our American guests. You'll see why when you start collecting the tips they leave. Every night, the Chief has an evening cocktail party. I prepare the drinks and you serve them. You're going to meet famous people from all over the world sitting right here: royalty, film stars, statesmen, anybody who is anybody, if they travel on this ship. You'll see them all right here in the Chief Steward's own exclusive little bar." And he was right: I did meet them all and my pockets began to swell, thanks to their lavish generosity.

Soon my job became quite routine and already I was becoming used to the glamor of the "Queen" and its passengers. The fifth day was docking day and I made my way to the top deck to meet Pete and Eric.

"She's beautiful, isn't she?" I said looking out toward the Statue of Liberty. "I love seeing New York again."

"Listen Ken. You brought a good suit with you, didn't you?" Pete asked.

"Of course, why?"

"Well, we want to take you out and show you the town," he said with a mischievous wink.

"I can't. I promised Mum I would visit my sister, Susie. I didn't have time the last time I was here. Maybe, tomorrow night."

I was surprised to see Susie: her resemblance to Mum was remarkable. I spent the first two hours in her apartment telling her all about Mum and the family back home. She was naturally very interested in learning as much as she could since she hadn't been home in twenty-five years when she left England as a girl to come to the United States as a student nurse.

"Do the English still dress so formally?" she asked looking at my dark suit, starched white shirt and neatly knotted maroon tie. "I'll take you to the store and make an American of you," she said taking her purse and starting for the door. Before I knew it, I found myself on my way to one of the best men's clothing shops.

I returned to the ship in the early hours of the morning, dressed in my newly acquired light blue gabardine trousers, pale blue shirt, hand painted tie topped off by a beige windbreaker. I felt very American as I climbed the gangplank looking down at my brown moccasins and yellow socks, vigorously chewing gum for the first time. What a transformation! But this was to be just the beginning: the next day I went with Pete and Eric and bought a whole new wardrobe: suit, shirts, socks, shoes, cufflinks, key chain, the whole works. Southampton, here I come! The old Ken Roberts has died: witness the birth of the new!

How quickly the months went by and how quickly the months changed me. Six months ago, I was the timid new commis finding his way around an ocean liner for the first time. Now, I was a confident man of eighteen making quite a sum of money for one so young. No longer was my wardrobe confined to that charcoal grey suit with the maroon tie. Now, I had a dozen suits and I couldn't count the ties. I was making at least two hundred dollars a week in tips alone and had a bank balance the envy of many an older man. I understood now why the married Cunarders owned the houses in the best part of town and lived at a standard much higher than other Englishmen. They drove flashy cars and had all the latest gadgets in their homes; many of which they brought back from the United States. No wonder the single Cunard steward was much sought after by the local girls who knew us by, "Cunard Yanks." We may have been popular with the girls in Southampton, especially those who were looking for a good time, but we were very unpopular with the local males: they considered us brash. We didn't consider them at all. Even my relationship with Johnny and Max wasn't the same. I began to think of them as dull, and they had already decided I had outgrown them. They had made this quite clear one night after I had been working on the QE for about three months.

We spent the evening in the usual way, arguing about what to do and then deciding on the pub and St. Theresa's. There was one difference, however, I never walked anywhere now; no matter how short the distance. I went by taxi.

"Bitterne Brewery," I said to the cab driver as the three of us jumped in.

"Why do you waste so much money?" asked Max with a shake of his head.

"Easy come, easy go," I replied pulling an extra inch of shirt sleeve down to expose an elaborate, expensive gold cufflink.

"You're not the same chap any more, Ken. And everyone notices it," John said.

"He's right, Ken. You know your mother is quite concerned about you, too. She's awfully worried," interrupted Max.

"Mum is always worried and concerned about me, but she needn't be. I'm no different, just older, that's all," I said as I took a cigarette from a gold case.

The taxi stopped: the fare was fifty cents. "Keep the change," I said as I handed the driver a five dollar note.

"Who are you trying to impress?" John said disgustedly.

"That's the smallest change I had and I didn't want to appear cheap, waiting for change," I explained, but it still came out boastful.

John and Max made their way to the door of the public bar. "Wait up, let's go in here," I motioned toward the lounge entrance. They both kind of shrugged and followed me.

About a dozen scattered people were reclining in the plush chairs, the coffee tables were filled with dishes of cheddar cheese cubes and nuts. Percy had graduated also: he was now in charge of the lounge bar.

"Haven't seen the 'Three Musketeers' in a while," he said leaning over the bar. "What will it be, three pints of beer?"

"Do you have chilled beer?" I asked.

Percy gave me a look of disgust. "No, this isn't New York."

"Then make mine Scotch," I called after him as he went to get the drinks. "On the rocks!"

"On the 'what'?" asked John.

"Ice cubes. You wouldn't understand. That's American," I said placing a ten-dollar note on the bar.

Johnny and Max looked at each other in dismay, then reaching for their beers, turned toward the entrance of the public bar. John stopped for a moment and looked back. "Go home, Yank!"

CHAPTER FIVE

"Lord, I am not worthy . . . ."
Lk 7:6

It was amazing: the English called us "Yanks" and the Americans called us "Limeys." "Cunard Yanks" was a good name for us: we weren't the real thing. We had American tastes with British accents. I soon began to feel like a square peg in a round hole, trying to impress everyone on both sides of the sea. My newly attained sophistication backfired on me several times: on one occasion causing Big Jack real embarrassment.

I had decided to visit Big Jack in Philadelphia. That evening, he and Molly took me to the home of a very important business associate that Jack was trying very hard to impress. He led me around the room, introducing me to all the guests, "I want you to meet my little English brother," he would say proudly. "Say something, Ken, let them hear how cute you talk." I felt like

59

a performing parrot as I entertained them in my best St. Mary's accent, which at the time, I was trying desperately to lose. Nevertheless, I really put it on to please Jack: I knew how important it was to him and how much it pleased him.

After dinner, the women and men separated for coffee and small talk. The executive sat down beside me and blowing a cloud of cigar smoke in the air, he turned and asked me proudly, "Well, what do you think of my little woman?" I pondered for the right answer. How can I best compliment her? She isn't attractive, so I can't say she is beautiful. She didn't cook the meal so I can't comment on her culinary talent. She opened her home to me and made me feel very welcome and because of her friendly way, I really felt "at home" in her house: a trait that would be very commendable in England. That's it! I know exactly what I can say. I turned to the gentleman who was smiling kindly, waiting for my answer. "Sir, I must say, I found your wife extremely HOMELY!"

Big Jack choked on his cigar and looked at me in amazement. The husband said nothing and a dead silence fell upon the room. What did I do wrong? Later, when I learned the American meaning of the word, I was as shocked as Jack. I made my apologies and Jack aided with an explanation to my American host. I never felt more awkward, too English to be American, and too American to be English. Soon, I was even becoming uncomfortable at home: like most teen-agers, I felt Mum and Dad just didn't "understand" me. As I look back, I realize they understood me better than I understood myself.

"Will you be home for dinner tonight, Kenny? We're having roast beef and Yorkshire pudding, your favorite," Mum asked as she poured the tea.

"I'll be here to eat, Mum, but then I have to take off early. I'm meeting Eric this evening for a few laughs."

"Why don't you call on Johnny and Max? They ask about you all the time." I could see concern in Mum's eyes.

"Not tonight. I promised Eric that he and I would give as many girls possible the pleasure of our company," I said jokingly, but then realized Mum didn't think of it as much of a "joke."

"I'm worried about you, Kenny. I never know if you're being serious or not." She sat across from me at the table and I had the feeling that she was getting ready to have one of those "heart to heart talks." Rather than upsetting her any more, I became serious and tried to offer her assurance.

"You needn't worry, Mum. You know I just like to tease you. Besides, you know I haven't missed one morning serving Mass on ship since the day I started." I saw a look of relief on her face, but I felt guilty inside, because although it was true I had been faithful to my daily Mass attendance, I knew it was more out of habit than commitment.

"I'm proud of that, Kenny, but I still worry about the way you act. You place too much value on material things, like always talking about the money you're making now and . . . ."

"That reminds me," I interrupted. "I forgot to tell you. Now since I'm eighteen, I'm eligible for men's rating on the ship. That means I can earn more than twice the money I'm making now. But here's the best part, Mum, Pete just received his first class rating and he was placed as a first-class waiter due to his present position, Captain's Commis." I rattled on excitedly, but Mum showed no reaction. "Don't you understand, Mum? I'm sure to get the same rating since I'm the Chief Steward's Commis. Mum, I can be earning triple the money

I am right now." Still no reaction. I tried harder to make her share my enthusiasm. "Mum, a waiter on the QE in the first class section is one of the most sought after jobs there are. Men twice my age are striving for this position and it's going to be mine. In just a short time I'll be working in the plushest restaurant on the sea, or the land, too, for that matter." She just looked at me and I had the feeling she was searching my soul. The more she stared, the more nervous I became and the more I kept talking. "If you could just see that first class dining room, Mum. The Queen herself, doesn't dine more elegantly . . . and the people that sit at these tables . . . the most important people in the world, film stars, celebrities, royalty, politicians . . . ."

"I must go now, Kenny," this time, she interrupted me.

"Where?"

"I'm going to visit the sisters and pray a while in their chapel. I can always think better there. I'll say some special prayers for you, Kenny . . . so that you find whatever you're looking for." She stood and walked toward me, then bent down and kissed my cheek. "I'll see you at supper. See that you're not late. Good-bye, dear. God bless," she said closing the door behind her.

"God bless," I called after her. I don't understand Mum. All this worrying and what for? I'm just not a kid anymore—Doesn't she realize?—I'm a man! I'm glad I'm meeting Eric tonight—Wonder what he has planned for a few laughs—

The next trip I overslept and arrived late in the chapel one morning. Then it happened. It was quite full and one of the passengers was already serving Mass. The priest was at the gospel so I stood by the door in order to disturb as few people as possible: I knelt there for the rest of the Mass. As I was leaving, an elderly American lady, elegantly dressed, stopped me. "Excuse me, young man. Can you spare a moment?" she asked with a gentle smile.

"Well, not exactly. You see Mam, I'm already late for duty," I said looking down at my watch. It was docking day and the chief ate early.

"Then perhaps you could come to my suite before we dock?" She wrote her room number on a business card.

After breakfast, I searched for her cabin. I wonder what she wants me for—I knocked on the door. "Yes," answered the stewardess as she opened the door. I showed her the business card and explained, "Mrs. Diskin wishes to see me."

When I entered her cabin, she was checking the last minute items to go in her small luggage, then she asked me to be seated.

"I hope you don't think me peculiar, young man, but something extraordinary happened this morning at Mass," she said as she placed her hands on the sides of her lounge chair. "Let me explain, . . . You see my brother was a priest, he was much younger than I and he died the beginning of this year." She looked at me very intently. "Well, I promised God to find a replacement for him at the altar and hence this trip. I asked the Blessed Mother to search with me and show me a sign when I found him." She paused for a moment. What is she telling me all this for? "I've watched you serve Mass every morning since I've been aboard this ship, but today you weren't there. This morning it happened. During the consecration a shaft of sunlight came through the window and you were kneeling right in it." She had a look of ecstasy on her face. This woman is a nut!—I better get out of here. "If you would give all this up and decide to become a priest, I will pay your expenses. What is your answer?"

"Well, I must think about it," I replied and made a quick excuse to leave.

"Promise me you will write and let me know your decision. I'm certain the Blessed Mother and I have 'found him in the temple.' " Those were her final words. I made my way to the door in a hurry.

Outside in the alley, Eric was passing. "There's a real nut in there!" I caught his arm. "You're not going to believe this, but this lady . . . ." I recounted the whole story and finished by saying, "A priest, can you imagine me, a priest?"

"Hell no!" Eric laughed.

I dropped her business card into the trash can, shook my head in disbelief and walked away laughing.

Before the end of the complete crossing, I decided to go to the writer's office and pick up my first class rating. I can see the slip now, KENNETH JOHN ROBERTS: —FIRST CLASS WAITER. I gave the clerk my name and waited as he went rummaging through some files.

"Roberts, yes. You have adult rating in your next contract," he said studying the open file.

"Could you tell me what the rating is?" I asked again, certain of his reply. After all, I knew French and hadn't I attended the best school in Southampton? And I had been Dizzy's commis for a year, meeting the most important passengers on ship—It was really stupid of me to ask.

"Tourist class waiter," answered the clerk. "Next!" he said resting his eyes on the man behind me.

"Tourist class waiter!" There must be some mistake. Tourist class, down with all those emigrants—cabin class would have been better, at least the majority of those passengers were still American, but "tourist."

How was I going to make a living from all those emigrants?

Mother was amused when I told her of my misfortune. "It will be good for you, son. You need to learn humility. You know what our Blessed Lord said about that: 'He that exults himself.' "

"Yes Mother, I remember." How could I forget when since I was small, she had been drumming this lesson over and over again. Like the time she brought a tramp home and made us wait on him, reminding us that what we did for the least of our brethren, we do for Christ. Or the time, when she brought home the drunken woman, filthy from head to toe, dressed in rags. She left our house bathed and dressed expensively in clothes and accessories donated by Mum. As she left, Mum said, "How good God is to us, son, to give us all these opportunities to show we love Him."

How could I forget what Christ had said, when Mum was a living example of humility? I guess I was a bad student, that's all.

I wasn't too excited about sailing day my next trip: the tourist accommodations were drab compared to the exotic luxury of the first class, which I became so accustomed to. The dining room was cramped with long tables that could have been appropriate for the scene of the "Last Supper." They seated twelve people, fourteen, if you used the end seats. One waiter was assigned to each table. I was miserable as I set the necessary silver. I don't even know any of the crew down here, either—This is like starting on a new ship—They told me I was assigned down here because I had no dining room experience and Pete had been waiting on the Captain's table for about two years—That makes sense—I'll just have to start at the bottom and work my way back up

—It's just going to take a little longer to become the Restaurant Manager or Chief Steward—It won't take long—I'll show them—

"First trip, mate?" asked a young waiter with a cockney accent.

"No, I've been the Chief Steward's commis in the first class for the past year," I answered disgustedly.

"Find it different down here, you will," he continued.

"Yes, I've already noticed," my St. Mary's accent contrasted extremely noticeably.

"Coo 'e talks posh, don't 'e?" said his companion. "You 'ad bettar get rid of those fancy ways down 'ere, mate . . . not 'ere to impress anybody, just serve the food," he added with a mocking grin.

"Sure had," the first waiter agreed. "My name is Bill. If you need any help, just yell."

How uncouth! If only there was somebody down here with some culture, I thought snobbishly.

I was used to serving drinks and I knew how to read a French menu, but I wasn't prepared for this. I had to serve fourteen passengers in one hour then serve fourteen more: and this was for all three meals a day. I hadn't even taken the dessert orders yet when the second setting was already crowding the glass entrance doors like a bunch of vultures. And the orders were another matter: even with the use of a pad and pencil, I never could remember who got what. My head was swimming as I fumbled with trays, becoming more flustered by the minute.

"Let me help you get this," offered Bill. "The next sitting is about ready." Thank God!

The doors opened and the second group stampeded like cattle, grabbing chairs and thowing orders at me like mad. Could Moon Mullins and Dizzy have started like this?

The second day on the job proved to be even more

disastrous. In a state of false confidence, I balanced a dozen different dishes on one tray and went through the exit instead of the entrance to the dining room only to be met by a waiter coming toward me at rapid speed. BAM! Up went the tray and the dozen dishes. He and I both, were covered from head to foot in tomato soup and Russian dressing, topped off with mashed potatoes and gravy plus many other delicacies. This started a chain reaction: other waiters bumped into each other, some falling on the slippery floor, depositing even more food on the already crowded exit: all this accompanied by the loud bangs and clash of falling silver and the choicest of Anglo-Saxon words. It looked like an old-time slapstick movie, but unfortunately, I was the stooge. I knew by now that I was a failure as a tourist waiter.

After six months, I had enough. I was offered the opportunity to work as a first class waiter on the *Andes*, a Royal Mail Ocean Liner. Regretfully, I said good-bye to the *Queen Elizabeth* and signed on the *Andes*.

The trip was not outstanding on the *Andes*: I had less to do on this ship than when I was Chief Steward's commis. I did the round trip to Argentina and Brazil and back with only five passengers to wait on, three times a day. The rest of the time I spent reading and sunbathing on deck. One big thing did happen: it took me away from the North American scene. I was no longer a "Cunard Yank" and with so much time on my hands, I had time to think and evaluate my life.

Every morning, I served Mass for my namesake, Archbishop Roberts, S.J., the Archbishop of Bombay. He was acting as chaplain for the round trip. With so little to distract me, the habit of daily Mass began to have its effect. By the time I arrived back in Southampton, I was nineteen and thinking along different lines. Perhaps

God was calling me to the priesthood after all? Was all this His way of showing me what I must do? Did He take me away from all the tinsel to let me see how phony my life was becoming? If only I hadn't thrown that lady's business card away—Maybe she wasn't a nut after all!

I was nervous when I approached the breakfast table that first morning home. "Good morning, Mum," I said kissing her on the cheek.

"Kenny, I want to talk with you before the others come down. You seem different, more content." She sat down beside me at the table and was about to continue when Dad came in. Roy and Jack followed close behind. Mum stood and began to set the food on the table.

"You look black. I'm sure all that sun doesn't do your skin any good," Dad said taking a chair across from me and unfolded the paper.

"He looks healthier than his usual anemic night-club color," added Jackie as he kissed Mum on the cheek.

"How's it going, Ken?" asked Roy as he reached for the pot of hot tea.

"Fine . . . I guess."

"You guess? Have you found a new ship?" Roy asked sipping his tea.

"No, I haven't looked for any to tell you the truth."

"Then what do you intend to do now?" Roy showed real interest.

"Well . . . don't laugh at me, but I've been thinking about the priesthood."

Dad dropped his newspaper and actually laughed. "The priesthood! If you make the priesthood, I'll become a Catholic, that is, if miracles still happen."

"Are you serious? You wouldn't joke about something this sacred, Kenny . . . Would you?" Mum looked at me searchingly and with just a trace of shock.

"I think he is, Mother," said Roy.

"If that's what you want, Kenny," then she added quickly, "If that's what God wants."

Jackie just sat there saying nothing turning his head from one side to the other as if watching a ping-pong match.

"For goodness sake, be practical, woman. Who is going to pay for him to go through college? Even if they would be stupid enough to accept him, where would we get the money," Dad shouted then turned to me. "Why don't you enlist in the army, that's a man's career and forget all this nonsense."

"I know we can't afford it dear, with you being retired and all, but if it's God's will, He will supply the means," Mother said softly.

"I wish I had saved my money instead of blowing it away," I added.

"Don't worry, Kenny. We'll start a novena (nine days of prayer) today. God will show us the way. Have faith son." Mum squeezed my hand as if to offer me confidence.

"You're all crazy, if you ask me," Dad got up from the table and threw his chair back in disgust.

"I think you would make a very good priest, Ken." Roy patted me on the back.

"You're really not kidding. I don't believe it," was Jackie's only contribution to the conversation!

I wasted no time in getting to work on what seemed to be the impossible task of contacting Mrs. Diskin. The Cunard office offered to forward a letter to her for me since it was a policy of the company not to give out the addresses of their clientele. It didn't take long for her reply: she reconfirmed her offer. Now, I had only to approach the bishop.

Father Walshe didn't seem too convinced, but he promised to arrange a visit with the bishop for me. In the meantime, Mum was visiting the Sisters who were now doubling up on their prayers for our special intention. In two weeks, at our parish picnic, Bishop King would speak at the opening ceremony. Father Walshe said I would be able to speak with him at that time. All I needed was his official acceptance!

Bishop King was a kindly old man in his seventies. Dressed in the red of an Archbishop, with white bushy eyebrows, red cheeks, blue twinkling eyes and a happy smile, he looked like St. Nick, himself.

"Well Kenneth, so you want to be a priest . . . ."

"Yes, your Grace, even if I am a late vocation," I answered nervously.

He laughed heartily. "Nineteen is hardly a late vocation."

I gave him an account of my life thus far then showed him the letter from Mrs. Diskin.

"I'll phone Father Tigar, the rector of Osterley College to interview you. It's a Jesuit House of Studies: Father Tigar trains all my students, what few I have. I'll let him decide on your suitability."

The Jesuits didn't waste any time. A week later I received a letter, brief and to the point:

> Dear Kenneth:
> Please report to me for an interview, next Saturday at 4 p.m., prompt.
> Clement Tigar, S.J.

The English Jesuits don't waste words!

Father Tigar was a well disciplined man: his eyes seemed to read my very soul as he stared at me intently while I tried to answer his many questions.

"Why do you want to be a priest?"

"To save my soul and the souls of others."

"You can do that as a simple Christian," he replied.

I didn't know the answer to that one: he never once showed any external sign whether or not my succeeding answers were correct.

"I would like you to wait another year, but keep in contact with me." He looked at his desk diary. "Yes, it's August now. Write me on August 15th next year, if you still want to be a priest." He raised his hand to give a blessing. The interview was obviously over.

I wasn't too disappointed: entering the seminary was a serious matter and I didn't want this to be a rushed romance. Besides it would give me time to prepare myself spiritually and I could earn some money to help defray all the expenses that Mrs. Diskin so generously took on herself for my sake. I took a job as a shoe clerk in a high class shop: the only salesman there, the rest were girls. I was very careful to avoid any involvement with any of them. My goals were set: nothing would distract them.

It was just like the old days, with Johnny and Max, except this time I influenced them for the better. They decided to become Catholic and Mum and I were their godparents. Instead of that last beer before going home, we made a visit to the chapel at St. Theresa's. I was happy, and although I was anxious awaiting my entrance to the seminary, I was content because I knew at the end of the year I would be beginning my studies at Osterley, the first step to the great day when I would be FATHER KENNETH J. ROBERTS.

On August 15th, I sat down and composed my letter

71

to Father Tigar as I had promised. I wanted to be as honest as I possibly could: I wanted to bare my soul to him so that he would realize my spiritual level. I hid nothing from him when describing the temptations and frustrations of the past year. Mum and I awaited his reply, talking constantly of the many things that had to be done before my entrance, both of us were so certain of his reply. Finally it came!

"Mum, it's here! It's here!" I screamed as I ran into the house with the half opened envelope. I pulled out the letter and unfolded it. When would I start?—What clothes will I need?—My eyes went racing across the printed copy.

> Dear Kenneth:
> Forget all idea of the priesthood. Serve God as an apostolic layman.
> Yours in Christ,
> Clement Tigar, S.J.

I couldn't believe it! The shock and disappointment were too much for me. I threw the letter on the table and ran upstairs to my room. I hadn't cried since that day at St. Charles. I knelt down and sobbed. God, no! Not another failure—LORD, I AM NOT WORTHY!

CHAPTER SIX

"I must also see Rome . . . ."
Ac 19:20

In three weeks I would be twenty-one, a man: and a man fought for what he wanted and believed. I wanted to be a priest and I believed God wanted it too, but how could I go about it?

"What do you intend to do now, son?" Mum asked as she pulled weeds from her lily bed.

"I wanted to talk to you about that. I was thinking perhaps I'll take a few weeks off and go to Rome and Lourdes. I've saved a little money for the seminary: right now I can't think of a better way to use it. It would be like my own private pilgrimage. I don't know what I'll achieve, but I feel I'll find something even if it's peace of mind. What do you think?" I stooped down to gather some of the weeds.

"A vacation would do you good, Kenny. I know how you feel son." She leaned over and picked up a long thin stick. "Hand me that string, will you dear?"

"Do you really know how how I feel right now? Mum, I was so sure that God wanted me to be a priest. It's like I wanted this more than anything in my whole life. . . . It was something inside me just bursting to get out . . . Mum, it's almost shaken my faith." I watched her fumble with the stick and string for a moment. "What are you doing with that?"

"See this lily, son. The bloom is so large that the stem can't bear the weight, so I'm letting this stick help support it." She finished tying it together then wiped her hands on her apron and looked at me very intently. "That lily is much like you right now, Kenny. The bloom is your strong desire and belief that the priesthood is for you, but that stem is like your faith. Right now it needs a little support: maybe this pilgrimage will be the 'stick.' Now, come along son, I'll make you some tea and we'll talk about your trip."

Within two days, I was ready to go: I packed a large brown back pack with a British flag sewn on the top

73

flap. I felt this would be very handy since I decided to hitch-hike once I reached Paris. Brother Michael from St. Mary's gave me a list of the cities where the Brothers had houses in Europe, along with a letter of introduction.

I boarded the cross channel steamer from Southampton to Le Havre: from there I took a bus to the station where the train left for Paris. I was exhausted from carrying the heavy pack, winding and weaving in and out through the crowd. It didn't take long for the rhythmic motion and hum of the train to lull me to sleep. "Ici Paris! Ici Paris!" cried a voice as the train came to a grinding halt. I slipped my arms through the supporting straps and climbed down the platform. Now I need only to find a taxi and I can make my way to College St. François Xavier, one of the houses designated by Brother Michael.

The Brothers couldn't have been friendlier. I was given a room and invited to eat with the small community. One Brother spent the whole day showing me the sights of Paris: Nôtre Dame, Sacré Coeur, Montemartre, Arc de Triomphe, the sidewalk artists and the street cafés. So this is Paris!

The next morning, I was up early for Mass, then after a quick continental breakfast of café au lait and bread rolls, I was ready for the road. The same kind Brother personally escorted me to the outskirts of Paris and dropped me off at a suitable place for hitch-hiking. I thanked him profusely and promised to pray for him at Rome and Lourdes. Now, my adventure would really begin!

I felt self-conscious with the pack on my back: people were staring at me. I wish I had left that flag off, I thought as I passed a bunch of noisy kids. They were all pointing and yelling, "Anglais!" I'll just walk for a while till I get past all these passers-by, then I'll hitch a ride—if I get the nerve—Maybe this idea of hitch-hiking wasn't such a good idea after all. If only they wouldn't stare so—The English wouldn't be so rude as to stare—Haven't they ever seen a hitch-hiker before? —Maybe it's just I've never been one before—I better start getting used to it—One advantage, I can speak the language—That's a comforting thought.

"Où allez vous?" [where are you going?] A voice broke into my thoughts.

"Rome, Italy," I said, hopefully.

"I'm not going *that* far, just ten miles down the road, but you're welcome," the driver said in rapid French reaching to open the door for me.

"So you are going to Rome?" He looked straight at me whenever he spoke. I wish he would look at the road.

"Yes," I replied nervously as the car swerved almost leaving the road.

He offered me a cigarette, taking both hands from the wheel, then he began talking a mile a minute illustrating his whole conversation with his hands. Why doesn't he watch what he's doing? I'm glad he isn't going very far—my nerves couldn't stand the strain. I was grateful when he dropped me off, not only for his generosity in giving me a ride, but that the ride was over.

I hoisted my pack again and began to walk. The air felt good as I walked briskly, looking over my shoulder at the rapidly passing traffic. If only I could bring myself to thumb a car: I still felt too self-conscious. A big army truck pulled up alongside me: it had USA markings and a GI was at the wheel.

"How far are you going, Mac?" he shouted.

"Actually, I'm going to Rome. I know you're not

going that far," I added stupidly, "but I would appreciate a ride no matter how short the distance."

"Hop in, Limey. I'm going as far as Fontainebleau. That should help you out some."

I really enjoyed the ride with the GI. He explained that he was stationed on a small base and had been in France for about four years. His knowledge of the customs was invaluable to me. One thing he emphasized was their manner of greeting.

"These French really go for the handshake here, everytime they meet and everytime they leave. Everybody shakes hands with everybody. It's wild!" He nodded his head in amusement, then continued, "And when they're really friendly or like you, they kiss." He turned to me and winked, "On both cheeks, of course!" We both laughed and compared our homeland customs with that of the French.

"Well, this is as far as I go. If you look on your map, you can see the next big city is Orléans. With a little luck, maybe you can pick up a ride and spend the night there. Good luck!"

I thanked him and waved good-bye: I was really sorry the ride was over this time. I wondered when I would have an opportunity to speak English again. Once again I began to walk.

It was late afternoon now: I must have walked quite a few miles. Wonder how far? I have to get over being embarrassed to thumb—How are cars going to know that I want a ride?—Well, they can see the flag on my pack—That should tell them something—Besides, it will be dark before long and I don't want to be stuck out here in the country for the night—My feet and back are beginning to get sore—I'll just stop for a short rest, then I'll thumb. Just as I was lifting the pack from my back, a small Citroën stopped by me. This time there were two passengers, both little old ladies. They told me they were on their way to Orléans. Thank God!

I began to climb in the back seat when the driver directed me to put my pack there and take my place in the front. How thoughtful of them!—The front seat in these small cars is always more comfortable and that sweet little old lady is going to give up her place for me. I take back all those ugly thoughts I had about the French when they were staring at me. I took my seat and smiled gratefully to the little old lady who had stepped out of the car. She smiled back then told me to scoot over. She must be kidding—The three of us can't possibly fit in here—No, she's not kidding, I thought as suddenly I was sandwiched between the two. They began giggling and chattering on and on, asking me a thousand questions: they were obviously enjoying themselves very much. I wished I could trade places with my pack!

Finally, we reached Orléans and it was already quite late.

"You may drop me off at a hotel, if you don't mind," I said kindly.

"Why don't you stay at our place and save your money," they offered.

"No, really I've imposed enough, but thank you all the same."

There was no response: we kept weaving in and out of one street to another. Where are they taking me? We already passed many hotels.

"Is there any special hotel you had in mind?" asked the driver.

"Yes, the next one we come to will be fine!" We went two more blocks. *"Voila un hôtel,"* I said emphatically. The car stopped at last and I grabbed my pack from the back seat hurriedly before they changed their minds and started off again. I thanked them and shook their hands vigorously: I remembered what the GI told me, so I stopped abruptly. I didn't want to be too friendly!

The next morning I arose early and attended the 6 a.m. Mass at a nearby church. It was quite nostalgic as I meditated that here I was in the city of St. Joan of Arc. After the usual continental breakfast, I was back on the road again: this time my destination was Bourges. If I could make it there by lunch, I may be able to get pretty far today.

I had only been walking a short time when a car stopped: this time a Jaguar. I welcomed the luxury after that cramped ride the night before. The driver told me he was going to Bourges: I was really in luck. After some conversation, he asked me why I was making this journey. He had already shown evidence that he too was Catholic so I told him of the events that led up to my trip. I was glad we hit on a common subject, but surprised to learn that although most of the French citizens claim to be Catholic, most of the working class in the cities did not practice, yet the people in the rural areas were very religious. He sympathized with my situation since he had a brother, a priest and two sisters who were nuns. I accepted his invitation to have lunch with him when we reached Bourges.

The luncheon was quite elaborate: much more than I was used to since I had started this trip. We had a cocktail before lunch, wine with the meal, and liqueurs afterwards. By the time he left me off outside the town about seven miles, I was beginning to feel a little drowsy. I couldn't resist the temptation to stop for a short siesta after I bid him farewell.

The chill in my bones caused me to stir. It was dusk and the sun was beginning to set behind the distant trees. I jumped up: I hadn't intended to sleep this long. I looked at my watch—6:30!—I've wasted the whole afternoon. I picked up the pack and marched off slinging it over my back. The cars whizzed by: they don't see me too well in this half light.

Four hours later, I was still walking and the cars were still whizzing by. There's no sign of life out here, no sign of a town in sight, not even lights—How I would welcome the sight of those two old ladies now— At least I'm not cold any more—That steep hill looks like a mountain—I hope something's over the top— anything.

I had worked up a sweat by the time I reached the top of the hill, but I was relieved to see lights in the distance. I judged it to be about two miles away—Thank goodness. I really have been lucky so far, though: I haven't really had to walk terribly long at one stretch until now—And all those people I have met—It's like an education. This has been a great way to learn about people, and really, I suppose they're the same all over.

Finally, I came to the town; actually it was more like a very small hamlet. I walked up the narrow street: there were a few small shops, a couple of bars and a church, all situated around a small square. Some men sat drinking at tables outside a sidewalk café. This place looks pretty good—There seems to be a boarding house set up behind this small drinking and eating area —Maybe, I'm in luck. I walked into the café placing my pack on the floor by the door.

"Can you accommodate me with a room?" I asked in my best French.

"For how long?" asked a fat lady behind the bar. Her French didn't seem to be the same dialect that I had been used to thus far.

"All night," I answered.

"Certainly." She turned and motioned to a young

girl, whom I presumed to be her daughter, then directed me to follow her.

"Could I have something to eat first?" I asked, flopping in a chair at one of the tables.

"You want to eat now?" asked the fat lady surprised.

It was difficult making conversation as my school French was devoid of any slang and although I spoke French quite well, I wasn't familiar with any of the dialect. Most of the conversation was unintelligible to me. They seemed to understand me quite well, but what they had to say to me didn't always make any sense.

I looked around the room: several girls sat around smiling at me. One of them winked. In England that would be considered flirtatious, I thought, but then we would never kiss each other on both cheeks as a sign of greeting either—Maybe that's the local custom here of greeting a stranger. I winked back.

The young girl rose from her chair and took a seat opposite me.

"What would you like to eat, some cheese?"

"I was hoping I could have something more substantial: I feel like I need to recuperate my strength. Could I have a steak?" She nodded "yes." "And perhaps some French fries and Camembert cheese." She began to walk away with my order. "May I have a bottle of Vin Rouge, too?" Again she nodded affirmatively.

The girls were laughing about something, but I couldn't understand what they were saying: I just looked at them and smiled. When the young girl came back with my food, she placed it in front of me, then sat back down again. These people are certainly friendly, I thought.

"Have you done this before?" she asked.

"No, the first time was in Paris just a couple of days ago," I answered, presuming she was talking about the hitch-hiking, since we had just finished retracing my trip thus far.

"You must be quite experienced now," she said winking at the other girls and they all began to laugh.

I wish I knew what is so funny. Perhaps, it's my accent, although the Brothers at Southampton told me my accent was perfect.

"Where are you going from here?" she asked again.

"To Rome, then Lourdes," I replied. "I'm making kind of a private pilgrimage." With this remark, their laughing became louder, but I was becoming annoyed.

"You are going to Lourdes?" The young girl was apparently amused.

"Yes, I hope to find a seminary that will accept me. I want to become a priest." I noticed the laughing and giggling suddenly subsided.

"A *Catholic* priest?" she asked raising her eyebrows in astonishment.

"Yes!" I was quite emphatic.

"And the Church lets you do this sort of thing in England?"

"Of course. What better way is there to broaden one's mind and learn about people. Already, I have learned a lot about the French and the local customs . . . I would never have had these opportunities if I had gone by train." She said nothing, just sat there staring. I wonder why she is so baffled about that.

I finished my steak and downed the last drop of wine. "Could you show me to my room, now?" I asked politely.

A few minutes later I realized the humor of the situation when she brought me to my room. This was no ordinary hotel and we hadn't been discussing "hitch-hiking." "You can't stay here. I'm going to be a priest!" I said to her as she began to undress.

The next morning, I made a quick exit. Many of the

local inhabitants had seen me enter the night before and a small crowd of young people were gathered near the door laughing as I left with my pack. There were several ladies on their way to church just a few doors away: they turned to look at the small commotion. Perhaps, it would be wise for me to skip Mass today— They would never understand.

My next big town would be Lyon: I headed for the highway. While walking I chuckled to myself as I recalled the humor of the whole incident. How could I be so naive? Why didn't I realize it immediately? The setting and situation should have been quite obvious— anyway, all's well that ends well—I must be more careful in the future, or at least, more aware.

An open convertible crowded with eight young people passed me then stopped a little way ahead. "Where are you going?" the driver shouted, smiling from ear to ear.

"Rome," I called back quickening my pace.

"We are going to Lyon. Do you want to come?"

"Yes, thank you. But do you have the room?" I asked.

"We'll make room!" And we took off down the road "like a bat out of hell."

This turned out to be one of the most enjoyable days on my whole trip. As we drove we sang and laughed: everyone seemed to enjoy just being together, sharing. When we reached Lyon, they invited me to book in the same hotel with them, then they would take me to Grenoble the next day. I accepted the invitation. We all attended Mass together the next morning: they were all members of the Young Catholic Movement. To see these young people enjoying life, every minute of it, yet committing themselves to a real cause, strengthened my faith in the Church of tomorrow. I was sad as I bid each of them a fond adieu: and I was very glad to exercise the French greeting with these happy people. A hand-shake and a simple good-bye would not have seemed sufficient for me to show how much I enjoyed being with my new friends.

In Grenoble, I decided I wasn't going to take any more chances when it came to finding lodging. I searched out a church and consulted the pastor. He told me of an old church which had an enormous crypt laid out as a dormitory for the mountain climbers. When I arrived, it was still early. A young priest showed me to the basement dormitory where I had the pick of fifty cots, all laid out close together. The only other person there was a Benedictine Monk from Holland: he was lying on a cot, fully clothed in his habit.

I turned in early, but I was awakened about midnight by voices in the crowded basement, men and women were running around in different stages of at-tire. One woman was clad only in her black underwear as she walked past me toward the bathroom carrying a toothbrush. The Dutch monk looked at my shocked ex-pression, then laughed. "This is France, son!" he said, then turned to his side to go back to sleep.

The next morning I served Mass for the Dutch monk and had breakfast with him. Once again, I headed for the highway: this time toward the Swiss border. Travel-ing was very slow and difficult as I was now in the mountain country. By late evening I arrived in a little town, Bourg St. Mauritz, on the French side of the Swiss border. I was tired from the long walk and mountain air so I went directly to the parish church to ask about lodging for the night. I thought it best to get some rest: I hadn't slept much the night before.

The priest looked at me somewhat suspiciously as I told him I was a pilgrim traveling to Rome and Lourdes. I was beginning to look more like a tramp. I skipped shaving that morning and my clothes were very unpressed. He led me to the church and up the spiral staircase to the bell tower. "I don't need free accommodations, Father. I have money." He said nothing: he just kept leading me along. Oh well, I don't want to offend him. I'll accept his hospitality anyway.

On the floor, directly under the bells, which were at a much higher level, was a mattress and a blanket. I thanked him and he left me. I heard him bolt the door that led from the tower to the church. Maybe, he's afraid of theft, I thought. Soon it was dark: I lay down to sleep.

DONG—DONG—DONG. I counted the heavy sonorous chimes as the tower vibrated, eight. It must be eight o'clock. Don't tell me this thing is going to ring every hour. It was worse than that. The DONGS, every hour, were answered by DINGS every fifteen minutes. Immediately my heart swelled with compassion for Quasimodo. I'm going to be built like him too, I thought, as I cramped my knees to my chest and gripped my head with my arms trying desperately to shut out the noise. In the darkness, I felt something furry close to my face. I put out my hand to brush it away. It feels like a kitten. I struck a match. There it was. A rat! In the light of the flame, both of us stared at each other hypnotized with fear. It can't be, "RATS IN THE BELFRY!"

Morning couldn't come soon enough. It didn't take me long to hop the first bus to Turin. Soon, I would be in Rome. The bus climbed the mountain roads: they curved almost in circles as slowly we reached a higher level, higher, higher, higher, and even higher. At last, we reached the summit. What a breathtaking view! The snow-capped peaks enveloped us.

When we started the descent into Italy, our speed increased as our bus hugged the cliff edge. I held on to the seat in front as the bus took each successive circular curve on what appeared to be two wheels. My anxiety increased as each oncoming bus missed us by inches as it passed. It was like the big dipper at Coney Island, with one exception: on that ride you knew you were safe. Here comes another bus towards us—I'll close my eyes—This one look like it's heading straight for us. The horn blared—This is it! "Oh my God, I am heartily sorry for having offended thee . . . ."

That night in Turin, I dined with one hundred and fifty seminarians visiting Italy from France at the Salesian seminary. I was happy to have their company for that morning when I reached Italy, I realized I had a problem I had completely dismissed until I tried to find this seminary: I didn't speak the language. For this reason, I decided to confine my mode of travel to buses and trains: hitch-hiking was definitely out.

Rome at last! I can't believe it. I jumped from the train onto the platform dragging my pack behind me. Everybody is so noisy . . . I can't wait to leave this terminal and take my first look at the Eternal City. I quickened my pace as my excitement increased.

The square outside was unbelievable. It was massive. The fountains sent up gigantic sprays which danced in artificial light. The buildings too were bathed in light like actors on a stage. And in this square, the station itself stood out in all its modern regalness as the lead character. So this is the Eternal City! I'm glad I arrived at night to see it dressed so formally.

After approaching four taxis, I finally found one with a driver who could speak reasonably good English. I asked him to take me to an English church: this was done with some difficulty, however. He kept saying "Turch?" and I kept saying "No, church!" Before I knew it I was using the exaggerated hand gestures as much as he. I tried to illustrate by arching my hands together and crossing my index fingers as if to form a cross on top a steeple. "Church! Church! E-N-G-L-I-S-H church!" I said nodding then waited for a sign of recognition. "Yes, yes," he said blessing himself and gesturing as if he were praying, "A TURCH!" Why didn't I think of that?

The driver was typical of all Italians. In the middle of conversation, one which I found extremely difficult to understand, he would stop to scream rudely to another driver, then continued where he left off as if he had never been interrupted at all.

The pastor at the English church told me of a very nice convent that took in short stay boarders: this time the driver had no difficulty in understanding his directions. The pastor told him where to take me in Italian, a favor I was grateful for. I sat back in the taxi and enjoyed the scenic ride. We passed the Colosseum, the Victor Emmanuel Monument, and every few blocks, the driver would point out a structure that still stood from the time of Caesar. I was completely fascinated. The driver was amused by my excitement, and I think he enjoyed my enthusiasm. Whenever he pointed his finger, I jumped up and peered in that direction waiting to find a new surprise.

We stopped at an intersection and he motioned for me to look straight ahead. A very pretty girl was walking slowly across the street. When we started up again, the car swerved and we almost ended up on the curb: the driver was still watching the girl.

"Very nice, yes?" he said as he twisted his index finger into his cheek, then he continued his account of the state of the Church in Italy.

My room at the convent boarding house was more than adequate, it was beautiful. I cleaned up hurriedly and made my way to the dining room. Two men and a woman were already seated: the men stood when I entered to introduce themselves.

"I'm Paul, an archeology student," said a young American with a crew cut. "And this is Mary, a magazine reporter . . . also American. And this is Don Guido, a priest."

"A suspended priest!" Don Guido added shaking my hand. I couldn't believe his strong resemblance to the film star, Charles Boyer.

"I'm Ken Roberts. I'm on a pilgrimage from England."

After sharing a delightful meal and an equally delightful conversation, Don Guido looked at me and half smiling, said, "You seemed shocked when I told you I am suspended."

I swallowed hard to cover my awkwardness, and took a sip from my wine glass. "I've never met an ex-priest before," I stammered. They all laughed.

"Don Guido is not an ex-priest, he is just suspended. He is still a priest. He is not allowed to say Mass or administer the sacraments, that's all," explained Mary.

"I see," I said, still confused and doubtful about my impressions of this man.

In the next two hours I learned the whole story about the complex little man. He was an army chaplain during the war and had seen quite a bit of killing and suffering: he spent the last years of the war with the underground fighters in Greece. They were a Communist group. After the war, he started working with the war-orphaned boys of Rome: there were thousands. Many of them had taken to a life of crime in order to survive. Out of such boys, he built up a flourishing community of self-supporting youth. Then came a bitter disagreement with the church authorities about how to organize and administer this community. The authorities relieved him of his charges by appointing another priest to fill his post. This led him to an irreconcilable state of conflict with both the Church and state authorities. The result was his present status as a suspended priest. It was sad because he was a man of God ahead of his time, a man who loved Christ and who truly saw the suffering Christ in mankind.

In the next two days, I came to know my new friends very well. Paul took me sight-seeing on his motor scooter throughout Rome. One day, we spent the whole afternoon visiting the catacombs. Don Guido and I spent many hours discussing religion. I told him of my aspirations for the priesthood and he said he would try to help me find a seminary, although in his present position, I couldn't see how. Mary arranged for me to obtain a ticket for a Papal audience. I was overwhelmed with the thought of seeing the Holy Father himself!

The atmosphere was tense with anticipation as about five thousand people crowded tightly into the small inside square in front of the palace in Castel Gandolfo. I was squashed in with a group of American Protestants.

"Where are you from?" asked a woman from the group.

"England."

"We are not Catholics. We have only come to get pictures to take home. The Pope is nothing to us," she said placing film in a camera.

Suddenly there was a great shout, "Viva il Papa!" The crowd shoved and pushed each other noisily, trying to get a better view. Everyone became ecstatic as a white figure appeared at the throne. It was Pope Pius XII. I felt a lump come into my throat as the vast crowd sank to its knees, including the American group of Protestants. The lady with the camera was visibly moved, as Pope Pius XII, successor of St. Peter, walked toward us blessing all in his path.

I spent my last dinner with Paul, Mary and Don Guido practically dominating the conversation: I related the account of the Papal audience starting with the very first minute to the last. Finally, Don Guido changed the topic with a surprising question. "How would you like to spend your last night in Rome taking me to a movie? I will translate for you. I've never been in a movie house before."

"Never been in a cinema? You're joking!"

"It's true, Ken. I've been a prisoner of a religious habit since I was a child of eight. Priests and religious are forbidden to enter places of amusement, scandal, you know." I was stunned. I listened closer as he went on to explain. "Here in Italy, you will see little children who can not be little children; teenagers, who will never be rebellious teenagers; and young men who will never be romantic young men because they wear a habit which they are not allowed to remove in public." He looked very intense, and picturesquely, he waved his hands to demonstrate his thoughts. "A whole world is closed to us. The world doesn't know us, and we don't know the world. Jesus knew the world and loved it. How can we change what we do not understand?" He concluded with a frustrated sigh.

"Yes, Father. I'll take you to a movie, any one you want to see," I said looking at him pityingly.

Don Guido looked funny as he skipped like a little child up the street whistling, his hands thrust deep into the pockets of his light blue slacks. His yellow shirt was open all the way to the third button exposing his chest. He passed a lamp-post and began to climb it. I was embarrassed watching a forty year old man act this way.

He let out a loud "Tarzan" yell as he swung from an overhanging tree branch. I hope nobody is looking at us. . . . They'll think he's crazy.

"You can't understand what it is to do these things, can you? This is freedom, freedom to be yourself. Freedom to walk down a street without people bowing to you, without people kissing your hands. Freedom to be unnoticed!"

I was amused. "Freedom to be unnoticed!" There won't be a soul in Rome that won't notice him if he keeps this up.

We came to the cinema entrance: he was like a little boy on a treat with his father as he looked at the billboard outside. "It's an American western," he said grinning from ear to ear.

I walked to the ticket counter. "Two," I said raising two fingers. I gave the tickets to Don Guido. He held them in his hand and looked about as if to catch everything in view as we entered the darkened cinema. An usher took the tickets from his hand and tore them in half. Don Guido grabbed the usher as if to hit him. I pulled him back just in time. "That man tore our tickets!" he protested.

"I'll explain inside," I said laughing as I led him away.

The next morning, I watched Don Guido as he knelt in prayer at Mass. He went to Mass and Communion every morning even though he couldn't say Mass himself. He looked so different in his cassock. I smiled as I thought of the night before. He is really a complex man, but I like him. Look how devoutly he prays and he thinks he is a cynic. Bless him, Lord. Help him be a proper priest again. A priest who can say Mass and forgive sins in Your Name. He has found you, Lord— Now, help him find himself!

After Mass, he came to my pew and sat down beside

me. "Well Kenneth, I hope you have enjoyed your visit to Rome and I hope I did not scandalize you too much." He paused for a moment then went on. "You see, Kenneth, I do love the Church and I do love being a priest. There are many holy priests in the Church and I will never do anything to harm my Church. That is why I remain silent now, and I will do so until the day comes when once again Holy Mother Church permits me to say Mass and administer the sacraments once again. I can wait. I have Christ with me too." He smiled sadly. "Your vigor and zeal reminds me of myself when I was your age and I want to help you. Here is a letter to my dear friend, Don Quay, who is a rector of my old seminary at Aosta. I have asked him to help you gain admission to the seminary." He handed me the letter then stood. "Now Kenneth, let me say good-bye here. I want to stay a while and pray."

"Give me your blessing, Father." I knelt at his feet.

He blessed me, then gave me an affectionate hug so natural to the Italians. "Pray for me, Father," I said clutching his hand.

"We'll pray for each other . . . Now, go, you don't want to miss your train." He smiled then turned to the altar and knelt once again. I thought I detected a tear in his eye when he looked away. I knew there was one in mine.

On the train, my mind was full of the events of the past few days. I was sorry to say good-bye to my new friends, and I was sorry to say good-bye to Rome too. Will I ever see Rome again?—If I do, under what circumstances?—Rome, I love you—I will never forget you, and I promise someday, somehow, I will see you again!

CHAPTER SEVEN

"Blessed art thou among women . . . ."
Lk 1:28

"Is this the train for Aosta?" I asked the official who was passing with a whistle poised ready, to start the train.

"Non capisco," he answered lowering the whistle.

By the look on his face, I knew he didn't understand what I was saying.

"Aosta," I repeated more deliberately as I pointed to the train.

"Si, si," he said as he opened the door of a compartment and ushered me inside. He gave a shrill blast on the whistle and the train pulled out leaving Turin behind.

I took a seat in the crowded compartment and sat back to ponder what new experiences the trip still had in store for me. It was impossible to make conversation as all the passengers were Italian, but I was amused at the constant babble. I wonder what they're saying— Wish I could speak Italian—At least then, I might understand all that "sign language"—Italians would probably be lost for words if they couldn't use their hands, I mused. The hum of the moving train was like a lullabye to my ears. I fell asleep.

"Aosta! Aosta!" a voice cried.

I opened my eyes. Where did everybody go—They

must have left earlier, I thought, as I grabbed my bag and descended the steps to the platform.

So this is the seminary where Don Guido started his studies for the priesthood: I hope someone here speaks my language. I rang the bell at the gate.

"Che cosa?" asked a priest in Italian.

"I don't speak Italian." I waited for a reaction to my English. Nothing!

"Parlez-vous Français?" I asked hopefully.

I was in luck, he did speak French. I asked him to take me to Don Quay.

Don Quay was a saintly man, tall, slender, and graying: his eyes and face radiated with an inner sanctity as he offered me his hands. I remembered what Don Guido said about kissing priests' hands in Italy, and even though it was alien to my British nature, I kissed his outstretched palms.

Don Quay spoke fluent French, but no English, so my French was put to the test again. I gave him the letter from Don Guido which he read with interest. He smiled kindly several times as his eyes glided over the words.

"So you wish to become a priest, my son," he said with emotion, "let us walk as we talk, I think better walking." He took my arm and led me out into the grounds.

We walked up and down passing many shrines. There was a beautiful statue of the Blessed Virgin: I couldn't help noticing how he glanced at it several times as if he were asking for guidance.

"You have had a very interesting life so far, my son. It would seem that our Saviour is really guiding you," he said placing his arm on my shoulder.

He's certainly very holy. I've never met a priest who

is so Christ-like. No wonder Don Guido admired him so.

"Do you know that Saint Anselm came from Aosta? Yes, he became a priest in this tiny town: he walked these small winding streets, he breathed this mountain air, and he meditated the glory of God, looking at the beauty of the Alps: but we gave him to England. He was Archbishop of Canterbury, you know. Perhaps that is a good omen . . . maybe England will give you to Aosta," he said squeezing my arm. "Perhaps you will become our Bishop," he added joking. "Let us return to the house and I will show you your room. We can talk again after supper."

Supper was a typical Italian meal washed down with a half bottle of local red wine. There were three other priests at our table, but only a couple of students at the other tables because the college was officially closed for the vacation and most of the faculty and boys were away for the summer. The other priests ate in silence as did the students, but Don Quay broke the silence to talk to me.

"Would you like to go into the town after supper and take coffee there?"

"That would be very nice," I said as I reached across for the cheese. One of the silent priests took the basket of bread and offered it to me smiling.

"Grazie," I said. One of the few Italian words I had learned so far.

The next morning, I attended Mass said by Don Quay. I had never seen a Mass said with more devotion: all his words, so distinct and his actions, so graceful, but mostly his face; it was almost transfigured with joy as he held up the host for me to receive Communion. He spent fifteen minutes after Mass in silent thanksgiving before the tabernacle. I wonder if he is a saint—Wouldn't it be wonderful if I met a real saint on this trip?—I'm sure Pius XII is, I thought, as I knelt in the pew gazing at the solitary figure kneeling at the altar

I learned to respect him a lot last night and I was very impressed with the way all the children gathered round him in the streets. They grabbed his hands to kiss them. He pulled a handful of candy from his pocket and threw it in their midst laughing delightedly as they pushed and screamed trying to retrieve the treasure. At almost every corner, a beggar would hold out his hand to receive a coin discreetly placed on it by the compassionate priest. Yes—Don Quay was a real priest: he really was what all priests should be—another Christ.

Don Quay made the sign of the cross, genuflecting before the altar and turned to me with his gentle smile lighting up his face again.

"Let's go, my son. You must have breakfast before you catch the bus to Grenoble."

He ordered two boiled eggs for my breakfast: he didn't think a normal Italian breakfast of coffee and rolls would be sufficiently sustaining for a long bus ride. After breakfast, we discussed the possibility of my entering the seminary at Aosta.

"This is not the major seminary here: our students are from eight to sixteen years of age, and I think you would find it very difficult living here with these younger boys. I would suggest that you try to enter a seminary where you would be with your own nationals or, at least, with students your own age. However, if you do not find such a place, I will gladly teach you here and prepare you for the major seminary, myself."

He took his large black circular hat from the desk and placed it on his head. "We must leave if we are to catch that bus."

When we entered the street, Don Quay was immediately besieged by a dozen little barefoot children. Again, he threw candy in their direction. The children scattered following the falling pieces, and we made our escape. The people nodded respectfully and the more devout took Don Quay's hand to kiss as we made our way to the bus station. We had a few minutes to spare before the departure of the bus and the saintly priest excused himself as he entered the gift shop. On his return, he placed a new leather wallet in my hand and slipped my bus ticket inside it. "This is a small gift, a souvenir cf our visit together." He would not let me pay for the bus ticket: he took my arm and led me toward the bus.

"Good luck and may God be with you, my son," he said as he raised his hand and made a sign of the cross over my head. I boarded the bus and watched him from the window as the bus pulled away, he was putting something in a beggar's hand and from up the street, a group of children were running towards him. "Goodbye, friend . . . good-bye, priest of God!"

Soon we would be climbing the Alps again to cross into France. Good-bye Italy, at least, for now!

Back in Grenoble again— a lot has happened since I was here last. It seems longer than two weeks since I slept in that church basement, I thought, as I booked into a small hotel. A quick meal and then to bed—I want to get an early start in the morning. It's a long way to Lourdes!

It was early morning when I began my walk along the country road, my pack slung over my back, and my old St. Mary's scarf around my neck. I was a little more confident now: I was no longer self-conscious as I turned to face the traffic thumbing with my right hand holding a large card in my left on which I had written in giant letters, "LOURDES." A car went by and then another. I said the rosary as I walked: that would be a good way to prepare for my visit to Lourdes. Besides, I didn't make much of a thanksgiving after Mass this morning: as soon as the 6 o'clock Mass was finished, I left the church to get an early start. I looked at my watch: it was still only seven thirty. Another car went by. I missed thumbing that one. I started the second decade of the rosary, the "Visitation." I began to meditate on the words of St. Elizabeth to Mary: "Blessed art thou among women, and blessed is the Fruit of thy womb. . . ."

A truck pulled up alongside of me.

"Vous allez à Lourdes?" said the young man leaning out the window.

"Oui," I answered, pleased by his question. I opened the truck door and climbed in.

"My name is Manuel," he said offering me his hand.

"Manuel?"

"Yes, I know it is a Spanish name. My parents were refugees from the Spanish civil war. Although I'm Spanish, I speak only French," he answered, anticipating my next question. "So you are going to Lourdes?"

"Yes, have you ever been there?" I asked hoping he would be able to tell me something about it.

"No, I don't believe in it, nor do I believe in God!" he replied with a leer.

How could such a pleasant person be an atheist? He doesn't look any older than I, either.

"How old are you?" I asked already feeling sorry for him.

"I'm twenty, but that has nothing to do with it. I have always been an atheist. When you are dead, you are dead. There is no life after death—that is just a story the priests tell you to keep you afraid and to keep them rich."

He increased the speed as we came to a long straight stretch of road.

"Are you a Catholic?" he asked.

"Yes, and obviously, I do believe in God," I answered looking at him to see his reaction.

He shrugged his shoulders and smiled sarcastically. He looks a lot like Peter—He has the same handsome features—He's a little darker, maybe—but his nose and mouth are the same. What a pity, he is so bitter.

"So you are going to Lourdes?" he repeated as he broke into a song: "Ave, Ave, Ave Maria—" he sang the Lourdes hymn in mock devotion.

He has a good voice, too, I thought. I hope the Blessed Mother enjoys it. He finished his mock praise and turned to me and smiled. Yes, he really does look like Peter!

"I'm going as far as Nîmes," he said pointing to it on the map.

"Can you see it there?" he asked.

"Yes, it is quite a good distance," I answered.

"I have to stop first to pick up a load in Avignon— You've heard of Avignon, of course?—city of the popes. You know, when there were three popes at the same time," he said smiling again.

"When there were three claimants to the title, that is not quite the same thing as three popes," I said trying to answer him.

"I can't see the subtle difference," he said.

"Well, does this truck belong to you?" I asked.

"No, it belongs to my father, why?"

"Well, suppose two other people said it was theirs, it wouldn't have three owners, merely three claimants to the title. It would still have only one owner. Get the subtle difference?"

"You're smart, I like you," he said offering me one of those awful French cigarettes with the black tobacco.

I took one and accepted a light from him. As I lit it, I replied, "You are 'not' smart and I like you."

We both grinned and drew on our cigarettes blowing the smoke out at the same time.

"Well, we have one thing in common—we both smoke," he said grinning again.

We continued to exchange views as we drove. He wasn't really rejecting God, but most people's idea of God.

"I believe in a superior force, an unknown energy, an 'X' or an 'it' which controls evolution, or perhaps is evolution itself. Maybe we are a part of this totality which is 'it.' Maybe the totality of all essence is this unknown power," he said philosophically.

"You are smart, after all, you do at least think, but think a little deeper. I'm speaking to you in French, my natural language is English and your father's is Spanish. In each language, we have our own word for this supreme being, God or Dieu or Dios, but it is the same being. You have invented other names, 'X' or 'it.' Do you get the message?"

"Yes, but my ideas of the 'X' or 'it' are not as big as your ideas of this 'God' of yours," he answered.

"Yes, but nobody's ideas of this God are exactly as He is."

By the time we reached Nîmes late that night, we found we had a lot more in common than a cigarette.

"It is late. Why don't you come to my home and eat with us? You can stay the night if you wish. I have six brothers at home and two sisters, plus Mama and Papa," he said as we entered Nîmes.

"Are they all atheists?" I asked grinning.

"Of course!" he replied laughing heartily.

"Then I will come, for any family that size, must be basically Catholic!"

We both smoked another cigarette, an English one this time.

Mama and Papa were wonderful characters; so were his brothers and sisters. All of them had a terrific sense of humor and we spent the evening laughing, singing, and eating in that order for the Spanish eat late at night. It was almost eleven thirty before we eventually sat down to eat a feast.

"Would you like to say grace?" said Manuel as we took our seats.

"Are you serious?" I asked.

"Yes, if you pray to 'X' or 'it,' " he replied with a wink.

The meal lasted two hours and we spent the time discussing politics. Who said you can't make friends if you mention the forbidden subjects?

Mama made me a bed on the floor of the dining room.

"I'll call you early in the morning for Manuel is leaving early for Montpellier and that is in the right direction for you to Lourdes," she said as she left the room.

It has been an unusual day, I told myself as I lay on the soft feather mattress. I must remember to pray for this wonderful family at Lourdes. If only all Christians could be as Christian as this family of atheists.

The next day, Manuel dropped me off in Montpellier at the entrance to the major seminary. "I'm sure the priests will accommodate a prospective seminarian and a pilgrim to Lourdes," he said.

"Can I offer you something for all your kindness, perhaps something for the gas," I said taking out my wallet.

"Please don't insult me," he replied looking a little hurt.

"I just wanted to give you something in apprecia-

100

tion," I told him putting my wallet back in my pocket.

"Well, if that's what you want to do, there is something. . . ."

"Yes, what is it?"

"I really like that unusual scarf you are wearing," he said.

"Oh this, this is my old school scarf." I took it from my neck and gave it to him.

If only Brother Michael could see a Spaniard from France wearing the school colors from our English school. I was happy that it pleased him. As I said "Adieu," I realized how appropriate the French farewell was. "*Adieu*—to God," . . . *Adieu*, Manuel.

I spent the night at the seminary: it was empty except for two priests and a student; the summer vacation, I realized as I walked to my bedroom. I'm really getting close to Lourdes now. Who will I meet tomorrow? Hitch-hiking is just as quick as the train, so far, and more exciting.

Once again, I was on the road, here comes a car. I held the "to Lourdes" card and thumbed. The car slowed and stopped. "I'm going to south of Bezier," said the middle aged driver.

"Thank you, sir." I climbed in.

My French is quite fluent: I'm thinking in French. I haven't thought in English for a few days now, I suddenly realized.

The ride was uneventful, so uneventful, I don't remember where he dropped me off. I know it was somewhere south of Bezier and north of Carcassonne.

I've been walking a long time—I wonder if this is the right road—There doesn't seem to be much traffic on it. I sat down by the roadside—I must have been walking for hours—I wonder where I am—Well, I'm certainly in the south of France—Look at all those beautiful grapes! I plucked a bunch of grapes from one of the vines. I sat on the bank eating them. I hope this isn't going to be one of those days that led to the night I found that "hotel"—No, I couldn't go through another day like that, or night either—Well, I had better get a ride soon, it's 4 p.m. already.

When I was finished with the grapes, I hoisted my pack and began to walk again. Another half an hour passed and the heat of the day was beginning to get to me. I must take a rest.

"Bonjour, Monsieur," I said to the farmer spraying grapes in the corner of a field.

"Will you do me a favor?" asked the fieldworker.

"A favor?"

"Yes, you see I am out of wine and I cannot leave this field. I want to finish it before dark. Would you take my flask to the wine merchant and get it filled for me?"

What a strange request, the man must be mad. I'm almost exhausted from walking, goodness knows how many miles, and he wants me to get his flask filled.

"I'm hitch-hiking to Lourdes, Monsieur, and I too would like to get going before it gets dark," I replied.

He looks very disappointed and very thirsty. Perhaps, I shouldn't have snapped at him.

"How far is this wine merchant?"

"It is not far, perhaps, a mile," he said holding his empty flask out to me.

"What about my bag?"

"Leave it here, it will be safe with me," he said pulling the bag from my back.

"You are English," he said catching sight of the British flag.

"Yes," I affirmed as I took the flask and the francs for the wine.

"Fill it," he shouted as I walked away.

I must be crazy. Here I am walking to fill this man's flask and I may miss my only chance for a ride.

I was very tired when I returned to the field. The little French fieldworker was shouting for me to hurry. *"Vite, vite,"* he cried waving his arms. It seemed like an hour since I saw him. What's that car doing by the curb? It looks like a Rolls Royce. It is a Rolls Royce! I began to run.

"Are you going to Lourdes?" asked the driver in English. "Yes sir," I answered dumbfounded.

"Well, give this chap his wine and let's get going."

I handed the flask to the smiling Frenchman who kept nodding as he said, *"Bien,* I get the wine and you get to Lourdes, *bien n'est ce pas?"*

I opened the door of the Rolls and got in beside the driver's woman companion. He introduced himself and his wife. They were going to Lourdes and stopped to ask directions from the fieldworker who explained that I, too, was English and going to Lourdes.

"That's why we waited for you. Good job, I could speak some school-boy French, what!" said the driver as he pulled away. "What part of England are you from, young man?"

"Southampton, sir."

"Oh yes, we sailed from there on a cruise once, didn't we dear?" he said glancing towards his wife for confirmation.

"It was twice, dear—no, three times," she said, now certain.

"Oh, was it?" he said indifferently.

"Where are you from, sir?" I asked.

"We are from the north of England."

"Yes, we are in cotton," said his wife proudly.

They ought to be in diamonds, I thought, looking at the luxury of the car and the expensive way they were both dressed.

"We are going to Lourdes to thank the Blessed Mother for the cure of our son," said the lady.

"We are just going to spend the night there and then we are moving on to Spain and the sun. England is so beastly, wet and dull. It does you good to get away from it all," he said offering me a cigarette. "How old are you my boy?" he asked as he pushed in the automatic cigarette lighter.

"Twenty, sir—No, I'll be twenty one in two days. I never realized it before. I will come of age in Lourdes."

"You don't look that old, are you a student?" the lady asked.

"I hope to be soon. I'm trying to get into the seminary."

The journey passed and so did the next two hours as we approached the Pyrenees and Lourdes.

In this city of hotels, the Rolls pulled up in front of the best. A uniformed man rushed forward to open the door.

"Where are you going to stay in Lourdes, Kenneth?" asked my genial host as he stepped out of the car.

"With the Brothers—I hope."

"Well, why don't you be my guest for tonight? Let my wife and me celebrate your coming of age two days prematurely."

We all three walked into the luxurious hotel together.

Later that night, I was wined and dined in the hotel restaurant. This place is very elegant, too elegant for a pilgrimage, but it is very nice and very kind of my hosts to be so solicitous. How falsely we judge people. They were rich, the kind of rich many people consider superficial. I had learned another lesson; they were genuine Christians too. I will never forget my twenty first birthday, thanks to them.

We walked down the hillside towards the Grotto. The streets were completely packed on either side with shops selling religious goods. The crowds flocked by in their thousands carrying candles for the night procession.

"Let's get three candles, dear," said my hostess as she handed one to her husband and another to me. "The little candle shades have the words of the hymns written on them in English." She pushed a candle through.

"Ave, Ave, Ave Maria. . . ." Thousands of voices were raised in song and prayer as the faces of the vast crowd were lit up from the glow of a sea of candlelight. The procession climbed the hill and wound its way down again the other side like a gigantic snake of fire. We stood and watched the faces of the people as each group passed led by an illuminated sign: England, Belgium, Italy, Ireland, Holland, Germany, and still the countries of the world kept coming by as they sang their praises to the Virgin, each in their own tongue: the chorus being the only thing in Latin: "Ave, Ave, Ave Maria. . . ."

The next day, I thanked my benign benefactors and made my way to the Brothers. There were at least a dozen of them at table and opposite me sat a young priest. We ate simply. I was not hungry after the feast of the night before. I spent the day between the grotto and the town where I bought rosaries, medals, and souvenirs to take back home.

That night, I went to a midnight Mass in a crypt chapel. The clock chimed the hour as it does each hour by playing the "Ave." It is midnight. When the clock stops chiming, it will be September 14th. I will be twenty one, a man at last. The priest asked me to serve the Mass as he walked by me to the side altar. Just the priest and I, and of course, Christ. During Communion,

I asked Christ to accept my manhood which now was officially fifteen minutes old.

At breakfast, next morning, I spoke with the young visiting priest and discovered he was not French, but Portuguese: he spoke flawless English. Father Placido spent the day with me at the grotto. I told him of my search to enter a seminary.

"I'm a professor and vice-rector of a private college in Portugal. If you would care to come to my college, I could prepare you for the major seminary. You can learn Portuguese, perfect your Latin and start your philosophy, then I will introduce you to my bishop who I know will accept you for we have a desperate need for vocations," he said as we walked down the many steps from the basilica.

I accepted his offer. My prayer is answered, the pilgrimage has been a success. What a birthday present!

We walked through the gates of the grotto and along the path to the cave of the apparitions. An English priest was leading a large crowd of kneeling people in a recitation of the rosary. It must be the pilgrimage from England. The priest's voice was loud and clear. We quickened our pace as he recited the *Our Father*. By the time we reached the group, he was starting the *Hail Mary*. We both knelt. "Hail Mary, full of grace, the Lord is with thee, Blessed art thou among women. . . ."

CHAPTER EIGHT

"And it came to pass . . . ."
Lk 2:46

I paid the cab driver and ran toward the door. Wait till I break the news to Mum—She will be as happy as I am—I can just see her face—

"Anybody home? I'm back!" I screamed, waiting for Mum to come running from the kitchen. There was no response—I'll bet she's in the garden. I ran through the house and opened the back door.

"Mum, you down there?" I called, standing in the doorway.

"Your Mum's at the butcher's, Ken," called a neighbor from the other side of the hedge. "How was your trip?"

"Great! Mum will tell you all about it. I'll walk up to meet her." I shut the door then opened it again. "Thanks!" I called back.

Mum was standing in front of the butcher's holding a shopping bag: she was talking to a lady with a small baby.

"Mum, I'm home!" I said as I hugged her, shopping bag and all.

"Kenny, I'm so angry with you," she said kissing my cheek and squeezing me harder with her free arm.

"What kind of a greeting is that?" I laughed.

"Why didn't you write?"

"I did Mum. Didn't you get my cards?"

"Did you send any?" she asked teasingly. She turned to the young lady. "Excuse me, this is my son, Kenny. He just returned home from Rome and Lourdes. You did get there didn't you?" she said facing me again.

"Of course. I have so much to tell you, Mum. Here, let me take that bag. I'll tell you all about it on the way home." I was so excited I didn't realize that I was being rude to the young woman, whom Mother had just introduced. "I'm sorry. Very glad to meet you, Ma'am. You sure have a pretty baby there." I knew that compliment would clear me.

Mum fixed me a big breakfast; something I missed very much on my trip. I spent the next two hours reading her the diary I had kept day to day of the entire trip. She didn't miss a syllable. When I finished, she sat back in her chair and just smiled.

"Well, what do you think?" I asked.

"Kenny, it sounds like a beautiful trip. I'm so happy for you, son. I think you've found the peace you've been looking for."

"I have, Mum. I really have."

"Now, you will be off to Portugal. Our prayers have been answered," she said smiling. "I'll miss you, Kenny, but if this is what God wants, for you to begin your seminary studies in a different country, then I must not be so selfish." She became very serious. "Kenny, do you have any idea how hard the Sisters have been praying for you since you left?"

"No, but I'm sure you made certain that they did," I said laughing.

"Kenny, stop it. I'm serious. You know it would make them very happy if you would take that diary to the convent and read them all about your trip."

"Alright, Mum. I'll go up there this evening, but this afternoon, I want to organize all my visas for Portugal."

I stood to leave. "I'll get busy on them right now, then I'll go straight to the convent." I stopped to kiss her good-bye: she looked troubled. "Mum, is something wrong?"

"No, nothing's wrong—It's just that—Well, you know, I don't think that perhaps. . . ."

"For God's sake, Mum. What is it?" I asked impatiently.

"Kenny, would you leave out that bit about that funny hotel, you know where you stopped to eat—that young girl and that? It may shock the dear Sisters!"

That evening, all the Sisters gathered in the recreation room to hear the account of my trip. When I came to the part about "that funny hotel," I began to flip over a few pages when one of the Sisters stopped me. "Read it all, Kenneth. It's so fascinating." Oh well, here goes. And I read it ALL. They laughed good humoredly, but not quite as much as the two French Sisters: they were hysterical. At the end of the reading, all the Sisters thanked me and excused themselves: Reverend Mother remained for a short visit. As I was leaving, she said to me in her quiet voice: "Your mother has been a constant visitor to our chapel since you've been gone. She is such a holy woman, Kenneth—and she loves you dearly. All she talks about is 'her Kenny.' "

"I know and I really must be going now. I just came home this morning and I have been busy all day lining everything up for the trip to Portugal. I really haven't had too much time to spend with her today." I stood to leave.

"Yes, you run along. I won't keep you any longer," she said rising from her chair.

I shook her hand and opened the door. "Thank you for all your prayers," I said. She seemed to become uneasy, like she wanted to say something, but didn't know how. "Is there something else, Sister?"

"No, I was just thinking. You should go home and read that fascinating diary about your trip to your mother. I know how much she would enjoy it." She hesitated for a moment. "But perhaps, you should leave out that part about the hotel, it. . . ."

"Yes, Reverend Mother, I know IT MAY SHOCK HER!"

On the way home, I met Dad just about to enter his regular pub.

"Dad! Wait up!" I called running toward him.

"Ken. Mother told me you were home. Where have you been?"

Before I had a chance to answer, he invited me in for a drink.

"Come in with me. You're twenty one now . . . I'll buy you a birthday drink—We'll celebrate your becoming a man!"

I can't believe it—Dad's inviting me to drink with him!

He took me from one table to another introducing me to all his friends. I think he's almost proud of me, I thought—That's a switch. My being a man now must mean an awful lot to him—

"What will you have, son, a pint of beer? I'm having bitter myself."

"Whatever you're drinking—I'll have the same," I said nonchalantly. I bet that impressed him.

One thing Dad was expert at was holding his beer. I'll show him I'm really a man and keep up with him— He may not have been too impressed with the grades I kept "up," but he'll be impressed with how many beers I can put "down." He lifted his pint glass and sank it down without stopping for a breath. I did the same. I felt a little bloated—never drank a beer that fast before.

"Same again, son," said Dad pushing his empty glass on the bar top.

"Same again!" I said boldly. I reached for my wallet.

"Put your money away. This is my treat for your coming of age."

Once again we sank down two more brimming mugs of beer. This stuff's not so bad after all!

"Game of darts, son?" The he looked at the bartender and said "Two more!"

This time we sipped the drinks between "throws." I was grateful for that. After the game, Dad motioned me towards one of the tables. "Sit down and we'll talk about your trip," he said taking the two empty mugs. He returned with two full ones, this time with a Scotch chaser. Dad sure is in a good mood. I've never seen this side of him before—He's even singing!—His face is getting a little red—I wonder if mine is?

"I'm proud of you, son. It takes guts to do what you did," he said placing the whiskeys beside the beers. "Of course you know, an old army man like me would rather see you be a soldier, but if you make the priesthood, you may see me a Catholic yet. . . . You think you can handle that?" He motioned towards the whiskeys then raised the glass to his lips. I did the same.

I wish this room would quit moving—I'm quite certain that it is, I thought, as I downed the whiskey and reached for the beer. I don't think I feel very good!

"One more, then we'll head for home. Alright, son?"

"Anything you say, Dad," I said in false confidence.

"Left, left, left, right, left—Pick up those feet!" Dad commanded as we marched together. He was as upright as a general on a battlefield and I couldn't stop giggling as I tried desperately to follow his commands. "A man

111

who can walk a straight line after a few drinks is a MAN, son," he said tracing the line in a sidewalk with his footsteps. Finally we reached the door. "Take off your shoes. You don't want to wake your mother." Quietly, he opened the door. "Shhh, quiet, very quiet," he whispered as we crept up the staircase very, very slowly and ever so very very quietly.

BANG CLUMP BANG CLUMP BANG I dropped my shoes down the steps.

"Damn it! Who did that? Now you'll wake your Mother!" he shouted, almost falling on top of me.

"Mother IS awake—and I'll see you both in the morning," said Mum from the top of the stairs; then she turned and shut her door.

Dad and I were a little late coming down for breakfast the next morning. Jack and Roy had already left the house. I had never seen Dad so docile, as he kind of hid behind his newspaper, glancing toward Mum from time to time, waiting for her to break the awkward silence. I wanted to say something, but I didn't know what. I know—I'll just pretend that nothing happened. "That breakfast was really good, Mum." That was her cue!

"Honestly, Kenny, I don't understand you," she said crossly. "You tell me you want to be a priest and I believe you, then the first chance you get you let your father lead you astray just when I thought you were finally becoming a leader. It doesn't make sense to me. Don't tell me all my prayers for you are going to be wasted." She stood by the sink facing us with her hands on her hips. She was obviously waiting for some explanation.

"Let me explain, dear," Dad said sheepishly.

DEAR! I had never heard Dad call anyone that in my whole life!

"It isn't as bad as it appears," he continued.

"Drinking to excess is always bad," Mother answered crossly.

"Elizabeth, he's a man now!" Dad was quite emphatic.

I was pleased to hear those words from Dad's lips. I was obviously a success in his eyes last night, but not in Mum's.

"Your idea of a man and mine are not the same," said Mum and she left the room.

Mum never could stay angry long and by that very afternoon, she mellowed. We even managed to get her to laugh a little over the comic sight the two of us must have been, but she was still a little reluctant to do so.

"Ken, your taxi's here!" Dad shouted from the bottom of the steps.

"I'll be right down, Dad," I shouted back. Roy was helping me pack a few last minute things. "Roy, take care of everything. And write and let me know how everyone is getting on, won't you?" I said awkwardly. I knew it was time for another "good-bye" and farewells have never come easy to me.

"Don't worry about a thing. You just think about getting on with this business of becoming a priest. I'll look after everything," he said taking one of my bags and starting for the stairs.

Mum was waiting at the door. She hugged me tightly: her cheek was wet against my face. "Be a good boy, do you hear? And don't forget to write, Kenny." She wiped her eyes and smiled. "God bless, son," she said as she made the sign of the cross on my forehead just as she did when I was small and she sent me off to school.

Jackie shook my hand and gave me a jab on the arm. "Guess you're really going through with it, huh, Ken?

Hope they don't make you study too hard. Good luck."

Roy was standing there observing silently. When I moved to him, he put his hands on my shoulders and said, "I always knew you would make it, sooner or later. Take care." He was always there to offer me the encouragement when I needed it most.

I bent down to pick up my bags. "I'll help you with these, son," said Dad picking up the two largest. We walked to the cab together while Mum stood at the window. I felt a lump in my throat—I must remember to be a man, especially in front of Dad. I swallowed hard.

"Well son, I'm happy for you—if this is what you want," he said and for the first time I could remember, he put his arms around me. I was grateful for these last three days at home. I came to know a part of Dad I had never known before: I wanted to tell him that, but I didn't know how. From the look on his face though, I felt he already knew.

"Rather see you going off to the army but nevertheless, good-bye and good luck," he said teasing, then stood at attention and saluted.

I saluted back and we both laughed. "Good-bye, son," he said again.

"Not 'good-bye,' Pop, just Cheerio."

"Good-bye, son!" The taxi pulled away: as I looked back from the rear window, he was still standing at the curb waving.

Father Placido José Lobo, the young Portuguese priest, met me at the train station in Guarda, Portugal. From there, we took a rickety bus to Pinhel. I wasn't very impressed with my first introduction to my new surroundings. The people all seemed so poor. I felt embarrassed as Father and I walked among them at the terminal: they were all dressed in peasant-type clo-

114

thing, black dresses and shawls and suits made of the cheapest material. Their apparel contrasted greatly with the well tailored suit and three quarter length jacket made of the best cloth Father was wearing. They bowed as we passed, and he nodded, almost condescendingly, I thought.

We stepped down in the little town's square. A very small boy, who looked about eight, tried to pick up my bags and place them in a truck. I tried to stop him: I thought he was too small.

"Leave him do it. He is one of your two servants. That's his job. His name is Evaristo and he will look after all your needs, do your shopping, wash your clothes, clean your shoes, make your bed, clean your room and wait on you at table. That's what he is paid for."

"He looks very young, too young for such duties," I said a little repelled by the thought of having a slave.

"He's fourteen and receives two dollars a month, a handsome sum when you consider he gets his room and board and if he did not have this job, he would probably starve," said the Portuguese priest in his Oxford accent. He even looked English with his fair complexion and blue eyes, but he was in fact, Portuguese.

The college at Pinhel was an old Bishop's palace: it looked like something from the Dark Ages. My room was on the second floor with the faculty's. I felt very "out of place" here, most of the students were high school age, and the language barrier created a new problem. My first task was obviously to learn Portuguese; how else was I to communicate with my fellow students. I hated the idea of being waited on by my two little servant boys, also. I began to spend more and more time alone in my room, trying desperately to learn the language. Soon, I was able to understand it somewhat, but I never had much opportunity to put it to use since two friends, John and Paul Petracchi, both students, always volunteered to interpret for me. These boys were Italian and English: I was happy to have someone to talk with in my native tongue, but I lazily relied on them to translate.

One afternoon, while John and Paul were away, a group of us were sitting in the dining room. They were all discussing the merits of the English soccer team and comparing it unfavorably with the Portuguese team. I joined in the discussion and angrily defended England's reputation. The boys turned to me in amazement. "You are speaking Portuguese!" one shouted. So I was. I had surprised even myself. That was the last day I depended on John and Paul to do the talking for me.

Time dragged slowly at Pinhel. I studied almost constantly. The strain of a rigid schedule began to show: the constant diet of fish and rice, which I hated, didn't help my overall well being either. I was glad to see the Christmas vacation come, if only to break the routine. I was very homesick and the prospect of my returning home for the holidays was impossible so I accepted the invitation of the Petracchi boys to spend the vacation with them. I knew they lived in Portugal, but I didn't really care where: one place is as good as another in Portugal, I thought.

"Then it's settled, you'll spend Christmas with us," said Paul.

"Fine, I'll be glad to go home with you. Where do you live?" I asked, not really caring.

"Fatima," John said as he was walking out the door.

Fatima!—They never mentioned the fact they lived in Fatima. I knew little about them except their Italian father was dead and their mother, who was born in England, now ran a boarding house hotel. I was about to see Fatima! For the first time since I arrived in Portugal, I felt excited about something.

It didn't take long for me to feel at home at Mrs. Petracchi's. She couldn't be nicer: she was happy to have someone from her homeland visiting since it had been twenty two years since she left England. She planned for me to go with John and Paul to meet the families of the three children who saw the famous apparitions of the Blessed Virgin in 1917, Jacinta, Francisco and Lucy. Lucy was the only one of the three still living and she was a Carmelite nun in Coimbra.

I was amazed to see the humility of the parents of Jacinta and Francisco: their dwellings were humble too, a poor tumbledown two room house with a small yard. They were both dressed in the common peasant clothing of Portugal. One hour later, I was in the home of Lucy; her parents were both dead so now her aunt lived there. Later, I became great friends with her son, a Salesian student.

"Tomorrow you must come with me to the seminary to meet the other English boys—" said Mrs. Petracchi at dinner.

"English boys?" I interrupted.

"Yes, they have an English novitiate at the Consolata seminary: there are only four boys in it, but they are all English. All the priests are Italian. It's an Italian missionary congregation."

This was a surprise I wasn't prepared for. The seminary was the newest, cleanest and most modern building I had seen since I arrived here. I was even more thrilled meeting the other English students who were around my own age. Father Peter, the Novice Master spoke fluent English: he had studied for a while in England after his ordination. I explained that I was studying at Pinhel to complete the required courses of Latin and Philosophy so that I could gain admittance to the major seminary there. He listened to my whole story then offered to do whatever he could, should I need him.

I hated returning to Pinhel. Father Placido had been taken ill so I was asked to assume his classes in English and French. It was an impossible task to prepare classes to teach and at the same time, devote as much time to study to complete my courses in Latin and Philosophy. Immediately, I settled back into the dull routine of constantly surrounding myself with books, books to study, books to read, books to teach, books, books and more books. I began to lose weight: my stomach could no longer tolerate the local diet. I felt tired and weak and it showed. My schedule didn't leave me much time for any relaxation or recreation, but the thought that all this would eventually lead me to official acceptance by the bishop, sustained me. More and more I looked forward to the letters from home: it was the only thing I really enjoyed. I would take them to my room and read them over and over, reflecting about all those things that were familiar in this new and unfamiliar environment.

It was towards the end of January: I had been feeling unusually weak and tired for several days. I had just finished teaching and was about to go to study hall when someone came with a special delivery letter for me. I recognized Mum's handwriting immediately. I'll go to my room and read it where I can be alone—I'll bet it's about the Christmas gift and pictures I sent her —I opened it excitedly:

Dear Kenny,
Your father died last night—

I looked at the date of the letter. It's too late—Dad's already buried by now—I must go home, just to be with her—She will have a difficult period of adjustment to make—I should be there to help her. My mind was racing: I felt confused, sad, anxious, everything. I looked down at the letter again. Dad is dead! I'll never see him again. I could picture him laughing and saluting

118

me that last day at home. "Good-bye, son!"—"Not good-bye, Pop—just Cheerio!"—"Good-bye, son!"—I wonder if he knew it was really a "Good-bye."

That same evening, I began to run a high temperature and they sent for the doctor. He told me I was too ill to travel. The following week went by without my being aware of much of anything; I was half conscious from the high fever.

I kept corresponding with Mother, trying to offer her consolation in my letters. I didn't want to burden her more by letting her know that I wasn't well; the illness had left me very weak. At Easter, the doctor recommended that I go away for a rest. I decided to go back to Fatima and apply for the English novitiate with the Consolata Fathers: I wasn't making any progress at Pinhel.

Father Peter assured me I would have no difficulty in obtaining acceptance when I applied for the seminary. I had only to wait for the official approval from the Provincial, Father Di Marchi, who was on tour in the United States. In the meantime, I stayed with Mrs. Petracchi and passed the days studying and showing tourists around Fatima as a guide. I came to know Fatima and the "families" quite well in the next two months. I felt I was making progress in my studies too. Lucy's cousin, a Salesian student, was teaching me Latin. We became good friends and he obtained a promise of prayer from Lucy on one of his rare visits to her cloistered convent. "I will remember Kenneth in my prayers," was the message she sent back.

I was becoming more anxious with each passing day. What is taking Father Di Marchi so long?—If only he would return so I could obtain the official acceptance and begin my formal education for the priesthood.

Then came the bombshell! I received a letter from

119

the Archdiocese of Westminster from the Cardinal Archbishop, signed by Monsignor Warlock. "Dear Kenneth, We regret to inform you . . . ." The letter stated that I must be accepted by the congregation before the end of the month or I would no longer be exempt as a bona fide seminarian and would be compelled to return to England for the draft. Now I had a deadline!

I waited and waited: the days came and went with no word from Father Di Marchi. Finally, the day arrived and my deadline was up. I had to return to England. As I packed my bags, I remembered Dad's words: "Of course, I would like to see you a soldier, but if you make the priesthood, you may well see me a Catholic." That would never be—Dad was dead and he did not become a Catholic—Did that mean that I would never make the priesthood?—And what was it Mum said to me that morning at breakfast when she was so angry with Dad and me? "Don't tell me all my prayers for you are going to be wasted?" Now it appears they are. I am returning to England a prospective soldier. Perhaps Dad got his wish after all.

The journey back to England gave me time to meditate about my life thus far. Even while I was on the QE, I was a daily Mass goer, and although I enjoyed playing the "big shot" for a while, I was sincere in my beliefs about my religion. Didn't I spend a year or more in prayerful preparation, once I decided to become a priest?—I was prepared to give my manhood to Christ as I promised in Lourdes on my twenty-first birthday —Why hadn't He accepted it?—Everything was going just right—Mrs. Diskin offered to pay for my education —I found a seminary that was sure to accept me—All those wonderful people were praying for me, even Lucy —I was so sure God wanted me to be a priest—But what was it Mum told me the very first time I mentioned my intentions for the priesthood—

120

"If that's what you want, son, but what's more important, if that's what God wants!"

"If that's what God wants—" Well, I guess He doesn't. I was confused and perhaps, a little bitter. Over two years of prayer and preparation for the seminary—This urgent desire to be a priest—Had all this happened for nothing?—Had it come, only to pass?

CHAPTER NINE

"Then the soldiers . . . ."
Mt 27:29

"Left—left—left, right, left. Pick up those feet you load of idle nig-nogs! I'll never make soldiers out of you rabble. Left—left—left, right, left. Pick up those feet! Squad, squad, halt. Stand at ease, stand easy."

The drill sergeant was barking out the orders at the top of his voice. What an enormous mouth he has, I thought, as his face became the frame for an enormous cavity. His voice was as loud and shrill and sudden as a factory whistle.

"Roberts, you blithering idiot, wake up!" he screamed in my ear.

"Alright, alright, you lot. Since you are all new recruits, I have a few basic things to drill into your stupid skulls. The first thing is . . . this square, you dummies are all parading on is called . . . what is it called Riley?"

"A parade ground, Sergeant!"

"Stand to attention when you speak to me," he bawled at the shaking recruit. The latter immediately brought his left foot up and banged it against his right, while simultaneously bringing his arms to his sides.

"Do you call that 'standing at attention'? Chest out, stomach in. You look like a pregnant duck! Stand easy."

Riley reverted back to an easy position, although nobody really felt "easy" as we stood in line in our brand new uniforms. What a sorry sight, and how desperate the drill sergeant looked as he continued to bark.

"In the British Army, the most sacred thing is the parade ground. It's more sacred than God—if that's possible. You never, I repeat, never walk across it unless on parade. At other times, you walk around it, even if it takes fifteen minutes longer. Point two! The Queen's uniform—Although on your lot, it looks like a uniform for 'queens,'—will be worn with dignity and respect at all times outside of the barrack buildings. To be properly dressed, means to have your head covered by your beret. You never, I repeat NEVER, salute with your hand unless you are properly dressed. Now—What does 'improperly dressed' mean, Jones?"

"Indecent expo—"

"Idiot! Listen! I won't tell you slobs again. Improperly dressed means to be in uniform without your cap or beret while 'outside' the barrack buildings. Johnson, what would you do if you passed an officer 'inside' a building and you were not wearing your cap?"

"Turn around and go back for my cap," Johnson grinned.

"Take that smile off your face and don't be smart with me. I can swallow you in one gulp, chew you up, and spit you out again. You little fink! If you pass an officer without your cap, you do an 'eyes left' or 'eyes right' with a quick turn of the head, like this." He im-

122

mediately demonstrated. "Now, don't forget, you idiots, you never, never, walk across the parade grounds and never salute an officer without your cap on. That's all I can expect you squad of osculating fairies to learn in one day. Squad, squad, tenshun—Dismiss!"

We turned smartly to the right and fell out. We had been drilling for two hours and we were feeling quite exhausted as we dragged our weary bodies back to the barracks.

"Soldiers! Look smart there. Shoulders back, chin in, chest out, stomach in. Look lively there," another sergeant bawled as we entered the building.

So this is the army—if only Dad could see me now!

"Boy, it's good to sit down," a young recruit said as he pulled off his heavy boots. We all threw ourselves into our bunks in a state of nervous collapse. We were not to be at peace for long—

"Okay, all outside! The headshrinker wants to measure your IQ's. I could save him the trouble, but that's what he's paid for," the sergeant screamed.

Once again we were falling in outside: this time to march to the medical center.

"Before you see the headshrinker, the MO wants to inspect you, just in case any gals managed to enlist by mistake. I could save him that trouble, too. Get stripped off," he barked again as we stood waiting in the medical inspection room.

We stood in two rows as the MO quickly passed down the lines, stopping at each man. He peered into our ears, looked down our throats, listened to our chests, and —"Cough," he said before passing on to the next man. "Okay, get dressed and move out to the next room," cried our unwilling host.

In the next room, we were handed sheets of test pa-

123

pers, which were supposed to tell the doctor of our degree of intelligence, or lack of it. For the next two hours, we relaxed physically, while we exercised our brains. "Okay, hand in your papers, finished or not. Fall in outside," said a corporal who seemed unusually polite, after the bullying of the drill sergeant.

This was my first week in the army. I had been drafted into the Royal Army Medical Corps, the only non-combatant force in the British army. They presumed this would be the right section of the army to assign a prospective clergyman. This camp was the initial training camp of the Medical Corps; the recruits spent only two weeks in it, being acclimatized before being sent to the larger basic training camp.

Two days later, on the way back to the barracks from the mess hall, I was stopped by the drill sergeant. "Roberts, come here, double!" he shouted. I marched toward him at the running pace required when the order "double" was given. I stood to attention as soon as I reached him. "Report to the Camp Commandant, immediately!" I did an about turn and marched off toward the office of the commanding officer. When I arrived there, I found others waiting in the outer office. I wonder what I've done wrong—I've only been in the army a week and I'm already on the mat!

"Come in," cried the colonel in answer to my knock. I opened the door and entered.

"Oh Roberts," he said glancing up at me. "Take a seat." He opened a file with my name on it. "I have just received the results of your tests. How would you like to go into the Intelligence Corps?"

"Intelligence?" I questioned nervously.

"Yes, the personnel selection office suggests that you be transferred to Army Intelligence. What are your views on it?"

Intelligence—That's all that cloak and dagger stuff,

124

parachuting behind enemy lines and being tortured if you get captured—even killed. I would sooner be a live coward, not a dead hero.

"I am quite happy here, sir, but thank you for thinking of me," I said politely and stood to leave.

"Sit down, boy. I haven't finished with you yet. You have no option. You've already been assigned to Intelligence. I just wanted to hear your views, and I've heard them. Sign here." He pushed some transfer documents toward me.

"What do they do in Intelligence?" I asked taking the pen.

"If I knew that boy, I would be signing that paper instead of you. Sign!"

I signed the paper as he pushed it toward me for the second time.

"Here is your railway warrant. Your train leaves for Uckfield in Sussex at 8:35 in the morning."

As I packed my kitbag, I began to wonder—What do they do in Intelligence—Why couldn't they leave me here with only a drill sergeant to worry about?

The train pulled into the station of the small town of Uckfield which is about forty miles from Brighton, an East Coast resort. On the platform were about fifty other soldiers, all of them recently arrived from all parts of the British Isles and belonging to different corps, regiments, and units.

"Get fell in," said a military policeman who shepherded us into orderly lines and then led us out to a waiting truck. Soon we arrived at the country village of Mairsfield which we passed as we went a little deeper into the country. "Here it is!" said our escort.

A high wire fence surrounded the camp and sentries stood guarding the entrance. A large board, close to the gate read: ARMY INTELLIGENCE DEPOT. NO ADMISSION

TO UNAUTHORIZED PERSONNEL. The truck stopped at the guard room while the guard commander went through a routine security check and we drove on to the main square of the camp. "All out," cried an even louder, shriller voice than the previous drill sergeant's. It was the voice of the Sergeant Major, a member of the Irish guards, a crack British regiment. He continued to shout and scream at us as we jumped to the ground and began to fall in. "We are going to meet the commanding officer. Look alive, there!" We were all led into the lecture hall. "Be seated gentlemen," shouted the Sergeant Major.

This is a change—At least, he calls us "gentlemen." This place seems to have class. It has more than class: it reeks of the status symbol beloved by the best English gentlemen. Almost all schools in England play soccer except the very exclusive schools of nobility, and some few schools that tried to ape them. These exclusives played rugby rather than soccer.

The door opened, and the commanding officer, a major with a bitter lemon accent and handle-bar moustache, entered. He sounded like an exaggerated Terry Thomas as he said, "Good afternoon, gentlemen. Be seated. A very, very good afternoon to the cream of the British Army. Now, you are all here because you are above average intelligence. Stand up, all those who play rugby." His eyes glanced eagerly at the faces of the standing men. "Good. Now each one stand and tell me your father's occupation and the schools you attended." His eyes rested on the first man as he nodded him to commence the litany. "President of a textile firm . . . Eton and Oxford," he said proudly. "Banker . . . Winchester and Cambridge," said another. "House of Lords . . . Eton and Cambridge." The litany of noble gentlemen continued until it reached the back of the second row. A young Scotsman answered, "Fish and Chip shop . . ."

"Your father is a catering executive?" interrupted the officer.

"No sir, he only works there. I was educated at St. Patrick's parochial school and State college."

The CO looked as if he had just been repelled by some horrible sight as his nostrils twitched while he stroked his large moustache. "Next," he said annoyed. The next day the young Scot was transferred to other duties.

All our instructors were quite polite except the drill sergeant whose job it was to make soldiers of us. The other instructors trained us in different branches of Intelligence work.

"Well gentlemen, this morning we're going to teach you what to do, by showing you what *not* to do. As you will have already been told, an Army Intelligence man is given a blank paybook without the inclusion of rank in it. This will enable him to assume any rank suitable to the assignment. Do not do this!" A curtain opened and a young man who looked eighteen appeared on the stage dressed as a general. The class laughed: the point was taken. "Do not assume a rank that would draw attention to yourself when you do not look the part." The instructor joked on. "Do not do what one Intelligence officer did during the war. He assumed the rank of a general, walked into Army headquarters in North Africa and gained access to a top secret document which he promptly posted back to the War Office with a little note that read: 'Look what I found!' They didn't like it and he was court martialed." Once again, the students broke up with laughter. This is quite interesting, I thought as I pictured myself doing all kinds of extraordinary practical jokes. The afternoon went quickly as we listened to our instructors and watched the demonstrations.

Most people think of only one thing when you mention Intelligence: they imagine espionage. I know nothing of that side of Intelligence, neither do I know a great deal of counter espionage except in so far as it was connected with Field Security, the branch for which I was being trained. This included interrogation of prisoners and all that it entails. Our main duties, however, were concerned with security of our military establishments and protection of secret and classified documents. If we were to spy on anybody, it was to be our own British personnel.

Not everybody in Intelligence looked the part. Maybe that's why we wore green shoulder flashes that had the words, INTELLIGENCE CORPS, written in black, otherwise, the world would never guess. At least it gave us a feeling of pride and demanded great respect wherever we went. It always created interest and we were amused as we watched the faces of the whispering onlookers, "Are they spies?"

(It may appear to the reader by this time, that I'm ridiculing the British Intelligence by emphasizing the humorous events, but due to the fact that I was compelled to sign an oath, a Government Official Secrets Act, I'm restricted to the nature of what I can write about at this period. It is for these reasons, I've concentrated on hte British Intelligence. I would like to add, that during my enlistment in the British Intelligence, I met very competent, intelligent men, capable of fulfilling their job efficiently: all of them earned my respect and I made many true and reliable friends among them.)

Christmas came at last, and we boarded trucks for the station: we were going home for our first leave. I was excited at the thought of being home again: it seemed a long time since I had seen it. I threw my bag up in the rack and leaned out the window of the train to watch other guys who were waiting on the station platform for other trains. "Don't get too drunk! Merry Christmas!" I shouted to a group of friends.

The station was decorated with Christmas trees covered with lights and the station speakers were piping carols to the waiting passengers: it was Christmas Eve. As the train pulled out to the singing of "Silent Night," I began to catch the Christmas spirit. How different from last Christmas in Fatima—Was that only one year ago?—Dad was alive then too—I must make sure Mum has a special Christmas and doesn't brood too much—The train rolled on towards Southampton.

One unique thing about being a member of the Intelligence Corps was that all of us would eventually be split up, as we would be assigned to different duties in different parts of the world. As the year passed and our training drew to a close, I finally received my posting. I was to be posted back to the Medical Corps for medical office training. This training was to familiarize me with the Army documents used in British military hospitals and headquarters: it consisted of a concentrated course of lectures and studies followed by exams. At last, the examination results were out and I graduated with honors as top student. Once again, I was waiting at the door of the commanding officer. Now, perhaps, I can get to where the action is!

"The CO will see you," said a young Corporal who ushered me in to the commander.

"Well, you did extremely well in your exams, Roberts. I am pleased to offer you a unique opportunity. You are an enlisted man serving two years, isn't that right?" he said looking at some papers on his desk.

I wonder what they are cooking up for me this time?

"Yes sir," I replied a little uncertainly.

"We are prepared to send you to Cambridge University for three years where you can major in Russian, but of course, that would necessitate your signing on for a seven year stretch in order for you to be of benefit to the army," he said picking up the papers. "You would be living in college and be on Army Lieutenant's pay and at graduation, you would automatically be given Captain's rank. What do you say?"

It seemed very attractive, but I didn't want an army career: I was anxious to finish my service and try for the seminary again.

"Thank you very much, sir. I'm very flattered, but you see, I'm hoping to join the seminary as soon as I finish with the army and I have only a little over a year to go." I hoped he wouldn't be too offended.

"I understand, but you are missing a golden opportunity, not everybody gets the chance at Cambridge." He put the papers down and picked up another set. "I was not expecting you to refuse the offer, but it so happens I have a general who is looking for a private secretary—"

"Do I have to take it, sir?" I asked before he could finish.

"No, you don't 'have' to take it, but it is a very easy, comfy job. The general is quite old and very inactive," he said a little surprised at my lack of enthusiasm.

"I would prefer an overseas posting, if that is possible. Perhaps I could be useful at NATO in Paris with my knowledge of French," I suggested.

It was clear the CO considered the interview over, so I stood to attention, saluted and excused myself.

It wasn't long before the postings were out: I looked at the board anxiously, scanning the long list of names. I was assigned to Army Headquarters in Germany at Luebbecke. Well, at least I was going overseas, even if

I didn't speak German. A friend of mine, who spoke German fluently and no French was assigned to Paris.

Luebbecke was a small town in Westfalia and I had to report at the district HQ's: I was amazed at the accommodations. We were all housed in commandeered civilian houses. Our mess hall was a hotel dining room also taken over by the military as was almost all the private property in town.

When they discovered I spoke no German, I found myself a student once more. I enrolled in the military language class which was directed by an eccentric Dutch professor who spoke German with a Dutch accent, and English with a German accent. He was constantly confusing German words with English words, and it was a miracle that any of us managed to learn the language under his direction. He wore black jackboots, riding breeches, a GI jacket and a French beret on a massive mop of unruly hair. He looked like the mad professor from a Frankenstein movie. I can still remember the early lessons and still recite the whole story of *Little Red Riding Hood* from memory.

After three months of constant study and application, I was ready for real duty. I reported to the HQ and was assigned to the Assistant Director of Medical Service (ADMS). I couldn't wait to find out the important responsibility that I was about to undertake. All these weeks of training and preparation: they must have something very special in mind, something real "top secret." I left the headquarters completely in awe of my new status. I don't believe it—All this training and I have finally been given the responsibility of all these classified documents, "the Venereal Disease Reports"!

During my tour of duty, I became very good friends with Major Brodie: he was in charge of Army Hygiene.

Eventually I became his personal interpreter acompanying him to many official luncheons and banquets. Through his influence, I was able to get many week-end passes to different parts of Germany, including Berlin, Hamburg, Hanover, Dusseldorf and Muenster.

Whenever I wasn't on duty, I was at his home tutoring his children in German. Soon I was an accepted member of his family. I seldom went out with the other men. One day, he said to me, "Ken, I feel I know you well enough to tell you this, as a friend and a doctor. You're too strict with yourself. Why don't you go out with the other guys and let your hair down. You're not in the seminary, you're in the army. Go out and get plastered. Relax and live!"

I did. And too rapidly, I began to change. No longer did I go to daily Mass, and although I still managed to get there on Sundays, many times I was absent from the Communion rail.

The time finally came for my discharge from the army and return to civilian life. The seminary at Fatima forwarded applications and medical examination reports to me, but I didn't feel they were any longer needed.

My last night, I had dinner with Major Brodie and his family: I was sad to say good-bye. "What am I going to do for laughs, and who is going to interpret all those VD reports for me?" he said and we both laughed. "Do you still think of entering the seminary?"

"I feel mixed up. I have to think about it for a while."

We said good-bye that night.

The Camp Commandant, Colonel Prior, drove me to the station, then helped me with my bags to the platform. "You weren't the world's greatest soldier, Ken, but you were a bundle of laughs," he said. As the train pulled away he stood at attention and saluted. It reminded me of another soldier who saluted in the same way at a different "good-bye!"

132

CHAPTER TEN

"If you love me . . . ."
Jn 14:15

"What do you plan to do now, Ken?" Roy asked as we sat at lunch.

"I don't know. I feel unsure about everything. Before I went to Germany, everything was simple, but now I don't even understand myself. One thing is for sure, I better make up my mind about something. I've already been home a month," I said uncertainly.

"I know just how you feel, Ken. I was the same way when I came home from the Navy. Of course, my problem was different somewhat, it wasn't the siminary I was uncertain about, nevertheless . . . ."

"What's this about the seminary?" Mum said as she opened the door. She had been working in the garden. We could both tell by the look on her face that she was hoping to hear a positive decision had been reached regarding my plans.

"Nothing really about the seminary, Mum. I was just telling Roy that I'm confused right now. Perhaps, it would be best for me to take a job and give myself some more time to think things out," I answered.

"Whatever you think is best, son. You know I only want what's best for you. God will show you the way, Kenny. You must be patient," she said trying to offer me comfort, in spite of the fact that I knew

133

she must be a little disappointed that I didn't return to the seminary, but she never once let me know how much it really meant to her to have a son, a priest. She trusted me to make my own decisions and I respected her for it.

"Will you boys be home for dinner tonight?" she asked.

"No Mum, I'm going out with Johnny and Max to a show We'll eat out after the movie," I answered.

"I won't be here either, Mother. I'm taking Claire out to dinner," Roy replied.

"Why don't you marry that girl, Roy? I know you never see anyone else, and I think she really loves you. You two have been sweet on each other since you were teenagers. If I were Claire, I'd be tired of waiting. You do love her, don't you, Roy?" Mother looked at him waiting for some reaction.

"Don't ask so many questions, Mum," Roy answered teasingly.

That afternoon I decided it was high time I went about the task of finding a job. The man at the Employment Bureau gave me a green card with the name and address of a plastics company that was looking for a laboratory assistant. I explained to him that I knew nothing of this kind of work, but that didn't seem to make any difference to him.

"You needn't worry about that. Just mention your background and schools and I'm sure they will be suitably impressed."

He was right. The personnel manager couldn't have been nicer.

"I see you were at St. Mary's, fine school," he added.

I was completely honest with him, but he assured me I had nothing to worry about. They would train me.

The next morning I was to report at 8 a.m. as a laboratory assistant in the plastics division.

"So you're going to be a lab technician," said Jackie at breakfast. "What do you do there?"

"It's much like my 'Intelligence' work, a big secret," I answered, then winked at Roy.

"I'd love to know what you really did in Army Intelligence. You probably made the tea at four o'clock, if the truth was known," said Jackie cynically.

"Actually Jackie, you will never know the great acts of heroism that I featured in. Unfortunately, I am sworn to secrecy," I said grinning. Roy was taking a lot of pleasure in listening to us "put each other on."

"Well, it's no secret that you know nothing about laboratories or chemistry. You don't even know what H^2O is!" Jackie grabbed his books and started for the door. He had graduated from St. Mary's and now he was a student as an apprentice for a shipbuilding firm: he attended school one day a week to learn blueprint reading and drawing. "See you, Dr. Pasteur!" He walked behind my chair and ruffled my hair with his hand.

I pushed his hand down and grabbed it pulling it behind his back. "You may be bigger than I am, but I can still lick you—and don't you forget it."

"Okay, okay," he screeched and I released his arm.

"You boys fighting again? You're a little old for that! Jackie you're eighteen, and Kenny, you . . . twenty-four, and still fighting!" Mum said as she came into the kitchen.

"I'm twenty-three, Mother," I said laughing.

"Just the same, act your age!"

"Mum, they were just fooling around," Roy explained.

"Just like Ken will be doing in that laboratory
135

today," said Jackie running for the door. He put his face to the window and looked in at me and grimaced, "See you, Dr. Pasteur!"

Jackie didn't know how right he was—I don't have the vaguest notion of what I'll be doing—I'll clock in early—That will be a good start for the first day.

The laboratory manager gave me a white coat like a doctor's and some instruments and a slide rule, then showed me to my desk. What am I to do with these?— I don't even know what they're called!

I needn't have worried so: the first week I was taught and aided by another lab assistant who showed me how to perform the many different tests on the new samples from the factory and how to make up a report on them, marking them either "reject" or "pass." I felt rather important knowing that thousands of factory workers couldn't start producing a product until I put the official "pass" on it. Too bad the pay isn't commensurate with the responsibility, I thought.

Besides the dozen or so laboratory assistants, there were about six young girls who assisted us by bringing and removing samples and keeping our instruments and desks clean. One of them, an eighteen year old, named June, was especially attractive. She looked very Italian, with her almost black hair, large brown eyes, fair skin and well formed body.

"What do you think of her?" asked one of the older men as she left my office.

"Very nice," I answered, a little annoyed at his intrusion.

"I'll bet you a couple of quid you can't date her," he said, then added, "she's very hard to date—ask the other chaps, they'll tell you."

I knew June must be a little interested since several times a week, she made a point to tell me all the good movies playing in town—And besides a couple of quid is about seven dollars—That's more than enough to cover the cost of a date to the show—One date can't harm anything—Whether or not I decide to enter the seminary can't be influenced by a simple date to the cinema—Besides, I need a night out, for a change.

"Okay Alf, I'll take your bet!"

I arranged to meet her at the movies: throughout the whole picture, I was the perfect "big brother." Afterwards, I invited her for some fish and chips. She accepted saying shyly, "That would be lovely."

We sat at the table making small talk, then suddenly she grinned.

"What is so funny?" I asked.

"I must remember to thank Alf tomorrow."

"Thank Alf, what for?" I was confused.

"I told him I wished you would ask me for a date, and he said you were a little shy, but he said he knew how to fix it up." She giggled.

"Oh he did, did he?" I answered, beginning to understand.

The next morning I overheard June talking with the other girls: she was discussing the date the night before. ". . . and I'm sure it will be no time at all till he asks me to go steady!" Where did she get that idea?—I'll show her—She is very nice and very attractive, but the last thing I want now is to become involved with any girl—I'll have to cool this down—Maybe, I'll just ignore her—I don't want to be rude.

The next few weeks went by. June kept suggesting dates and I kept rejecting them. Finally one day she just boldly asked, "Don't you want to take me out? I thought you enjoyed our date together!"

"I did, but I'm rather busy. When I want to take

you out, I'll let you know," I answered without even taking my eye from the microscope.

About an hour later, Alf came into my office. "Look Ken. It's none of my business, but you can't treat that little girl like that. She is really sweet on you and you treated her very badly. Right now, she's out there crying. Why don't you sort things out?"

I felt guilty: I hadn't intended to make her cry. Perhaps I'll invite her to dinner tonight, then I can explain my situation, about the seminary and all—I'm sure when I tell her that, she'll understand my position.

"So you see June, it doesn't make any sense. The more often I see you, the worse it will be. You're eighteen and I'm almost twenty-four. I don't want to get serious with any girl, and I'm still seriously considering the priesthood. This is the main reason why it just would not pay for us to continue to date. You can understand that, can't you?"

"I don't see how it would do any harm if we just went out occasionally, would it?" She began to cry again.

"I don't suppose it would . . ." then I added, not knowing whether I was trying to assure her or myself, "providing you do understand my position. Nothing serious could possibly come of this."

"Are you going somewhere special tonight, dear?" Mum asked as I came into the kitchen for dinner.

"Well, not really special. June just wanted me to meet her mother and father, that's all," I answered taking my chair.

"She visited me several times now, Kenny. She seems to care for you very much." Mum took a chair opposite me. Another one of those heart to heart talks, I bet.

138

"Yes, she mentioned it." I tried to sound indifferent.

"I hope you know what you're doing, Kenny." Mum was very serious.

"Mum, June and I have an understanding. She knows the situation, I set her straight on that from the very start."

I was glad Jackie and Roy came in: the conversation ended.

The weeks slipped by: soon the Friday dates became Monday, Wednesday, and Friday dates. She began to visit my home quite often, sometimes just to sit and talk with Mother. I was beginning to feel quite differently: this time I was the one who wanted to have one of those talks.

"Mum, what would you say if I told you I was no longer thinking about the priesthood?" I asked.

"Son, marriage is also a sacrament of the Church and a holy vocation. If you feel that God wants this for you, then I will be very happy. All I pray is that He will let me see you three boys settled in whatever state you choose before I die."

"I was afraid you would be disappointed if I didn't go on for the priesthood," I said relieved.

"Kenny, I would be disappointed if you did anything that did not make you truly happy. Do you think you would be happy with June and the married life?"

"I know there are obstacles. I'm twenty-four and she is eighteen but I don't really believe that is a problem. June has already told me she wants to become a Catholic . . . ."

"Let's pray about it. I'll go right now to visit the Sisters and ask them to get started on a very special intention," she said taking off her apron, then continued to rattle on. "One sister still says a rosary for you every day and I was telling her just the other day . . . ."

Mum kept talking, but I wasn't really listening. My mind was somewhere else; I was thinking of June—Is this what they call "love"?

On Christmas Eve, after midnight Mass, I presented June with an engagement ring. Everyone was very happy for us. Her father said he approved of the marriage, but he would only give his consent after I had sufficient money to buy a home and keep her in comfort. Roy and Claire announced their engagement New Year's Eve, so we had two weddings pending. There was a lot of excitement during this holiday season, but when it was over, I settled down to doing some serious planning for "our" future. The sooner I could earn more money and save for a home, the sooner June and I could be married.

"I think your idea of finding a job with a better future is good, Ken, but why don't you look for something using your own profession?" Roy asked over my shoulder as I was paging through the want ads.

"My 'profession'? What are you getting at?" I asked puzzled.

"Something like this." He pointed to an ad. "Look here, BOAC is advertising for young men your age and older with catering knowledge who are qualified linguists. That would certainly be a job with a future. BOAC is Britain's largest airline, and with your ability to read, write and speak French, German and Portuguese, you have it made."

"Do you think I stand a chance?" I became excited.

"If you landed a job that you knew absolutely nothing about, I'm sure you won't have any problem getting one for which you are qualified," Roy assured me. He always seemed to be there when I needed him most.

Three weeks later, the letter arrived from BOAC requesting that I go before the selection board at 3:30 the following Friday. I was to meet them at London Airport in the BOAC office. Yippee! London, here I come!

The London Airport was enormous and I had some difficulty in finding my way to the right office. By the time I finally walked up the stairs to the building of the selection room, it was 3:40. The anteroom was full of young men: all the chairs were taken and some of the applicants were squatting on the floor.

"Are you Mr. Roberts?" asked a man in uniform.

"Yes sir," I said as I ran into the room puffing and stumbling over my own feet.

"You're late! You'll have to wait until the end. You have lost your turn!"

One by one the prospective candidates were called as each in turn entered the interviewing room. Each interview lasted about ten minutes: at the end of that time, the candidate was asked to wait outside while the interviewers discussed the merits and demerits of the applicant, then they were asked to return and told whether or not they had been accepted. During the waiting period, we talked among ourselves and learned a lot about each other's qualifications and backgrounds. I was very impressed with the standard of the applicants. By 5:00, ten had been interviewed and rejected. Each was given a different reason for failure to impress the board. One was told that as a non-drinker, he would not be a good social mixer, necessary to a successful air-crew member. Another didn't have the right school background. Another was too tall: another was too short, or too fat. One was too nervous. One didn't speak with the correct cultured accent. I was becoming less confident about my own

141

chances. I was starting off with a strike against me. Perhaps, I would be considered, "too late"!

I was becoming quite anxious. So what, I still had my job in the laboratory—I'll just go in there with a nonchalant attitude—I'll interview them to see if I want the job!—I'll put my "Intelligence" training to work—Wasn't I trained as an interrogator? I know all the tricks—I'll just imagine they are prisoners and I am going to break them down—

"Roberts, the board will see you now," said the uniformed official.

I walked into the carpeted interviewing room where three men, one in uniform with gold rings on his sleeve, sat waiting at desks. I shook their hands and introduced myself.

"I'm sorry I was late getting here, I came from Southampton as you know, and I'm not familiar with the layout of the Airport."

There were two hard back chairs and two easy chairs in front of the desks. I took one of the easy chairs and relaxed, or should I say, "appeared" to relax.

"We see here on your application form that you have had quite an unusual career so far . . . . Why do you wish to work for BOAC?" asked the uniformed interviewer.

I took my time answering: I reached for my cigarettes and said, "May I?" They nodded their approval, then I proceeded to answer their question. "I like traveling." I lit my cigarette and drew in deeply.

"We are not a free travel club," answered an elderly gentleman to the left.

"I realize that sir, but you have no objection if I do travel, supposing of course, I do get accepted," I replied smugly.

The uniformed man smiled. "Can you read a French

142

menu?" He handed me the menu: I translated it and handed it back. The third gentleman handed me a magazine and asked me to translate a piece into German.

"Do you want a translation or an interpretation?" I asked glancing at the difficult passage.

"What's the difference?" asked the first gentleman.

"One will be accurate and the other won't!"

The uniformed gentleman smiled again. "I see from your application that you learned Portuguese while in college in Portugal. What were you doing there?"

"I was hoping to study for the priesthood, but I presume I was not worthy because I didn't make it," I said trying to change the subject.

"Not worthy?" asked the uniformed gentleman again. "May I say, Mr. Roberts, that we on BOAC, also require a high moral standard."

"Yes, but do you require the vow of chastity?" I answered grinning.

They all broke up with laughter. "Wait outside, Mr. Roberts. We want to discuss your application."

Five minutes went by, but it seemed like five hours. What is taking them so long?—Perhaps, I was a little too audacious—Oh well, it's too late now—Me and my "intelligence"—I was a bit much!

"Mr. Roberts, you can come back in now."

I closed the door behind me and took the same seat.

"The board has agreed to offer you a position with BOAC," said the uniformed gent again. "You have the qualities we are looking for, however, I must stress the need for punctuality, a very necessary quality for an organization which specializes in service to others. We must live up to our motto: BOAC TAKES GOOD CARE OF YOU! We are now offering you admission as a student to our training school. You will, of course, receive sufficient payment during the training

143

to cover the costs of your London accommodations. Does this meet with your approval?"

"Yes, sir!"

After three months of training in all the many, many things an air steward must know, from first aid to passenger psychology and from mixing drinks to desert survival, we were ready for graduation. I received my elegantly tailored dark blue uniform and "wings." I was "air-crew" now and I felt quite proud, prouder than I ever felt before in any other uniform I had worn, so far. This one I really earned. Soon, I would receive my flight instructions and I could take my first flight in an aircraft!

After the ceremony, I walked briskly through the airport terminal. I was on my way to a swanky party that Mike, a fellow crew member and somewhat of a playboy, had planned for us. I know this is the happiest I have ever been in my whole life—I feel alive! Exhilarated!—More than that—It's love! I looked around the crowded terminal—That's it I'm in love— I'm in love with people—I want to throw out my arms and scream from the top of my lungs. "WORLD, YOU ARE MY PLAYPEN!"

CHAPTER ELEVEN

"Carried up into Heaven"
Lk 24:51

"Mum, I'll be in the garden in case you need me," I shouted as I walked out the back door. Mum was busy cleaning so June and I decided to get out of her way, besides I could tell June was troubled about something.

"I thought maybe you wanted to talk and it's so pleasant out here. Mum's flowers are beautiful aren't they?" I said trying to start a conversation.

She looked around the garden and nodded in affirmation. "Ken, did you meet many girls in London?" she asked.

"Just the ones at the training school. Why?"

"I was just wondering. They're all quite beautiful, I imagine. All the air stewardesses that I've ever seen are very pretty, don't you think?" She looked like she was waiting for the "right" answer.

"I guess. Never paid that much attention." I could tell by the look on her face that was what she wanted to hear. I was flattered to know she was jealous. "Now tell me, what do you want me to bring you back from my first flight? How about a little something from each place? It will be like a souvenir from each of the countries where I will travel on my first trip route. . . . First there's Tripoli, then Kano, then Lagos. Would you like that?"

"Yes," she said still smiling. Suddenly her expression changed. "I wish we had more time together before you leave. You'll be going the day after tomorrow and it seems like you just returned from London."

"I'll only be gone nine days, and I promise I'll write each time I land," I said taking her hand.

"Kenny, Kenny! You're wanted on the telephone. It's London Airport," Mother called from the back door.

The telephone at this time was considered a luxury in most homes in England, but with my new job it was for me a necessity. I had instructed Mother on how to use it.

I went flying through the house to the drawing room

145

only to find it replaced on the receiver. "Mum, I thought you said I was wanted on the telephone."

"You are. I told them to hang on," she said coming into the drawing room.

"But Mum, you put the receiver down. You cut them off!"

"I didn't. All I did was to tell them to hang on and then I put the telephone back on its little stand."

"That's not a stand. It's a receiver. When you put it down, you cut the other party off."

"You didn't tell me about that, son. I don't know much about these modern things!"

"I hope they call back," I said as I began to pace the floor like an expectant father.

"Kenny, sit down and relax. If they want you, they'll call back." Mother shook her head and gave me a look that said she was glad she was born seventy years ago. "I'm going to visit with June for a while." She left the room still shaking her head.

Within minutes the phone rang again. I was quite relieved. The voice on the other end said that a strange thing had happened; after he had placed his call and reached the number, he was disconnected. I smiled at the humor of the whole incident: I was too cross to appreciate it earlier. He then informed me that my flight time had been changed. I was to leave a day sooner, but the itinerary remained the same.

I didn't rest well that night—Why is it I can never sleep when I need sleep most?—I'm too excited about my first flight—What if I get sick?—Those planes travel over three hundred miles an hour—If I could stand those waves and storms at sea on that freighter, I can stand anything, I hope—Tripoli is an Italian possession in North Africa—I wonder if it's like Rome—I wonder what North Africa is like?—They still have tribesmen

146

there; I remember reading about them somewhere. I reached for the bedroom light and turned it on. TWO THIRTY!—I must get some sleep. I'll try counting sheep—All I can see are planes—I'll count them!

"You look smart in your new uniform, son," Mum said as she walked me to the taxi.

"Say good-bye to Jackie and Roy for me. It would be heartless to wake them so early," I said throwing two large bags in the trunk and placing a small handgrip in the front seat.

"Don't you think you have a little too much luggage for such a short trip, Kenny?" she said.

"I must take formal clothes, sports clothes and a spare uniform in case of accidents."

"Don't speak of accidents, you'll have me nervous," she said looking a little frightened.

"No Mum, that sort of accident is referred to as an 'incident,' " I said explaining the crew jargon, but still not offering her much consolation. "You missed the 6:30 Mass this morning, Mum."

"No, I'll make the eight o'clock one instead. I'll pray extra hard for you, Kenny. God bless." She kissed me, then made the sign of the cross on my forehead.

The chief steward showed me the small tourist class galley. "This is where you will be working." I was already quite familiar with it, having worked in a mock version of one in the training school. "Check all the trays, there should be fifty-four. Don't forget to check all your supplies and make sure the ground staff loads a sufficient number of frozen food dishes into the ovens. Report to me when everything is completed."

The stewardess was rushing up and down the cabins checking cushions and straightening drapes.

"Okay, the passengers are coming," shouted the

chief steward as he posted himself at the entrance of the first class section with the second steward beside him. The stewardess took up her position in the tourist cabin with me at the forward entrance.

"Fasten your seat belts, sir," I said to a stout American tourist who couldn't find his seat belt. "This is your seat belt, sir," I lifted the flaps from under a ton of camera equipment.

"Would you help me fasten this, young man?" asked an equally stout American lady.

I made the necessary check of passengers then reported to the chief steward who in turn made his way to the flight deck to report to the Captain. The captain acknowledged the report as he made his own checks aided by the first officer and engineer.

The Chief steward then picked up the mike and began:

"Ladies and Gentlemen, welcome aboard BOAC. Our flying time to Tripoli will be six hours and ten minutes. We shall be flying at a height of 30,000 feet, but you will have no ill effect as the cabin is pressurized."

When he finished in English, he handed the mike to me: I reported the same thing in French then handed it over to the stewardess who repeated it in Italian. The plane began to move slowly down the runway as the stewardess and I made a final check of the cabin. An old lady, white with fear, grabbed my hand.

"I'm very frightened, I've never flown before!" she said.

I suddenly remembered—neither had I! I said a few words of reassurance, hoping they would help me too, then made my way to a vacant seat and fastened the seat belt. I held tight to the armrests as the roar of the engines increased; the plane rushed down the runway and I blessed myself!

When the seat belt sign went off, we immediately

prepared the trays. Within twenty minutes, we were ready to start serving. The whole meal took only an hour and a half from start to finish.

"You'll get quicker with experience," said the stewardess as she passed the last used tray back into the container.

"Quicker? You mean it can be done quicker?"

She laughed and went to answer a call from the flight deck.

"The seat belt sign is on," the chief said as he walked through the galley to the flight deck. The stewardess made the "descent" notice in English and Italian and I repeated in French. We were about to go down. I peeped out at the old lady in the cabin: I decided not to wake her as her seat belt was still fastened and her seat was in an upright position. I felt a deaf sensation in my ears as the plane turned its nose downward and we lessened our altitude.

"Please extinguish your cigarette, sir," I said to the stout American who looked a little bloodshot.

I took my seat in the galley, and the plane touched down with a gentle kiss. We had landed: I had just completed my first flight!

The crew prepared to leave the aircraft: all the passengers whose final destination was Tripoli were asked to remain on board until the transit passengers had disembarked. Soon the relief crew was coming up the steps.

"Hi Ken, what sort of flight did you have?" said the steward who had come to relieve me.

"Mike! I didn't expect to see you so soon. Did you get pushed up a day ahead too?" I asked shaking his hand.

"Yes. Ken, wait till you see the life you're going to live, talk about heaven on earth. This hotel is out of this world. You have a suite of rooms . . . there's a casino where you can gamble away the night, and a beautiful beach club where you can sun away the day. All on BOAC. They sure live up to their motto. BOAC 'took good care of me!' "

"What about pocket money in a place like that?" I questioned.

"They give you that too. It's crazy, man. They pay all the bills, even membership in the best clubs. Besides the generous salary they pay into our bank account each month, we get extra money for flying, extra money for being overseas and now she gives us ground expenses too. I tell you, it's heaven on earth."

"Sounds too good to be real," I said putting on my cap to leave and join the rest of the crew who were waiting.

"Wait till you see the company you're going to be keeping. There's a whole film cast in the hotel with you. And the girls, that's something else again. I don't know if it's the uniform or what, but I never had it so good. I don't know which I enjoyed the most, the girls or the booze. I'm afraid I'll wake up and find it was all a dream."

"I have to go, the crew is waiting for me," I said laughing at his enthusiasm.

"Wait Ken. I have this one chick's phone number. You want it?"

"Not interested. Did you forget? I'm engaged," I answered righteously.

"So what? You're not married!" he said as I walked down the steps.

"No thanks," I called back. I knew Mike had a reputation for living the fast life and was quite a playboy, but I couldn't help but like him. I must even say, I enjoyed being with him: it amused me to watch him operate.

Everything Mike said about the hotel was true: I felt like I was back in the first-class section of the *Queen Elizabeth*, only this time I was the guest: they waited on me! All the crew went to the bar, except the stewardess: she went to change into something more comfortable and joined us later.

The hours went by and the number of empty bottles began to increase in our little circle. The bar was beginning to move—I must have drunk sufficient. "I think I'll turn in, gentlemen, good night!"

"Don't leave now, the party hasn't even started!" one of them cried out as I turned away, making my way, staggering a little, to the elevator.

"Where to?" asked the elevator operator.

"To the top, straight to heaven!" I said as I braced myself like an astronaut ready for the blast off.

The next day, I spent bathing in the sun luxuriously, drying out.

The evening came too soon and we were ready to board the airline bus for the Airport again. There were sandstorm warnings and the crew didn't seem quite as lighthearted as they had the night before. We sat drinking coffee in the lounge waiting the arrival of our aircraft.

"It's off the runway!" shouted the captain. Everyone rushed out towards the flash of light. Can't they put it back on?—I was innocent of the term. It took me a minute, then I realized this was an "incident." The plane had crashed. Before I knew it, we were all helping with the rescue operations: about a third of the passengers were rescued. The stewardess and my opposite number were killed; he was one of our classmates, the one that was supposed to have had a different flight time. He had the flight that I was originally scheduled for. It should have been me!—A very sobering thought for one who had been considering heaven only yester-

151

day. We returned to the hotel early the next morning: my uniform was bloodstained and filthy. I was tired, dirty, unshaven and depressed. The luxury of the hotel surroundings didn't seem to matter as I checked back in again.

Two days later, we were off for Kano in Nigeria. The crew was still subdued, even Mike was a little docile when he met me getting off the plane. "Terrible about the incident in Tripoli. You were lucky you got that call to move up a day. It must be a weird feeling knowing it was almost you!" he said.

And it certainly was!

The accommodations in Kano were first class, but simpler in style. Our days, three in all, were spent around the hotel, and our evenings in bars and clubs. The second day there was Sunday. I went to Mass at a very large mission church conducted by English priests. It was a strange sensation when I realized I was the only white in the whole church. I felt self-conscious. I suppose this is how a black must feel in our white society. I wonder how we whites would feel if our roles were reversed. Even here in Africa, where the blacks are an overwhelming majority, they are still treated like slaves by the whites. How much humility these people must have: they have so little and still they seem to be thankful for so much—I was moved by their faith, but repelled by their poverty. That evening, as I sat in the plush atmosphere of the bar, sipping an expensive cocktail, a flash of realism hit me. That morning I couldn't wait to get out of that church and the morbid atmosphere that surrounded it, to return to the luxury and "class" of the hotel and people in it—Could this be an indication that perhaps I'm beginning to put values on the wrong things?

152

When we arrived in Lagos, we checked into the hotel and spent the few hours there, eating lunch, having a few drinks at the bar, taking a short siesta, then a quick sunbath by the side of the pool. The stewardess and I were in deep conversation about the economy in England versus Africa, when she reminded me: "Are you going to Mike's party when we reach London?"

"No, I'll probably go straight home to Southampton," I said a little reluctantly.

"That's too bad. I was hoping you would be there." She looked a little disappointed. "All of Mike's parties turn out to be a real blast. If you've never been to one, you don't know what you're missing!"

She's very pretty. June was right: all the air stewardesses I've met are extremely attractive. Suddenly I was sorry I would miss it.

At Lagos airport, there was an African woman dressed in the most colorful native dress and enormous headgear: the air crews referred to her as "Bloody Mary." She sat by her stacks of bananas, pineapples, and other fruits waiting for customers. I was very amused watching her in operation. She was bickering with the navigator: she was asking fourteen shillings, and he was offering ten. After ten minutes of arguing back and forth, the navigator paid her eleven shillings and walked away with the huge basket of oranges. Then her attention turned to me. "Hey, handsome (she called everybody 'handsome')—You want to buy something?" I showed no interest: I just smiled and nodded my head. "Hey, you is new . . . I never see you before. I make you a special offer, thirteen shillings!"

I didn't answer. I was grinning and nodding, but she kept right on talking. Fifteen minutes later, I was still standing there as she kept right on bargaining, and I still hadn't uttered one word. I enjoyed just watching her: her black face and thick lips were like ebony, her skin glistened in the sun and she rolled her large black eyes over and over. When she smiled, she revealed her beautiful white teeth. She was very picturesque in her bright green and orange costume: an appropriate scene for any post-card, I thought.

"I will give you four pineapples, besides the oranges. What you say?"

What could I say? She worked very hard to make this sale, while all I did was nod and grin.

As I walked through the airport carrying the huge basket of oranges and the pineapples propped on top, the navigator rushed over to me and laughed. "We should have warned you about Bloody Mary. You have to really bargain with her, or she'll steal you blind. I paid only eleven shillings for a basket that size. How much did she get you for?" he asked confident that I was about to quote an enormous sum.

"Seven shillings! Sometimes it pays to keep your mouth shut," I said smiling and walked on.

The next two days in Kano, I spent getting a real bronze tan; and my evenings were spent the same way, in the bar. Since I wasn't accustomed to drinking, I always seemed to tire out before the parties began. The crew never missed the opportunity of telling me what I missed, but I always felt they were exaggerating and pulling my leg, so I just laughed it off.

Soon we were airborne again as we soared through the sky on our way to Tripoli.

"Here I am again, Mike. This is the last leg for you," I said handing him the order book.

"You're coming to my party, aren't you, Ken? I have some air stewardesses lined up," he said nudging my arm and grinning from ear to ear.

154

"Sorry, I can't make it. I want to get back home," I said reaching for my cap.

"Don't give me that 'engaged' business again," he said with a slight trace of disgust.

"Sorry," I smiled and left the plane.

"You don't know what you're missing!" he shouted after me.

Oh no! Not that line again. I dismissed the thought and joined the rest of the crew.

As soon as my plane landed in London, I made my way to the terminal and hailed a taxi: I felt conspicuous standing on the curb with all my luggage and the huge basket of oranges and pineapples. As I was about to help the driver load the car, Mike pulled up in his Jaguar.

"Say old chap, . . . hop in!" he said then dismissed the taxi driver.

"You can give me a lift as far as the train station, if you don't mind," I said putting my gear in the car.

"What are you doing with all those damned oranges?" he said laughing. "Let's get them in here then we'll head for my apartment. Tonight's the night, old boy! The party's getting ready to start."

"I can't waste time in London, Mike," I explained again.

"I promise you, if you spend the evening at my party, your time won't be 'wasted'! Get the message?"

"I've already told you, I'm engaged," I said beginning to be annoyed.

"I know you're engaged," he said as the four pineapples toppled to the floor of the car. "Do you run a fruit stand in Southampton too? What are you doing with all those damned bloody oranges?" he asked again.

"I thought Mother would enjoy them and the pineapples. . . ."

"Never mind the damned fruit. Let's get going on to the party," he insisted.

"The party is out, Mike. I told you I'm engaged, besides I prefer the simple life at home. Your life is too flamboyant for me. Now will you take me to the station or shall I get a taxi?" I was emphatic.

"I'll drop you off at the station."

As I was unloading the car, I thanked him and apologized for spoiling his fun. As I was walking away, he called to me.

"Your plane has landed, old boy . . . . Get out of the clouds. Face life as it is. Don't be hung up with convention. Come on down to earth, AND LIVE!"

CHAPTER TWELVE

"Gain the whole world"
Mt 16:26

"Is that you, Kenny?" Mother screamed from the top of the stairs.

"Yes Mum, hurry down, I've got a lot to tell you." I struggled through the door with the huge basket of oranges, balancing the pineapples on top. On a table, in the kitchen, was an assortment of groceries: Mother always tried to have our favorites on hand when we were home. My eyes fell on the large box in the middle: it was full of oranges!

Throughout the whole meal, we talked of nothing but

my first flight: Jackie and Roy had a million questions about the countries I had just visited, but Mum had none. She wasn't interested in what I saw; she was interested in how it affected me. After Roy and Jackie excused themselves, she poured another cup of tea. "I hope all this luxury and glamor won't go to your head, Kenny," she said seriously.

"Mum, I'm not that easily influenced," I said, then I told her about the opportunity I had to stay in London with Mike and how firm I had been in resisting the temptation. That seemed to console her a little, but not completely—

"You were sure of yourself once before, but look what happened, remember the *Queen Elizabeth*," she reminded me.

"I'm older now, Mum, and I hope more mature."

"I know you think I'm just a worrisome old lady, but I couldn't help feel you were attracted in some way to this new life and your new friends. Take this Mike, for instance. Why does he live away from home? Doesn't he get along with his family?"

"It's not that, Mum. Some fellows need to feel independent, free, away from the constraint of an over-protective family. Some need to have room to grow," I tried to explain.

"I hope you never feel a need to 'grow' in London."

"Don't worry, Mum. I'll never leave home, not until I marry, that is!"

I picked June up that evening and since both her parents were home, we decided the only way we could talk in private was to go for a walk. We walked and walked and talked even more. "Let's stop in here for a drink," I said motioning toward a pub. June looked hesitant for she was a non-drinker. "You can have a babycham. It's a mock champagne and it tastes like pop," I said open-

157

ing the door to the lounge bar. She took a seat at a table as I ordered the drinks.

"Ken, do you mind if I ask you a question?"

"No, of course not," I answered. I wondered what was on her mind.

"What was the air stewardess like?"

"She was very attractive and quite intelligent. Why do you ask?"

"I was just wondering," she seemed to hesitate.

"Wondering what?" I was becoming impatient.

"Well,—did you?"

"Did I *what*?" I realized I was raising my voice as several people turned to look in my direction.

"Did you go out with the air stewardess?" she said in a pouting whisper.

I shrugged my shoulders Italian style. We were having our first jealous quarrel. "If you can't trust me . . . ," before I could finish, she was interrupting again.

"Alright dearest, I'm sorry. I won't mention it again."

I suppose I should be flattered that she is jealous— June really is attractive—I guess I'm glad I'm engaged, it keeps me away from bad company—If only she trusted me—

I was home a week before I received my next flight instructions: this time to Nairobi, with a whole four days in Rome and four whole days in Cairo. Rome, I can't wait to see you again!

"What do you intend to do when we land?" I asked the stewardess as the plane circled Rome's International Airport.

"I don't want to waste all my time in bars as we did on the way out."

"No, that was really a wasted two days, spending the

158

first night touring one bar and club after another, just to spend the next day in bed catching up on our sleep so we could do the same thing the next night." I agreed. "What would you really like to do, Marie?"

"Let's play the tourist and take in some sights, want to?" she asked excitedly.

"Sounds great. We'll make the first stop, St. Peter's Square. We'll start early tomorrow and spend the whole day touring."

Within thirty minutes after we checked in the hotel, one of the most deluxe on the Via del Corso, I was singing away in the shower. I was really looking forward to a quiet dinner and a few drinks with Marie and not the usual barhopping that was quickly becoming a steady routine.

I dressed formally as we were having dinner in the hotel restaurant. I was brushing my hair when I heard a knock at the door. "Come in!"

"Are you decent?" a female voice shouted from the other side.

"Yes."

"Then I shan't come in," she joked as she opened the door.

"You look gorgeous!" I said as I gazed at Marie in her very expensive and fashionable cocktail dress.

"Where are we congregating for drinks?" she asked.

"The chief's room. He told me to bring a glass . . . better take two," I said gathering up the glasses and taking Marie by the arm.

An hour later, just the two of us were sitting at a table in the plush dining room. The candlelight complimented Marie's beautiful face.

"I must compliment you on your will power to say 'no' to an evening that would have turned out to be just one round of drinks after another. For a minute there, I

159

didn't think they were going to let us get away. They will still be up there drinking three hours from now," she said as the waiter came to our table to take our orders.

"Champagne now, and we'll have. . . ." I gave him the order and nodded for Marie's approval.

"You know just what I like," she said a little surprised.

So I do! That's strange—We have only been together a little over a week and already I know Marie's tastes from the outward trip—In fact, I feel I know her better than June!

"They're having a big aircrew party when we reach London," she said, sipping the champagne slowly. "I promised another air stewardess I would go since she is helping to organize it," she added. "Are you going?"

"I've been thinking about it," I answered looking into her eyes. They were sparkling from the glow of the candle. Maybe I should see what I've been missing—Perhaps I will spend an extra few days in London after all—

The weeks passed on and soon I was an air veteran of three months. Southampton was the only part of my life that wasn't changing: the same old city, the same dull routine. Each time I came home, June wanted to go on those same dull walks and talk about her small, dull little world of a dozen lab assistants and Alf, or her mother and father and always the endless questions about the air hostesses. "Did you? . . . Did you? . . . Did you?" I always managed to be evasive, but no matter how clever I considered myself in avoiding the subject, she always ended the evening crying. I can't stand this dull routine—Everyone here is so provincial in their outlook—I must get an apartment in London as soon as possible!

160

"I'll take you home, June. I'm sure you need to get to bed early to get to your 'very interesting job,' " I said as we walked toward the carpark where I had parked my newly acquired car.

I pulled up in front of her house. "Are you coming in?" she asked as I led her to the door.

"I don't think so . . . I need an early night too," I replied yawning.

"Why have you been having late nights on this trip? Been out with those air hostesses?"

"Are we going to start that again? Goodnight June," I left her at the door and returned to my car. "I'll see you tomorrow. I don't intend to fight tonight, I'm too tired."

"Mum, I've been promoted! Remember that exam I took last trip? Well, I've been promoted to second steward. Isn't that great? That means more money too," I said as I handed her the letter to read.

"Son, I want to talk to you. Let's sit down and have a cup of tea together," she said walking toward the stove.

Good. She wants to talk. This would be a good time to tell her about taking a London apartment. Maybe this promotion will help convince her. "Fine Mum, we haven't had a good talk in a long time."

"Kenny, I don't want to upset you, but I'm worried about you. You're changing too rapidly. You're all wrapped up in material things. You never go to Mass except on Sundays and I never see you pray when you are there. Why do you always stand at the back? Have you become too important to kneel?" She didn't wait for an answer: she was just trying to prove her point. "And I know this is just between you and our Blessed Lord, . . . but Kenny, I have seen you at Mass, but at times, not at the communion rail. You're not that teen-age boy on the *Queen Elizabeth* who liked to ruffle his feathers.

161

You're a man and the games men play are far more serious. Even when you went through that period on the QE, you were at Mass every day."

"I am at Mass, am I not?" I answered defensively.

"You're there, son, but you never get there on time and you leave early. I don't think you even hear Mass. All this luxury, Kenny, . . . you know what our dear Lord said, 'What does it profit a man . . . .' "

"Yes, I know all about it," I interrupted. "What a pity the Church doesn't practice what she preaches!"

"Kenny! There was a time when you would never have said anything like that," she said hurt and a little shocked.

"I'm sorry, Mum." I took her hand: I felt ashamed that I had hurt her. "I just don't want to hear any sermons, I wanted to discuss something with you." I paused to find the right words. "With this new promotion, I thought it would be easier on me if I kept an apartment in London. Sometimes, my schedule is such that it would really help. It wouldn't mean that I wouldn't be home at all. I would be here just as much, but if I had my own apartment in London, it would be nearer my work for standby duty. So can't you see? I do need this apartment."

"Why Kenny? . . . *to 'grow'?*"

I was halfway through my second year with BOAC, when Uncle John, Mother's only brother came to live with us. There was no problem in finding room for him since the majority of my stand-off days were spent in London in my apartment with just a few days in Southampton squeezed in. June and I were still planning the wedding: it was decided that we would marry after her twenty-first birthday. That was another thing her father insisted on, however I was quite happy with my situation as it now

162

existed. While flying and in London, I was living the fast life, but in Southampton, I was trying desperately to keep up the image of the faithful fiancé and loving son: an image that Mum could see right through, for although she never once talked about it, she constantly reminded me that I was on the top of her list of "special intentions."

It was June of 1957, and Claire was finally going to be a "June Bride!" Roy and Claire were getting married in the chapel of St. Mary's College and I was their "best man." Brother Gregory was playing the organ. I went to him to make sure he had all the instructions about the songs selected for the ceremony. Before I had a chance to greet him, he looked up and said, "Hello September 14th!" How can he possibly remember that, I thought, as I stood there stunned by his salutation.

The Mass began and we knelt before the altar: I tried to concentrate on the liturgy, but my thoughts were racing back to when I was just a teen-ager here in this familiar setting. Nothing had changed: nothing except me, that is. I looked at Roy and Claire: they looked so happy and content—They are really taking the final step—No backing down now—That thought made me twinge—Am I ever going to be ready to take that same step with June?—I'm not being fair to her—or to Mother—I'm becoming more selfish by the minute—What have I actually done for someone else, other than myself?—I watched the priest take the wine and pour it—Wine!—There was a time when the first thought that would come to mind at the sight of wine was the Mass, now it's a "party."—God, I have changed!—I still believe, in my own way, I guess—Didn't I "defend the faith" just the other night in a deep discussion over religion? But even then it was done over a bottle of Scotch. My eyes roamed the sanctuary; it was as if I were trying to shut out the realization I had just found by focusing on something else. My eyes rested on the statue of the Blessed Mother: it reminded me of the time I was chastised by Brother Michael and felt compelled to write a poem of apology to Our Lady. How ironic, that one line: "Make not a hypocrite of me!"—I felt sick inside. The priest was beginning to distribute Holy Communion to the wedding party, soon he was standing over me. I lowered my head giving him the cue to pass on. Just a little while later, as we were standing getting ready to proceed from the chapel, I looked at Mum. She was crying: her eyes told me the tears were not those of happiness. Her eyes showed sadness: she was looking at me!

A few days later, I decided to really surprise Mum with something extra special; perhaps it was out of guilt, but nevertheless, I went about my task in a big way. I arranged for an interior decorator to come in and completely modernize the first floor. Everything was done in the brightest of colors. The parlor was transformed into my Chinese den, with furnishings and decorative lamps and fixtures from Hong Kong. Mum referred to it as "the opium den." The dining room was carpeted in thick red wool and the walls were a brilliant gold: the furniture was all modern. This Mum referred to as "the caravan." And the kitchen was completely changed: washer, dryer, modern stove, and large refrigerator, but this Mum referred to as "a joy!"

Just as the telephone was considered a luxury, so was a refrigerator, since the English do not chill their drinks and the food is chilled enough by the natural temperature. Mum looked about the kitchen. "I hope I can learn to work all these new fangled gadgets," she said shaking her head, but I knew she was obviously very pleased. I was happy for the conveniences also, as I was used to having all my drinks chilled since I had acquired many American tastes.

The morning after all the appliances had arrived, I went to the kitchen and opened the door of the refrigerator only to find everything warm.

"Mum, have you turned off the fridge?" I called in bewilderment.

"Of course I did, son. I didn't want that light in there burning all night wasting electricity!"

I laughed heartily and Mum laughed too, although she didn't understand why. After I explained it, she laughed all the more: Mother had a rare virtue, the ability to laugh at herself—Perhaps, some would call it "humility."

By the time I was twenty-seven, I was looking forward to my next promotion as Chief Steward. I had taken the exams and I expected the news any day. Finally, I received the call to report to headquarters, as there was a new assignment waiting for me. Although I was expecting the promotion, I wasn't prepared for the position offered me. I was to be sent to Gibraltar as the catering officer in charge of feeding and accommodating all the trainees. I had no officials looking over me: I was "The boss!"

"You will be in full command of all the trainees. Your job is to see that they are well fed and have the finest of accommodations. All our trainees are to be treated as first class passengers! Any questions?" the superintendent asked.

"Yes, how much am I allowed to spend?"

"I repeat, Mr. Roberts, 'they are to be treated as first class passengers!' You know our motto: BOAC TAKES GOOD CARE OF YOU!"

As soon as we arrived in Gibraltar, we went directly

165

to the best hotel. I was amused by the twenty-five train-ees: they were in complete awe of the luxurious sur-roundings. That evening, in the very elegantly furnished dining room, I directed the waiter to let them all choose from the deluxe menu, and since I was becoming some-what of a connoisseur, I selected the wines and liqueurs. Everyone was treated cordially, except for me—I was treated regally; I was the one signing the tab. I enjoyed this role, too. Every employee in the hotel bowed when I passed and all of them were waiting to meet my every need.

Never before had I so much time on my hands; dur-ing the day we spent all our time on the beach, swim-ming and sunbathing, as the students had their trainee flights only at night and my only task was to plan their inflight meals.

After a few weeks, I was becoming bored. As I sat on the beach, I realized I might even be a little home-sick, something I hadn't felt in a long time. I wish I was walking down a country lane, or sitting at a pub with Johnny and Max—Fish and chips would taste good right now—I wonder what's wrong with me?—I'm bored with elegant dining rooms, wine lists, liqueurs, caviar, "Yes sir," "No sir," "Anything you wish, sir" —I'll even be glad to listen to June's questions and opinions—Of course, this time, she won't be able to ask the usual: "Did you? Did you? Did you?" There aren't any hostesses on this trip—Could that be one of the reasons I'm so bored?—The sun is beginning to feel un-comfortably hot—I'm even bored with the sun! I thought as I picked up my towel and walked toward the hotel—What I need is a drink—No, I'm even bored with that—

I was happy to see London airport again. Two months is a long time to be away—I think I'll just go straight on to Southampton—I picked up my bags and started for the terminal when one of the airport officials stopped me.

"Mr. Roberts, the Superintendent wants to see you before you leave the airport."

I entered the superintendent's office, and before I had a chance to make a move, he shouted, "Did you come in a Rolls Royce?"

"A Rolls Royce?" I said puzzled.

"Yes, you could have bought a number of them and charged them to the company. Have you seen these bills?" He threw a stack of papers on his desk and continued to shout until he finished in a state of exhaustion.

"You told me to treat them like first class passengers," I replied meekly.

"Yes, but not 'Royalty!' You have been transferred to the Britannia Fleet and you will return to normal flying duties. Good afternoon!"

Well, I did it again—"gained the whole world"—For what? Mum was right—"What does it profit a man if . . . ."

CHAPTER THIRTEEN

"What is it you seek?"
Jn 1:38

I was a little stunned and ashamed, but most of all, confused, as I drove home from London to Southampton. What am I looking for?—Surely a good job, money, prestige, friends and lots of material comforts are all a man needs for security and a feeling of well being—But I have all those things—There is nothing I want that I don't have or can't get. Even in Gibraltar, with all that affluence and influence, I was bored—What do I want? —I was better off when I had nothing—

I pulled up at the red traffic signal and waited for the light to change; a lady was pushing a pram across the street smiling at her baby as she walked. Maybe, that's what I need—I need to get married and back to flying again, back with the aircrews and all the fun of different cities day after day—I won't be bored then: I'll have balance in my life: the high life away from home and the quiet home life of a family man in Southampton— I'll have the best of both worlds!

I don't know why I'm worried: this transfer is still a promotion. The Britannias are the latest planes out and the crew is double that which I'm used to flying. Being a Senior Second Steward on the Britannia fleet is prestige enough—for now anyway.

Mother was in the front garden cutting the hedge when I pulled up: I gave a few blasts on the horn.

"Kenny!" Mother dropped the shears on the hedge and ran to open the gate. "Why don't you let me know when to expect you. I like to have things ready for you."

"I thought you liked surprises." I picked her up and swung her around. "You're looking good, Mum."

"Put me down," she said laughing, then took my arm and led me into the house.

"Jackie isn't home. He's away playing soccer this week. There's just Uncle John and myself. Things are so quiet when he's away, but they won't be for long, now that you're home. You will be home for a while, won't you Kenny?" she asked hopefully.

"A few weeks this time, Mum. Are you glad?"

168

"You know that I am. When did you get to London?"

"Just this morning; I came straight home from the airport," I said putting down my luggage.

She looked at me very surprised. "You mean you didn't even stop off at your apartment?"

"No Mum, I wanted to get home right away. Why are you so surprised? After all, I've been gone for two months. Naturally, I would want to come home and relax," I said trying to be very casual.

"This is the first time you've come straight home from a flight, since I can't remember when . . . there's nothing wrong, is there?"

"Mum, why should anything be 'wrong'?" I realized I was being evasive, but Mum realized it too.

"You may think me a silly old lady, but I can't help but feel something is bothering you. You see, Kenny, I know YOU!"

I never could hide anything from Mum—for long, anyway. We sat down and I gave her a full account of what happened regarding the Gibraltar assignment. "So you can understand now, Mum, that's why I was a little upset."

"Kenny, I don't want to hurt you, but I must say this. I'm glad this happened to you. You were beginning to believe your tinsel world was really living. Perhaps, this will be a lesson to you." She reached across the table and took my hand. "You can't keep taking out of life, you have to put something in it."

"Maybe you're right, Mum. All I know is that I'm confused. I'm not sure of anything right now. Well, that's partly true, I am sure of one thing . . . I'm glad I'm home."

"It's good to hear you say that. You haven't said that in a long time. One more thing, Kenny, . . . why don't

169

you start to pray more. Perhaps we could go up to the Sisters' chapel and . . . ."

"Mum, I know you mean well," I interrupted. "I said I didn't know what I wanted, but I do know what I don't want, and that's a sermon!"

She looked at me very hurt. Why did I have to say that?—She was only trying to help—What's wrong with me? I tried to smooth everything over, by taking her arm and leading her to the parlor.

"Come on. Let's wake Uncle John up from his nap. Then, we have some serious talking to do. We have another wedding to plan, remember?"

"I missed you so, Ken. I hate you being away so much, but at least this time you weren't with any air hostesses! What about those Spanish girls, they are really beautiful, aren't they?" June said as we walked.

"I missed you too, June. I really did. But you know you really have to accept the fact that this is my job and I love it. I couldn't stand any ordinary job, getting up at the same time, coming home at the same time . . . ."

"You used to do it once," June interrupted.

"Yes, but I've changed since then," I tried to explain.

"That's what worrries me. You have changed. Will you be able to settle down to married life, Ken? Besides, you'll be gone so much of the time . . . ."

"The time balances out. I'll be gone a month, then home three straight weeks. Don't worry, June. It will all work out," I said in an effort to change the subject. She was beginning to sermonize, too.

We were passing a pub. "Let's go in for a drink." I led her to the door.

"I don't care, if that's what you want, but why do we always have to go into pubs every time we go out? You know I don't like to drink and I hate pubs!"

Couldn't she try to please me, or just go along with

something I wanted to do my first evening home in two months?—Well, I guess it works both ways: I could have passed up the pub. I know she doesn't like them —It's true, though, I did miss her while I was away— But was it because there were no air stewardesses around? No, not really. I do care for June, and I need to put some substance in my life—Will she think differently about my job after we're married?

"What are we going to do tomorrow night, Ken?" she said as she sipped her drink.

"Well, you know, I thought I might give Johnny and Max a call. I haven't been out with those guys since . . . ."

"But Ken, you just got home, and you've been gone so long this time. I was hoping we could spend the first few days together. Why don't we have dinner at my house and visit with Mummy and Daddy for a while, then maybe we could go to a show. Wouldn't you like that?"

"Okay June, whatever you say." I downed my drink and went to the bar to order another. Nothing I'd like better than spending the evening with "Mummy and Daddy," I thought as I took a big gulp from my second drink and returned to the table.

I spent the next week catching up on some rest, visiting Roy and Claire, watching Jackie play soccer and listening to Uncle John snore. Although Uncle John was six years younger than Mum, he looked much older: his hair was white; Mother's wasn't even gray. He was over six feet tall, but his droopy slow walk took inches off him. Mum was little, but she walked as straight as a soldier with short rapid strides. I was glad Mum had Uncle John to keep her company, although he slept most of the time: still, it was someone else Mum could look after and that's what she liked doing best.

One afternoon, as I was returning home from Roy's, I was met by a delivery man carrying a TV set out instead of in!

"What's the trouble?" I asked him.

"The lady of the house won't accept it, sir," he answered.

"Take it back! I paid for it. She'll accept it," I ordered.

The man followed me into the house carrying the TV. "Where do you want it, Mum?" I called. TV was another one of those luxuries that was just beginning to catch on at this time.

"It's not going anywhere, but out that door. It's a waste of money. I don't know how to work it and neither does Uncle John. Even if I did, I'm not going to waste my time playing that thing all day and sitting around in the dark," she said as she began to look a little annoyed.

"Mum, you don't play it, and you don't sit in the dark either. You've never seen a television, but I know you will like it if you once watch it. Now, just sit down . . . please."

The man plugged the set in and waited for the picture to come. It would only be a test pattern as the BBC was only transmitting from 4 p.m. till 11 p.m. and it was not quite 4 o'clock. At this time, England only had one channel. A picture appeared on the screen: it was a series of contrasting diagrams and the picture was accompanied by background music. Mother and John looked at it for a minute. "I prefer the radio," Mum said getting up from her chair. "Besides, I can't waste time sitting here all day looking at all that modern art stuff!"

Uncle John sat mesmerized by the picture laughing and giggling like a child each time the test card was

172

changed. At last the children's hour started, a puppet show. The announcer, a woman, started:

"Good afternoon, children."

"Good afternoon!" answered Uncle John enthusiastically.

"Are you all watching, children?" continued the announcer.

"Yes!" was his snappy reply.

"Do you know what we are going to do today?" she asked.

"No! I don't even know what you did yesterday. Get on with the show," said Uncle John impatiently.

"Who are you talking to, John?" asked Mum coming back into the room.

"This daft dame who keeps asking a lot of stupid questions," he replied, not taking his eyes away from the screen.

Never again was Uncle John to sleep after 4 p.m.! And within a week, Mum was converted too.

I spent every evening with June. All we seemed to talk about was the wedding. I didn't agree with her elaborate plans: they were her mother's, and so we usually ended up in a tiff. Southampton was beginning to get on my nerves.

"When are you going to give up your London apartment, Ken? It really isn't necessary, is it? Besides, that money you are spending for rent could be put to better use now, with all the expense of the wedding. And then there's the furniture, and the down payment and . . . ."

"It's necessary for stand-by duty. We aren't married yet!" I said emphatically.

"I don't think you want to give up that apartment. What do you do in it all by yourself? Don't you get lonely? I thought you liked people?" she asked prying.

173

My thoughts returned to some of the wild parties we had at my apartment and I grew restless. I had an idea—

"June, how would you like to meet some of my BOAC friends?"

"You mean I get to meet them?" she said, hoping to be taken to London. "Daddy won't let me stay the night in your apartment, but I could get a room . . . ."

"Never mind the apartment. I'll invite them down here. We can have a party!"

"A party? Who is having a birthday?" She was becoming enthused.

"June, no one has to have a birthday just to have a party and have a good time. We'll have it at my place, in the 'Chinese' den. Mum would get a big kick out of cooking and getting everything ready. It would be just like the old days with the house full of people laughing and enjoying themselves." I was getting excited as I started rattling off a list of names to invite. "So you like the idea, huh?" I said lighting a cigarette.

"You smoke too much!" June complained as she pulled the cigarette from my lips.

I controlled myself. After all, she was happy about the party. I took out another cigarette and lit it. She didn't remove that one.

"Okay, let's do it," she said as we walked toward my car.

Mother was as happy as I was as she greeted the guests and showed them into the den where I was mixing drinks at the bar. With each new batch of cocktails I made, I took a sip to make sure they were alright. The room began to fill with people and smoke. I was enjoying myself so much: I didn't realize Mum wasn't in there with us, until someone said there was a knocking

174

at the door of the den. I could hardly hear above the noise and laughter. I opened the door.

"Mum, what are you doing out there? Come in here and join the fun. Let me fix you a small glass of sherry," I said as someone placed another drink in my hand.

"No dear, I'm going to bed. It's quite late and I have to get up early for Mass. There is plenty of food in the kitchen, just help yourselves. Good night and God bless you all. It was a pleasure to have you in my home, boys." She stretched to kiss my cheek, then turned to leave only to stop. "Where's Uncle John? I saw him come in here about an hour ago." I looked around the crowded room. There he was in the corner snoring. "Wake up, John! It's time to go to bed," she yelled in his ear.

Uncle John jumped. "No need to scream. Just shut me eyes for a second!" He stood, staggered for a moment, then followed her out of the room grumbling. Mum just smiled and led him along.

I was having a ball exchanging stories about some of our flights and laughing at the many funny imitations given of different BOAC personalities. Once in a while, some stewardess' name would pop into the conversation and I would cringe, then look toward June, who was sitting in a corner pouting: I'd just nod and smile. I'd give her that "throw me a kiss from across the room" kind of smile, but she wasn't sending any back. Soon, I became so wrapped up in having a good time and drinking, that I forgot she was even there.

"Ken, take me home . . . please," she whispered as I served up more drinks.

"What do you want to go home for? We're just starting to have a good time. Sit down and enjoy yourself," I half shouted, then returned to a group who were fumbling through some records.

About fifteen minutes later, somebody yelled, "Hey, someone's ringing the doorbell!" I went to answer it.

"Did you order a taxi, sir?" asked the driver.

"Nobody here ordered any taxi," I explained confused.

"I did!" said June who came running to the door.

I grabbed her arm and held her back. "What did you order a taxi for? I can take you home, if that's what you want," I said becoming angry.

"No, you stay with your FRIENDS. You're more interested in them than you are in me. You've been ignoring me all night. I've seen a different side of you tonight, and I don't think I like it. Why do you have to show off so? And you drink too much!" she screamed and slammed the door.

I stood there for a moment looking at the closed door. I'm not going after her—She didn't even try to have a good time—If she can't accept me and my friends, then that's too bad—She'll get over it—

"Don't worry about her, Ken. She'll be fine tomorrow. That's how women are. If you start bowing down now, you'll be doing it the rest of your life," Mike said as he gave me a fresh drink. I gulped down the old one and led him back to the den.

"You're right! Besides we're having this party for the sake of a good time, so let's have one." I walked back to the bar to make up some more of my "special" cocktails. "Hey somebody, change the records!" I shouted above the noise.

The drinking and laughing continued through the early hours of the morning. The last thing I remembered was picking up a spilled drink when I became so dizzy I couldn't stand. When I opened my eyes, a small shaft of light was peeping through the shades, but to me it was like an airport spotlight piercing my pupils, shattering

176

my head to bits. I closed my eyes, held my head and turned on my side taking a deep breath. The smell of stale liquor and smoke pricked my nostrils and sent a wave of nausea through me that made me shake. I didn't want to move a single muscle in my body. I didn't think I could. I lay there for a few moments trying to get up the nerve to open my eyes again. Finally I looked around the room. There were two figures sprawled out on the floor, the others were sleeping in chairs. Cigarette butts and ashes were all over the floor from the dropped ashtrays. Glasses and bottles were strewn about on their sides. I propped myself up on one elbow. My shirt was stained with tomato juice from a misplaced "Bloody Mary" and my tie was draped around my neck like a stole. I made my way to the bar and opened the ice bucket, stepping over the sleeping figures and holding on the arm of the couch. My mouth felt like cotton. When I reached my hand in, there was nothing there but a soggy ham sandwich floating in the warm water that had become a putrid yellow from the mustard. I knew I was going to be sick: I felt a great urgency to make it to the john. Each time I gagged, I thought my head would surely explode. I threw some cold water over my face and weakly made my way back toward the den, when I saw Mother standing at the front door.

"Mum?" I said still staggering.

"Good morning, son. I'm going to Mass. When I get home, I'll fix you and your friends a nice breakfast. Why don't you go to bed for a while and get some sleep. You don't look so good."

I tried to open my red swollen eyes. She was just standing there looking at me. I started to tuck my wrinkled shirttails in my trousers. "Let me drive you, I'll just . . . ."

"I must go, I don't want to be late for Mass and

177

you're in no condition to drive." She turned to open the door, then looked back at me again. "I'll pray for you, son."

I leaned back against the wall. I felt sick all over again, more than that I felt ashamed. I had picked up something in Mum's eyes I had never seen before, disgust. I feel so humiliated—If only she would get angry, or shout at me, or lose her temper—or something. It's hell, living with a saint!

CHAPTER FOURTEEN

"Unbind him, and let him go"
Jn 11:29

I spent the next few days being over solicitous to Mother, although she never once mentioned the party, not even when she had to clean up the mess we had so carelessly made. June was a little harder to get around: it took a couple of visits and some fast talking before she agreed to wear my ring again.

"Is there any mail for me?" I asked Mum at lunch.
"No son. You're anxious to get your flight instructions, aren't you?" she asked searchingly.

It was true: I was becoming more anxious each day to get back on another flight. I felt like I was suffocating in Southampton.

"Yes Mum, I guess I am. I get bored with nothing to do."

"Is it just that, Kenny, or do you feel that you don't fit here any more?"

"I don't know what it is. I'm just restless." I tried to change the subject. "Would you like me to take you somewhere, or perhaps, you could just go for a ride?"

"You could take me up to the convent, if you don't mind, and while you're there, maybe we could stop in to make a short visit to the Blessed Sacrament."

"I'm happy to drive you there, Mum. But please, don't ask me to come in with you. I'm not in the mood," I said trying not to be harsh.

"Are you ever 'in the mood' to pray any more, Kenny?"

"Please, Mum . . .," I said imploringly.

"Alright Kenny. The Blessed Mother lost her Son for a while and she searched until she found Him. I'll just have to wait till you find us!"

At last the flight instructions for the Britannias came. The "whispering giants" were to take me to the Far East. Tokyo and Sydney were the main destinations, but Rome was still the major stop-over. I was all too willing to leave Southampton and return to the glamor and high living of far away places.

The months slipped by and too soon it was a new year, 1959. June's twenty-first birthday came and went: still we were not married, but at least we agreed on a date. We were to be married in June! June was busy taking the last part of her religious instructions: soon she would become a Catholic. I'm sure that it was Mum's influence that made her so devout at this time.

"What do you want to do this evening, how about dinner, then a show?" I asked as we walked toward the car.

"You really want to know what I want to do?" she asked.

179

"I wouldn't have asked you if I didn't," I said impatiently.

"Then let's go to Rosary and Benediction!"

"I prefer the show," I insisted and got my own way for once.

The next day, I was back in Rome again. Two hours after landing, I was changed out of uniform and dressed in an expensive suit made especially to my tastes by my tailor in Hong Kong. I was ready for action! I picked up the phone and in my best Italian asked to be put through to the stewardess' room. "Hello, Pat? Is that you? . . . Champagne in my room in ten minutes . . . bring a glass." Having gone through the same procedure with the other two stewardesses and five stewards of our crew, I sat back and waited. I was ready for another "good time."

The second night, we were all feeling a little jaded so we decided to dress casually and have a quieter bar crawl. I was waiting in the lobby of the hotel for the rest of the crowd when I saw a chief steward friend of mine from another flight. He was dressed formally and he was alone.

"Hello Bob, where is your crew?" I asked.

"They have all gone to Capri and won't be back until tomorrow," he replied.

"Why don't you come with us? You're quite welcome," I suggested.

"No thanks, old boy. That's not my kind of night. I've outgrown them. But you're welcome to join me if you dress for dinner," he said looking at my sporty attire.

I felt sorry for him being alone, so I excused myself from our crew and returned to my room to dress formally.

180

"What are we going to do this evening, then?" I asked as we hailed a taxi.

"We're going to a very expensive night club on the Via Veneto. 'Madam Bricktop's,' " he told the driver as we drove off. Our taxi headed for the most chic street in Rome.

"What's so special about this place, Bob?"

"The owner! She's an extraordinary woman. Wait till you meet her. You're Catholic, aren't you?" he asked.

"Yes, why?" I was puzzled at the sudden switch in conversation to religion

"Bricktop, the lady who owns this place is Catholic too. She does a lot of work for the Catholic charities. She is really a devout woman . . . . Very well known in the Vatican circles. You meet all sorts of famous people throughout the whole world at her place. She's famous in her own right, too . . . . Really a fascinating person, Ken. You'll like her.'"

"It seems strange, a night club owner on the swankiest street in Rome mixing in the Vatican circles," I said amused.

"She's a convert to your faith, too. I'm telling you, you're in for an evening you'll never forget!"

Most of the guests at the club were Americans: you can always tell the Europeans by their formal dress. We made our way across the carpeted floor and found two seats at the bar: we ordered our drinks and sat back to enjoy the show.

"Hello honey, how's things?"

I turned to look towards the voice. A very large, jovial and extremely vivacious woman was greeting my friend with real gusto. She was smoking a cheroot and in her other hand she held a glass of cognac. She had a distinct southern drawl.

"Ken, this is Madam Bricktop," said Bob. "Bricky, this is Ken. He's with BOAC, too."

I stood up to be introduced.

"What are you drinking? It's on the house," she said motioning me to take my seat again.

"Ken's Catholic, too," informed John.

Her face lit up. She took a seat next to me and in minutes, I found myself completely wrapped up in conversation with this fascinating woman. I couldn't resist asking her about that strange accent. She explained that she was an American from the southern states. She told me all about her conversion to the Catholic Church, and when she spoke of her religion, she seemed to be aglow. Just listening to her, I realized my faith used to be like hers. It was like placing a new penny next to an old one. One thinks the old one is bright until its dullness is shown by the new.

Before long, I caught myself telling her about my mother's strong religious upbringing of us children and she became more interested with each word. I told her about things I hadn't thought of in years, my daily attendance at Mass when I was young, my desire to become a priest early in life, my pilgrimage to Rome and Lourdes, my subsequent application to the seminary in Portugal, the offering of Mrs. Diskin to pay for my education, and finally my draft into the British army. I even told her about how as a child I would sling a tablecloth round my shoulders and raise bread wafers before the crucifix in my room pretending to say Mass. And the one occasion when Mum walked in and asked what I was doing. "Practicing for when I become a priest," I said. This was a secret I hadn't remembered or shared with anyone till now. I don't know why I felt compelled to tell her all of that: it just seemed to come out. Perhaps, it was the Scotch, or maybe it was because she was a good listener. She seemed to hang on my every

182

word. I finished my account of my life by saying laughingly:

"But as you can see, I was not cut out to be a priest."
I finished my drink and ordered another.

"Why do you say that?" she asked very sincerely.

"Well, it's quite obvious. This is the life for men. I'm too attracted to the world. I enjoy the fast life. Some kind of priest, I would have made. Besides, I'm engaged!" I said almost as an afterthought.

"But you aren't married . . . ," she added.

"No, but I will be next June. I'll have to settle down a bit then I suppose." I laughed again. but I noticed she was quite serious.

"Let me pray for you, Ken," she said very intently.

"You sound like my mother. She prays for me constantly."

"Perhaps you were meant to be a priest. Do me a favor." She reached over the bar and took a piece of paper. "Do you have a pen?" she asked.

"Yes, here it is." I was confused as to what she wanted.

"Write down on this paper these words: 'Please show me whether I am to be a priest or not.' "

"This is silly. I have no intentions of becoming a priest. That is all behind me now. Now what?" I questioned.

"Nothing, you don't have to do a thing. We'll let the Blessed Mother handle everything. I'll put it before her shrine tomorrow," she said folding the paper.

It was 4 a.m. when I left the club. As I sat back in the taxi, I still felt overwhelmed by this woman and her deep faith—She is really fascinating—Truly in love with Christ—I remember when I used to have that same glow, too—Of course, I was young then, I didn't really know much of life—But I was happy, happier than I am now—That's funny because now I have ev-

183

erything any man could want, the adventure of travel, a good position, high living, plenty of material things— Soon I'll be married, and when I'm not living the fast life flying, I'll have the security of a nice home and family —I really do have everything—But something is missing!—This is ridiculous: I'm not going to take all this seriously—Although, I laughed at Mrs. Diskin too and she really was sincere—If God wanted me to be a priest, He would have seen to it then, I imagine—The whole thing is stupid. I'm not going to think about it anymore—How do I get involved with people like this? —or should I say, "WHY" do I get involved with people like this?

The next morning, it all seemed like a dream. Did it really happen? I couldn't get Bricktop off my mind, like when she looked at me and said, "You won't get married, the Holy Spirit has His hooks on you, boy, and He won't let go!" Why did I have to go to that damn club anyway—It's so unrealistic—How could I even consider a priestly vocation, when I'm not even a good Catholic?—I haven't been to confession in ages—And I don't want to be a priest any more—She's probably some religious nut!—I thought that about Mrs. Diskin too and look what happened—Yes, look what happened, NOTHING! The phone rang. "Hello! . . . Mike, when did you get in? . . . What's your room number? Okay, I'm on my way. I'll bring a glass. I could use a drink right now!"

Our next stop was Beirut: our hotel was very impressive; it was situated in the modern suburbs of the city. Usually we checked in, changed into casual dress and headed for the bar across the street.

"I'll see you fellows later," I said to the crew as I walked into the elevator.

"You're going to the 'Golden Bar' with us, aren't you?" asked the first officer as he followed me into the elevator.

"Not now, I'll be over later. I want to get a little fresh air." My mind was cluttered with a million things: I wanted a little time to kind of sort things out. I felt like just taking a long walk: I had no place special in mind to go, but just getting away from a hotel room and the phone would be a relief. I knew if I stayed around, I wouldn't have the will power to refuse an invitation for a drink, and tonight, I didn't feel the booze would drown my thoughts. It's time I brought them to the surface.

It was a beautiful evening as I walked through the quiet streets. I could see a big church at the end of the street, and vaguely I could recognize the strains of organ music. As I walked closer, I found myself humming the Latin hymn. They're just beginning Benediction—When's the last time I heard that?—I have plenty of time, I think I'll go in.

The altar was surrounded by dozens of lighted candles and flowers. A priest in a gold cope was putting incense into the thurifer, aided by two very Arabic looking altar boys. The priest stood to intone the prayer, "Panem de caelis . . . ." A great silence fell upon the church, broken by the ringing of the bell. The priest replaced the monstrance on the altar and began the "Divine Praises" in Arabic. It was strange to hear this familiar prayer in an unfamiliar language. The word, "Catholic" struck me: for the first time I really understood what it meant, "universal." The mood and the setting made me want to pray desperately, but it had been so long since I really prayed with meaning that I had to search for the right words. All I could think of was, "Lord, forgive me. I am a sinner."

I noticed a light over one of the confessionals. I was

very nervous as I entered—What if the priest doesn't speak English?—Maybe he speaks French—I knelt in the darkness and the little sliding door opened.

"Father, do you speak English?" I asked.

"Yes, my son," the voice answered.

"Bless me, Father, for I have sinned. It has been over a year since my last confession. I would like to confess the sins of my whole life . . . ."

The priest was patient as he listened to my long story and many sins. Finally I reached the end of what it took me so long to tell him: I felt like I was belittling my labors as I said simply, "That's all, Father. For these and all the sins of my past life I am heartily sorry."

The priest waited for a moment. He was a very kind and compassionate man: his voice was gentle as he spoke. "It seems, my son, this work of yours is a constant source of great temptation to you, a permanent occasion of sin. You should give serious consideration to seeking other employment, if you value the salvation of your soul."

"But Father, this would be extremely difficult for me at this time." I tried to explain my situation, how I felt I could never be happy in any routine job, and how the money I was making was important to me with my impending marriage. He listened very closely.

"I understand all this, my son. But let me explain. There is much more at stake than your future. You must think of the life of your soul! If you were sick and you knew for certain that something was endangering your very health, surely you would give it up for the sake of your over-all well being. As of late, your soul has been sick. Would you keep exposing it to that which threatens its very life, and eternity! Think about this, and pray for the strength to do what you know is right. Now for your penance make a good act of contrition and say five rosaries. *Ego te absolvo . . . .*"

186

I left the church with a light feeling of peace and joy. The only thing that marred this was Father's words, "The salvation of your soul." He's right; my soul has been sick up until now and I must get away from the source of contamination—But look at Bricktop. She is constantly surrounded with the glitter and tinsel, yet she has managed to keep her faith alive, even spread it within those surroundings—Could I ever do the same? Could I have the courage to be different?—"The salvation of your soul"—So help me God, I'm going to try!

I returned to the hotel: I decided to turn in early, besides I wanted to keep reminding myself of all that Father had just told me. As I was walking toward the elevator, one of the crew stopped me.

"Hey Ken. Nobody's up there. We're all across the street at the bar. I'm just going back over. Come on, I'll introduce you to the two new stewardesses from the other flight."

"Thanks, but not tonight. I want to turn in early," I explained.

"Well, just come over for a couple of drinks. It's not late."

"No, I don't feel like drinking, but thanks, just the same," I said getting into the elevator.

"Hey, what's with you? You sick?" he called after me.

"Not any more!" I smiled as the doors closed.

It was late spring and all the wedding plans were finally settled. In just a few weeks, I would be a married man! I was a different person now. Whenever possible, I started the day with Mass and Communion. It wasn't easy, but I was managing to live a good Catholic life as an air-crew member without being anti-social. My usual

187

drink was substituted by Cokes, and I excused myself early from all parties. My friends respected my wishes and I learned to respect them more, too.

June and I were to meet for lunch and go over some final items for the wedding. I wasn't looking forward to this meeting, since the last day I was in, twenty one days ago, we had a bitter argument. I was early so I decided to go to St. Joseph's church for a visit: I was becoming apprehensive as the day was drawing closer. I needed reassurance that this marriage was the right thing: I hoped I would find it through prayer. I knelt before the statue of the Blessed Mother. "Holy Mother, am I doing the right thing? I'm confused and a little afraid. I wish I could have a sign." I knelt there for a while longer—Funny, even as a child, I always came to kneel before the Blessed Mother to pray. Like when I was at St. Mary's and I wrote that poem. The last line hit me. "Let me be chosen by your Son!" Why should I think about that now? I can't be married and a priest too— Even if I wanted to be a priest, which I don't, what about June. I guess all grooms go through this time of indecision, I thought trying to console my anxiety. I genuflected before the altar and left the church.

June was waiting at the door of the restaurant when I arrived.

"Hope you weren't waiting long," I said as I took her in my arms to greet her.

"No, I just got here myself," she answered. She felt all tensed up as I released her.

We took our usual table in the corner and waited to be served, glancing at each other periodically in awkward silence. Something is the matter—Maybe she is still angry over the argument from my last trip.

The meal dragged as I tried desperately to make conversation. "Is everything ready for the wedding reception, June?"

"Ken—I don't know how to tell you this," she said nervously.

"What is. the matter with you? Can't you look at me?" I asked as she hung her head.

"Ken, I've been out with someone else while you were away," she started to cry.

I felt guilty. Here she was crying because she had a date with someone else when I had been living it up all the time, before. I tried to console her. "One date, June, I'm not going to get upset over that. I understand, really I do. After all, I'm away so much and . . . ."

"No Ken. You don't understand at all." Without looking up, she took the ring from her finger and placed it on the unused plate. "I'm sorry, Ken. I really am." She ran from the table crying.

I was stunned—What does all this mean? My God, what will I do now? I looked down at the plate where the diamond glistened. I don't understand all this—What will I do now?

Bricktop's words came back to me. "You don't have to do a thing. We'll let the Blessed Mother handle everything!"

CHAPTER FIFTEEN

"Coming down from the mountain"
Mk 9:8

"Kenny, you have been moping around this house for the last three days and it's not helping you, son. Can't you accept the fact that what happened to you and June was God's will?" Mum asked.

"Mum, I'm not all that upset over the split up. I'll get over that. What does bother me is, 'What is God's will?' " I tried to explain without mentioning even the slightest hint about the priesthood.

"We don't ever know what God has planned for us, son. All we can do is pray that we learn to accept it. Do you mind if I make a suggestion?" she asked. I could tell by her eyes that she was deeply concerned for me. "Why don't you go back to Lourdes and Fatima? You found what you were looking for there once before, maybe you will again."

"Perhaps you're right. I have over two weeks till my next flight instructions come—besides, I need time to think many things out."

I spent the next two weeks touring Lourdes and Fatima: there were many times I didn't feel like praying, but nevertheless, I did. I was hoping to gain inspiration or perhaps, contentment. And although I did feel more content, I felt that I still needed more. When I returned home, Mum told me she and the Sisters were very busy while I was gone, praying for me again, of course!

"You look so relaxed and refreshed from your vacation, Kenny," she said as she laid out my shirts. I was packing: I had to leave for London that afternoon for my next flight.

"I am relaxed, Mum. Now, what was it you wanted me to do while I'm in Calcutta?"

"I promised those friends of Claire that you would visit their daughter, you know, the nun. They worry about her so, Kenny, living in the midst of all that poverty and filth."

"I promise I'll call on her the first thing after I arrive. Her uncle is the Chief Customs Officer. I see him every trip there, and he tells me she is happy and getting along very well," I said as I placed the last few items in my suitcase.

"Kenny, isn't it marvelous though, the way that girl left all that wealth here and gave her life to God to do His work in that God-forsaken place? How unselfish she must be!"

"How unselfish!" Those words stayed in my mind and provoked the facing of another truth about myself. Could I ever give up my job and all the enjoyment that went with it to give myself completely to God? That's a decision I shall never have to make—He's not asking me to—Is He?

"Kenny did you hear what I said?" Mum asked again.

"Yes Mum, I was listening. You're absolutely right. She has certainly been generous with God. She's quite beautiful, too, Mum. She has the kind of beauty that is seen from within as well. It's like her love of God shows right through her and warms everyone with its glow."

"Why Kenny, I never knew you were so poetic!" Mum looked startled.

"There's a lot of things you don't know about me," I said laughing, then followed her down the stairs. I was a little embarrassed when I realized I was speaking my thoughts.

"Take care, son . . . and God bless," Mum hugged me, then turned to Uncle John who was snoring away. "John, wake up and say good-bye to Kenny, he's leaving now." She screamed at him. He was very deaf.

"Good-bye!" was his only word, then he went back to continue his nap. It was still too early for the "Children's Hour."

I didn't find the peace of mind or inspiration at Lourdes there, but during the drive to London, it hit me.

I never felt this way before or since. God's presence felt so real that the world seemed unreal. I felt a feeling of love so intense that I thought my heart would break. I was delirious with happiness. Now, I understood what people meant when they said they were "in love with Christ." No words could ever describe my state of joy at that moment. This state of euphoria lasted for the rest of the week. It was so easy to pray: it was so easy to love people. Everybody was beautiful: I wanted to hug the whole world. At the end of the week, God in His wisdom saw fit to withdraw this feeling of His presence. I had to come down from the mountain and face the reality of humanity, especially my own. I knew in my heart that I should be doing something about seeing whether I had a vocation or not, but with the withdrawal of this feeling, came the old pull of the world. How can I give up this wonderful job? Surely I can serve God and continue as I am, an apostolic layman. That is what Father Tigar, the Rector of Osterley had suggested so many years ago in London.

A week later, we were landing at the Calcutta airport. I hated Calcutta: I could never get used to the poverty and the ungodly stench. The only thing that made this short stop-over tolerable was my friend, the chief customs officer and uncle of the nun. I could escape the horrors of India, by visiting with him and his family in his home. I even hated staying in the hotel there. The luxury inside, made the destitution on the streets even more shocking. People strolled through the corridors in expensive clothes, smoked the best cigars, drank the finest liquors, and ate the most elaborate meals, only to leave through the front door and be besieged by starving children lying half dead in the streets begging for food. His home was like a sanctuary to me. Here, I could escape both extremes.

192

It took exceptionally long to go through customs: I had never known them to be so thorough. I couldn't wait to get through the line and away from the crowded terminal. India has a smell all its own, a combination of unwashed bodies and cow manure for both filled the crowded streets where the "sacred" animals are left free to roam at will.

"Ken, it's good to see you again. Please sit down," the nun directed me as she took a chair. "I'm glad I was in when you called. I've been quite busy with going to the University during the day and working at night," she said in her distinct Oxford accent: that was the school she attended before entering the convent.

"Working at night?" I said puzzled.

"Yes, we sisters leave the convent every evening and bring back the sick and the dying here to the convent. Unfortunately, we can't accommodate all who are in need, but we have managed to save quite a number, the rest we can at least offer the dignity not to die in the streets." She was truly beautiful. Her white, blue edged sari draped about her face. One couldn't help but picture her on the holy cards depicting the Blessed Mother. "Let's talk about something more pleasant," she said. "You should be getting married soon, what day have you planned?"

I quickly filled her in on the situation, then changed the subject. We talked for a half hour or more then I excused myself.

"I must be going, Sister. It was so nice seeing you again. I'm to have dinner this evening with your uncle, and I am running a little late. Do you have any message for me to give your folks?"

"Tell Mummy and Daddy that I am very happy here doing God's work and not to worry," she said walking me to the door.

"I'll give them your message, good-bye Sister."

"I'll pray for you Kenneth, I really think you were meant to be a priest."

"Good-bye!" I didn't want to pursue that suggestive line any longer. Not her, too!

Later that evening, I was in for quite a shock at her uncle's home.

"The customs were unduly severe today at the airport," I said reaching for a glass of water.

"Yes, unfortunately we have to be extra severe with the air crews: our intelligence is learning a lot about an organized gold smuggling ring which is bringing the gold in large quantities into India and we have reason to believe they are using aircrew members to do it. If you want to make yourself a pile of money, you should keep your eyes and ears open. We're offering a large reward for information that would lead to the discovery of the organization."

I took an extra gulp from the glass of water. This is a dangerous situation to be in—I know quite a lot about the organization already! I thought back to my second visit in Hong Kong. There, I was invited by a crew member to dine at the home of a Hong Kong millionaire who entertained the aircrews lavishly. Three years ago, on my first visit to his penthouse, he spent the evening showing me albums of photographs, most of them were of aircrew friends who visited him from time to time. He said his hobby was amateur photography. He offered to take my photograph and I accepted his kind offer. I remember how well we dined and drank and how he sent us back to the boat that would take us to Kowloon in his chauffeur-driven Rolls Royce. I had been very impressed. There were many such visits until I had reason to suspect that his motives were not "unselfish generosity." I also discovered that several aircrew members were smuggling watches to Tokyo. I wonder if my association with him could involve me with the organization!

Three days later, we were in Singapore, an Oriental city that was modern and clean and where we could eat the best Chinese food. What a pleasure to live in the luxury of air-conditioned hotels after the sweltering heat of Calcutta where a fan merely moved the hot stale air and kept the flies off the ceiling.

"Are you coming to the pool, Ken?" the first officer said on the other end of the phone.

"Yes, I'll be down in a minute." I hung up the phone, changed into shorts and a sports shirt, grabbed a beach bag and threw in my cigarettes, suntan lotion, trunks and a towel. When I entered the lobby, the rest of the crew was standing around looking very sullen. "Okay gang, let's go!" I shouted. Nobody responded: one of them handed me a newspaper. The headlines read in bold black print: BOAC GOLD SMUGGLERS ARRESTED IN CALCUTTA! I sat down to read the full front page story. I knew the two guys who had been arrested.

"What idiots! Who would be fool enough to take gold into Calcutta; the normal guy would be scared to smuggle beer into that country. Their first class hotels are bad enough: what must their prisons be like?" Nobody appreciated my humor. I apologized: it was in poor taste.

Each day the newspapers were full of stories of more and more dismissals from BOAC. The two arrested stewards in Calcutta must have talked and talked plenty. Our millionaire friend's home in Hong Kong was raided by the police. Still more arrests were reported and the number of dismissals from BOAC was soaring. BOAC was getting very short of stewards and I found myself doing a double shuttle to Sydney from Singapore.

195

After four weeks, we were landing at Calcutta once again: the customs were even more severe this time as each of us was required to strip for inspection. We were taken to a special office where an official was checking our passports against a list of names on his desk. One by one, we filed past as he scrutinized the passport, our face and list. "Okay, you can go," he said to me as he handed back my passport. Thank God we only had a night in Calcutta and were leaving in the morning for Karachi.

I was beginning to piece together a lot of the news about the whole operation. Evidently a steward with a load of gold to deliver to a contact in Calcutta had his aircraft redirected to Karachi because of bad weather and his plane overflew Calcutta, so he found himself in Karachi with no contact. Thinking he was outsmarting the organization he sold the gold privately and made himself a pile of money in the process. When he arrived in London, he resigned from BOAC and bought himself a restaurant. He didn't have it long: the next week, he was found dead in it. The police suspected murder and Interpol was called in. The fellow who was arrested was shadowed because of his heavy spending, which was well above the standard of his salary. Once they caught him with the gold, it wasn't hard to get him to talk.

One week later, we touched down at London Airport. The plane taxied to a standstill: the passengers left and then the Security Police boarded the aircraft. "Mr. Roberts?" said the taller of the two plainsclothesmen.

"Yes, what can I do for you?" I said efficiently.

"Please come with us to Security!"

The inspector was a very experienced interrogator. But that's not going to scare me—I put my Intelligence training in interrogation to the test once when I landed this job—If it worked then, it can work again—I'll just

196

remain calm and poised—I'm sure the right answers will come to me.

"Do you know Mr. X in Hong Kong, Mr. Roberts?"

"Of course, I'm a frequent dinner guest at his home."

"I'm glad you decided to cooperate. You see we have proof you were there. Do you recognize this?" He produced the photograph of me taken at the penthouse.

"It's a good likeness, but I have a much better one at home taken at the same time." I handed the picture back, then reached for a cigarette.

The inspector stood and walked to a desk. "It's good enough for our purposes."

"Sir, do you mind if we do not take too much time. Please get to the point. I'm in a hurry to get home."

The inspector turned back from the desk holding a closed file. "Very well, Mr. Roberts, were you aware that your friend in Hong Kong was the head of the international smuggling ring?" His voice became louder and more emphatic. He's trying to make me nervous—

"Yes!" I replied. He looks startled. He wasn't expecting that.

"I suggest, Mr. Roberts, that you were smuggling for him."

"You may suggest all you want, Inspector." Now I'm making him nervous.

"We have proof!" he said opening his file with a look of triumph. He produced some photostatic copies of checks made out to me and cashed by me from the Hong Kong millionaire. "What do you think of that?" he said with a smile, waving them in my face.

"I don't think anything. If you look at the dates on those checks, Inspector, you'll find either September or December, my birthday and Christmas presents." I drew deeply from my cigarette.

197

"For such large amounts?" he shouted and it was quite obvious he was becoming rattled.

"Large for a man of your means, Inspector, but not for a millionaire. Really, I am in a desperate hurry to get home so let's bring this interview to a quick conclusion."

The inspector was pacing now: it must be hard interrogating so many crews everyday. I was beginning to feel sorry for him.

"If you take the trouble to investigate, you will also discover I frequented the home of the chief customs officer in Calcutta, a person you seem to have neglected. I'll supply you with photographic proof if you need it."

"I don't see the relevance . . . ." He looked puzzled. I think I'm succeeding in convincing him, at least I have him listening, and confused.

"You don't see the relevance? There was a reward offered by the customs in Calcutta twenty times larger than the amount on those checks. Am I correct?" He nodded "yes." Now I have him answering me! "If I am as greedy for money, as you have suggested, why should I smuggle and risk a prison sentence when I could have obtained twenty times that amount with no risks? All I would have had to do was tell my friend in customs my suspicions. You already have proof that I had the necessary information and if you contact Calcutta, you can receive proof of the chief customs officer." I leaned forward in my chair to put out my cigarette.

"You're very smart, and everything you said makes sense. Now, will you sign this statement?"

"Certainly," I said as I took the pen and signed the record of our conversation. He thinks I'm smart—I knew this interrogation was going well, but I didn't expect a compliment.

"You may wait outside. It won't take long. I know

you're in a terrible hurry to get home!" That last remark sounded a little sarcastic.

A short while later I was called back in the room: this time the General Manager and Corporation Lawyer of the airline were present.

"Good day, Mr. Roberts," the manager said cordially.

"Good day, gentlemen."

"Mr. Roberts, we have your signed confession to 'associating with smugglers,' a fact to which you confess knowledge. You have broken a clause in your contract that forbids such behavior. Will you sign this, please?" The manager handed me a sheet of paper.

"What is it, sir?"

"Your RESIGNATION!"

CHAPTER SIXTEEN

"Seek and you shall find"
Lk 11:9

"Roy, I tell you this is beginning to get to me. Every time I apply for a job, they check my last place of employment and that's that. This BOAC thing has caused such a scandal, everyone is scared to hire anyone ever associated with it in any way. My resources are running low; it's been three months now. I must find something soon."

"I understand your concern Ken, but don't panic like this," said Roy trying to console me.

"Roy, do you realize I'm almost twenty-nine years old and I don't have the slightest idea of what the future holds in store for me. I can't help but panic."

"Ken, none of us knows what the future is going to be for that matter. Keep things in the proper perspective. You're out of a job, that's all. Besides, maybe all this is part of a plan."

"Plan, what plan are you talking about?" I was confused.

"Ken, it's none of my business and if you want to tell me to keep my mouth shut, I will, but I've been thinking a lot about your situation . . . ." Roy seemed to be probing for the right words.

"Roy, I've never kept anything from you. Out with it . . . what's on your mind?" I was very interested to hear what he had to say. Even though I was not a little boy anymore, he still felt like my "big brother" and whatever advice he volunteered, I always considered.

"Well, remember when you told me about Bricktop?" he paused again.

"What has she got to do with it?"

"Ken, she was so sure you were meant to be a priest. And every obstacle you had that prevented you from considering the seminary has been removed. Your engagement flopped, that pull to the high living on BOAC is gone, and you are living a Christian life. Maybe all these things happened to show you what God really wants you to do, be a priest."

"Roy, don't think I haven't been thinking that same thing, but I would never enter the seminary now, or even consider it under these circumstances," I explained.

"What circumstances?"

"Roy, try to understand. What would I be sacrificing right now if I did pursue the priesthood? Nothing. I don't even have a job to give up. If I went into the seminary right now, I would never be certain that I wasn't doing it on the rebound, a last resort. In other words, Roy, I don't want to commit my life to God as a 'second choice.' "

"Little brother, you look much bigger to me today!" I knew Roy understood, he always did.

With Roy's help, I obtained a job the next week as an encyclopedia salesman. I hated the job, but I had to get something. On my very first call, I met a family who later became my very good friends. That first night selling books was my last. Mr. O'Keefe not only bought a set of books, he offered to help me regain my seaman's book: he was one of the bosses at the Seaman's Union. I was more than grateful, I was overwhelmed. I had always loved the sea, now I was to be a part of the world I thought I would never know again.

The Cunard office was very cordial as I made my application as an interpreter.

"What languages do you know?" said the personnel official.

"I read, write and speak French, German and Portuguese. I also speak some Spanish and Italian."

The official took my papers and went to an inner office. When he returned, I was praying silently, but at the same time, trying to give the impression of indifference.

"Yes, Mr. Roberts, we can offer you a position. How would you like to return to your old ship, the *Queen Elizabeth*?"

"Mum, you didn't have to fix such a big breakfast. I hate to see you get up so early. Look, it's still pitch black out," I said raising the shade in the kitchen.

"You need a nice meal before you start your first day. Now sit down and eat before it gets cold."

"I'm anxious to see if any of the old gang are still

travelling on the QE," I said taking a sip of the hot tea.

"You're really thrilled by this new opportunity, aren't you, Ken?"

"I am and you know Mum, even though I'm starting in the tourist section, with a little hard work and drive I can work my way up to the first-class again." I was becoming more enthused by the minute.

"Ken, we're not going to go through that again, are we?" I could see a little anxiety in Mum's eyes.

"I'm a little older now. Don't start worrying before I even set foot on board," I laughed.

"You are a very lucky boy, son. Most men are offered only one opportunity in their lifetime, but you . . . just look at all the wonderful chances you've had."

"Yes, Mum and when I become first-class interpreter, I will say to the whole world, 'I owe it all to my loving Mother and the dear Sisters!' How do you like that?" I teased.

She laughed then became serious once again. "Kenny, do you ever think of the priesthood any more? I know you never mention it, but I can't help wondering if the spark isn't still there."

"Mum, the only spark I have or need is the one that will get me to my ship . . . I'm running late. I really have to go." I left the kitchen and gathered my luggage. Mum was waiting at the door.

"Kenny, good luck. I'm so glad to see you this happy . . . It's been a long time. Take care son, and God bless." She made the sign of the cross on my forehead then kissed me good-bye.

The first day on duty, I tried to help the tourist waiters with the menus for the foreign passengers, but it didn't take me long to realize I was just in the way. It was easier for them to bring twelve roast beefs, then

202

wait for each individual to have the menu interpreted for them and make a different order.

I began my second day with early Mass: I wanted to start this new job off on the right foot. I spent some extra time in the chapel after Mass making my thanksgiving.

"Roberts, what have you been doing all these years?"

I opened my eyes and looked up. "Mr. Mullins!" We clasped hands in a warm greeting. I bet that was the first time "Moon" put out his hand and smiled when he felt it empty, I thought. He took my arm and led me up the aisle away from the praying passengers. Outside in the lobby, he looked me over.

"Do you want to see my fingernails, Mr. Mullins?"

"No, but you could still do with a haircut, 'Pretty Boy.' " We both laughed. He really has a good memory.

"I see you're an interpreter now. Where are you working?"

"In the tourist, but I don't get much of a chance to interpret."

"We have a very good choir on board now, they sing Mass every Sunday, at 9:30. Why don't you join?" He paused. "But I don't suppose you could get away at that time, could you?"

"No, I would be on duty then," I replied with disappointment.

"We'll see . . ." he said leaving me in suspense.

The next thing I knew I was in the chief steward's office.

"Mr. Roberts, how would you like to work in the first-class? The present interpreter is Polish; however the Chief Purser and I agree that perhaps it would be advantageous for us to employ a British subject to handle all the translating in the first-class dining room."

This is too good to be true. My goal was five years to make first-class and here I am on my very first trip—I must hurry to thank Mr. Mullins!

I felt very elegant that night at dinner as I strolled through the first-class dining room in my formal dress uniform with starched dickey and cuffs and black bowtie. Although I was no stranger to the glamor of extravagant living, this palatial setting never ceased to thrill me. Ladies entered in their formal gowns and mink wraps accompanied by their formally dressed escorts through the huge glass doors held open for them by equally well dressed doormen. There they were greeted by Mr. Mullins as he stood bowing solicitously. It was as regal as the first night at the opera and Mr. Mullins looked like the conductor of a great symphony as he waved his arms directing the head waiters to escort the guests to their tables.

A fat American lady with a fist full of rings and a full chest smothered in diamonds called me to her table. Her long silver evening gown sparkled in the glow of the candles. "Can you help me with this menu, young man?" I proceeded to translate.

"Doesn't he speak cute? I just love his accent. He sounds just like James Mason!" said her even fatter but equally rich companion.

"I don't really need you to translate. I just like to hear the way you pronounce the words. They sound so 'French,' " the first lady said and they both giggled girlishly.

A waiter walked toward me and asked if I would follow him to a table where the wine steward was having some difficulty in understanding one of the guests. I was surprised to see this sought after job was now held by

Bill, the tourist class waiter who helped me when I began my first day of waiting tables. He was as stunned as I. After accommodating the gentleman at the table, Bill and I exchanged a few words. Later that evening I joined him in the crew's bar and he filled me in on many of the guys I sailed with before. Unfortunately, most of them were serving on different ships now, but a few still remained on the QE.

That evening I was walking along the promenade deck and a gentleman stopped me. "Hey feller, can I ask you something?" He had a distinct Texan accent. He was looking at the badge I wore on my chest pocket; it listed the languages I was qualified to interpret; it read: FRANÇAIS, PORTUGUES, & DEUTSCH.

"Are you referring to this?" I pointed to the badge.

"Ya, how do you pronounce your name, anyway . . . Francis Porrr . . . ."

"That's not my name," I answered. "These are the languages I speak. I'm an interpreter."

"Ohhhh . . . I see . . . ," he grinned.

I wonder if he's smiling at his mistake or was he pulling my leg. I walked away. Either he is extremely stupid or I don't understand American humor!

I was anxious to share the good news of my promotion with everybody at home. I called Mum when the ship docked to tell her I was on my way. When I pulled up in front of the house, she was waiting.

"Tell me all about your trip back, Kenny," she said as I entered through the gate.

"Wait till I get through the door," I laughed.

Uncle John was standing at the back door as we entered: he was on his way out to meet the cab.

"You can go back inside now, John. He's already here," Mum said.

"Did you bring me any American cigarettes?" asked

Uncle John walking slowly in front of us and speaking without turning his head.

"Yes, Uncle John, I brought you a carton."

"Good. Let me have them before Jackie gets his fists on them."

I gave out the gifts to Jackie, Uncle John and Mum then I filled them in on my fantastic promotion. Jackie and I teased each other a while in our usual way of belittling each other until Mum put a stop to it. She was always afraid our remarks would become too cruel and the joking would become anger, but Jackie and I understood our own special humor. Jackie excused himself and left for a date. Uncle John was snoring away so that left just Mum and me to talk.

"Aren't you surprised about my news?"

"Not really son. I knew our Blessed Lady would answer my prayers. I must remember to keep my promise to St. Anthony, too," she said with decision.

"What did you promise St. Anthony this time?"

"To increase my donations to his home at Salisbury . . . which reminds me, I must take you to my other orphanage at Nazareth House to meet the Sisters."

The next day I found myself keeping Mum's promise to St. Anthony as I handed a check to the Reverend Mother. Mum continued to preach to me. "You see, my son, our Lord's words are true. You did all that worrying and He told us, 'See the lilies of the field . . . .' " And I was given a full text and sermon on trusting in the providence of God.

Six months on the QE passed very quickly. I loved my job and my bank account was beginning to flourish. I met all kinds of interesting people, film stars, statesmen, royalty, to some of whom I was assigned as personal interpreter on many occasions. I was more than satisfied with my position. I was content knowing this was my life's work. I was a daily communicant once again and through the influence of Mr. Mullins, I was also assistant sacristan preparing the vestments and altars for the many priests that traveled. On one trip, I became very friendly with an American Dominican priest, a theologian, Fr. Thomas Donlan, O.P. We spent many hours chatting and discussing religion into the night. He was on his way to Rome with an American pilgrimage he was leading.

The following trip, outward bound to New York, there was only one priest on board, Father Desmond Wilson: he was traveling with his mother. That Sunday, as we waited for Father Wilson to vest, I didn't realize how he was to change my life. There had been only one other trip when we had less priests and that was Easter. On that trip, I officiated at a Scripture service on Easter Sunday. I must have impressed someone, for that individual, an Irish waiter, and member of the choir, had been trying to convince me of a vocation ever since.

After Mass, I saw this same waiter in deep conversation with Fr. Wilson. I thought nothing of it at the time. Later that morning, my friend told me he had made an appointment with Fr. Wilson for me: I was to see him at noon. "Fr. Wilson is a very intelligent priest. He's the spiritual director of a seminary, St. Malachy's in Belfast!"

I kept the appointment, although I didn't know why, and spent a pleasant hour with Fr. Wilson who questioned me about my life. "I think you're fighting a vocation. It would seem to me that God has given you ample signs of His will. Many arrows have pointed the way since Bricktop. Don't you think?" he added.

I wasn't convinced: and I wasn't about to give up the hard earned security of this job.

"Since you are so hard to convince, will you at least take my advice?"

"Yes," I replied.

"Since our Lord has promised to answer prayers of those who seek, I want you to do nothing, but pray. Give yourself a deadline, let's say one year from this date. If you are not in the seminary by then, forget all idea of the priesthood; if however, a bishop or religious order approaches you with the suggestion, accept it as God's guidance and know that God is calling you!"

"Is it likely that a bishop will approach me?" I asked.

"No, it is very unlikely; bishops just don't do it unless you ask them first. That's why I'm suggesting something with such enormous odds against it. This way, if it happens, you may have no doubt," he said concluding his advice. As I left the room, he repeated, "Don't forget, one year!"

The next trip from Southampton was doubtful: there was a great likelihood that the QE would not sail as the *Queen Mary*, her sister ship, was on strike and it seemed likely the QE would join her in sympathy. About a third of the QE's crew did, in fact, join the strike. Mum was quite concerned that I would also join the strike which she believed was Communist inspired and without the approval of the Union. She threatened men with expulsion from home. Although I knew she didn't mean to keep her threat, I realized that it did cause her great concern so I joined the other two thirds of the crew and sailed. I had a selfish reason for sailing also: I knew that Fr. Tom Donlan would be returning on this voyage and I had promised him to continue our talks on his homeward trip.

As the ship sailed from Southampton, we had about a hundred and forty priests and about fourteen bishops returning from the Eucharistic Congress in Munich, and of course, Rome. Once again, I was involved as assistant sacristan and served three bishops at three consecutive Masses each morning. Fr. Donlan told me that he had prayed for me at Rome and gave me a blessed medal and chain. He asked me to serve his Mass next morning. "I'll offer it for your intentions," he said. As I was leaving the chapel after Mass, I felt a peace and contentment I hadn't felt since my return from my last pilgrimage to Lourdes, when I began to change my way of living on BOAC. That lunchtime, I was approached by another Irishman, this time, a bedroom steward.

"Mr. Roberts?"

"Yes," I replied startled.

"Bishop Gorman wishes to speak with you. Could you come to his cabin at 4 p.m.?"

"Yes, but who is Bishop Gorman?" I asked.

"He's the bishop of Dallas and Fort Worth in Texas," he said.

I was at the bishop's cabin promptly at 4 p.m. I knelt and kissed the bishop's ring as I greeted him in the British manner, "My Lord."

"I see you are a linguist," he said looking at my badge. "Do you also know Latin?"

"Yes, my Lord." I didn't know that Americans didn't use this title.

" 'Bishop' is sufficient. It isn't usual for a young man at sea to be a daily communicant. What schools did you attend?"

Question followed question and once again, I was completely bewildered as I stood outside his door. In my hand was his business card. Father Wilson's words came back to me, "Set a deadline, one year from today . . . the chances of this happening . . . ." That was less than two weeks ago! The bishop's words came back again loud and clear, "If you decide you would like to become a priest, I will accept you for my diocese!" He will accept me and here I am standing outside the bishop's room after telling him, "I'll think about it." Well, I've thought about it and this time, Lord, it's for real—

I know it. I looked around the plush surroundings—I really have something to sacrifice—I can look up and say, "I'm ready, Lord, and You're 'first choice!' "

CHAPTER SEVENTEEN

"Woman, behold thy Son"
Jn 19:26

I was apprehensive as I handed in my letter of resignation: I don't know why, because I was sure I wanted to be a priest now more than anything else in the world. But to actually take the first step was a little frightening. It was like on a hot day when the water looks so good that you're dying to go for a swim, but when you first get your feet wet, the chill makes you have second thoughts, once you decide to jump right in, you're glad you did. That's how I felt as the official took my resignation: I had cold feet. When I walked out of the Chief's office, my doubts turned to peace and joy. From here on out, it's up to you, Lord—I wish I could share all this with everyone I meet—I want to shout to the world, "Come on in, the water's fine!"

"Well, it's good-bye again," said Mr. Mullins. He sounded like a prison warden saying farewell to a habitual convict whom he expected to be back. "I hope I don't see you again, not as a crew member anyway," he said smiling and shaking my hand.

I walked down the gangway while two commis waiters assisted me with my baggage and a huge life size teddy bear that I had brought home for Roy's new baby. I tipped the boys and waved good-bye to the *Queen Elizabeth.*

I went to the back door and tried to squeeze through it tugging the teddy bear and dragging my luggage behind me. Uncle John was dozing in his usual chair and Roy was sitting at the dining room table drinking tea with Mum.

"Hi gang!" I shouted. "Where's the baby?" I was still holding the teddy bear with one arm.

"Hello son," Mum rose from her chair to welcome me. "Claire's next door with Christopher: she wanted to show him to the neighbors."

"Is that Ken?" shouted Jackie from upstairs.

"Yes, come down and help him with his baggage."

Jackie rushed down the steps at break-neck speed shouting, "Where are they Ken?" As he entered the room, he stopped and looked at me for a second then grinned. "Who's your friend?"

"What?" I was puzzled until he motioned to the teddy bear I was still holding.

"Did you have a nice trip?" asked Roy.

"Very nice. I'll tell you about it later. You're staying for dinner, aren't you? I have to have some time with my new nephew. You think he'll like this?" I held the teddy bear outstretched.

"At a few weeks old, Ken, all he's interested in is eating and sleeping, but I'm sure when he's older, he'll love it," Roy said laughing.

I looked at Jackie who was rummaging through my large suitcase. "Where are they?" he asked.

"Where's what?"

"The cigarettes . . . let's have them before he gets his mitts on them," Jackie said nodding to Uncle John who

211

was snoring with his mouth open. "TV is on, Uncle John," shouted Jackie teasingly.

John immediately sat bolt upright, rubbed his eyes and looked in the parlor at the set. " 'Tisn't! . . . Think you're funny, don't you?" He adjusted his cap, which he wore indoors and out, sat back and closed his eyes. "Hello Ken," he said with his eyes still shut.

I thought I'd wait till dinner to break the news: we would all be together then. I might as well shock them all at one time.

"Go on Roy, . . . ask him," said Claire at dinner. I wondered what she was talking about.

"Ken, are you planning anything this Sunday?" Roy asked grinning.

"No, why do you ask?"

"How would you like to be a godfather? We would be very happy for you to sponsor the baby at Baptism."

"I was planning on it. I'd be offended if you hadn't asked me. Why do you think I hauled that teddy bear all the way from New York?" I joked.

"Actually, the only reason I asked you was because we figured you were the only one who could afford a decent gift," Roy teased back.

"You call that huge thing a decent gift?" Jackie chimed in.

I was still looking for the right moment to tell them, but I just couldn't find it. Finally, Mum said, "Kenny, do you have something on your mind? You look as if something is bothering you." Roy didn't say anything, but I could tell he sensed something was up.

"Are you on a trip off this time?" asked Jackie, helping himself to some more apple pie.

"No Jackie." Perhaps this is the right time. "You see . . . well, actually . . . ."

"You haven't lost your job, Kenny?" Mother said very apprehensively.

"No, Mum. I've resigned. I'm going to be a priest!"

"Great Ken. There's not a thing I can think of that would be funnier than that. You really pulled that one off," Jackie said laughing convulsively.

"Don't joke about something so sacred, Kenny," said Mum crossly.

"Mum, I wouldn't joke about it, not now anyway." I brought them up to date on the events that took place. Uncle John shook his head in disbelief.

"You look for months for a job and you land a chance in a lifetime and you're really serious about giving it up?" Jackie questioned. He was no longer laughing, in fact, I had never seen him so serious.

"You must be nuts!" was Uncle John's only reply.

"I think that's nice if that's what you think you really want," Claire said still looking a little dazed.

"This time, Ken, you're going to make it. I'd bet my life on it," said Roy. "If there's anything I can do to help, just let me know, anything at all."

"Well Mum, everybody else has had something to say, what about you?"

She was looking down at her plate throughout the whole conversation never uttering a word. Finally she looked up at me, but she still didn't speak. Everyone waited for her.

"Mum?" I coaxed.

She was crying, but smiling. "What can I say, but 'thank you'? 'Thank you God,' for answering my prayers, and 'thank you' Kenny, for making me very happy."

I relaxed around the house the first week at home, or when the weather permitted, I sat reading in the garden. I was accustomed to this quiet life long before this trip. June was the last girl I dated steadily and since BOAC, I hadn't even dated casually. As for friendships, Johnny and Max were both married and Max was no longer living in Southampton. Other than reading or swimming, the cinema was my only recreation. Sometimes, I would even convince Mum to see a good show with me and as Uncle John never needed convincing, all three of us would take in a movie and dinner.

The postman came and handed Mum a letter. "Is that for me, Mum?" I asked anxiously.

"No son, it's only a bill."

"I wish the Bishop would answer my application. Supposing he has changed his mind and I resigned my job for nothing." I was becoming more anxious with that last thought.

"Son, don't worry so. The letter will come, but you sitting around waiting for it won't make it get here any faster. I have an idea . . . ."

"I know. 'Let's go up to the Sisters' chapel and pray about it.' Isn't that what you were going to say?" I teased.

"It's a good thought, but actually what I was going to suggest was perhaps, you could take another short trip to Lourdes. You could make it a retreat in preparation for the seminary. What do you think?"

"I think you must be getting a commission from the hotels in Lourdes, you certainly help their business by sending me there every chance you get," I laughed. "But I think your idea is a good one."

"And by the time you get back, your letter will be here," she assured me.

"You really believe it will?" I was becoming anxious again.

"Kenneth (and she never called me 'Kenneth') have you so little faith?"

It was so peaceful in Lourdes as I walked through the silent throng of pilgrims on their way to early morning Mass. Teen-agers from different nations were pulling sick trolleys on which lay invalids and the dying. An old lady lying on a stretcher and propped up with pillows was passing me. Her fingers moved slowly over the beads of her rosary, her lips were moving silently as her eyes looked heavenward. Her eyes showed that same peace I so often had seen in Mum's. If only an artist could put eyes like these on canvas and give them to the Blessed Mother, maybe we could really understand Mary's role. What mother and child were ever so close? Mary's humanity brings the Divine Jesus to the world: Mary's humanity can bring the world to the Divine Jesus. That is her greatness, her humanity, that being human, she was found worthy by God to become the mother of His Son. What greater title can man give her when God has already given her the greatest, "Mother of God."

A priest was leading a group of pilgrims in the rosary. It sounds more devotional in French, I thought, as I stood to walk back to the basilica. The French priest was giving a meditation on the motherhood of Mary. "She is not only the Mother of Christ, she is the Mother of mankind. Didn't Jesus give her to the disciple, John? 'Woman, behold your son.' " As I walked away, I looked up at the image of Mary and asked her to continue to be a mother to me.

It was a beautiful sunny day when I arrived back in England, a pleasant change from the usual rain. Mother came running up from the bottom of the garden to meet me. "It's here, son! It's here!" I gave her a hug and we entered the house together. She rushed to the mantle-piece and grabbed the long white envelope. It was an official envelope of the Bishop of Dallas. Mum looked on with anticipation as I opened it. I'm sure the expression on my face told her all she needed to know, but she asked anyway. "What does it say, Kenny?"

"I am accepted and the Bishop has given me the choice of seminaries. He suggests that as I prefer to study in England, I apply to the Westminster Archdiocesan seminary. He already has a student studying there."

"What is the name of the college, son?" Her voice was quick with emotion.

"St. Edmund's College," I replied. I began immediately to go through a long line of things I would have to do to present myself to St. Edmund's, then I realized I was talking to myself: Mum had left the room. I went to the kitchen where Uncle John had just come from the garden. "Uncle John, where's Mum?"

"Just left." Uncle John was always stingy with words.

"Where did she go?" I asked confused.

"Sisters' chapel . . . . Said she had to pray." Then he turned to me quickly, quickly for Uncle John that is, "bring any cigarettes?"

"That was a good meal, Mum. You're the best cook in the whole world," I said as I wiped my lips on the napkin.

"You can't be serious, with all the fancy cooking in those luxury hotels that you've been used to," she replied.

"Yes, but there's nothing like home cooking and your Yorkshire pudding is something special."

"You'll be living on bread and water in that 'cemetery,' " said Uncle John helping himself to seconds.

"The word is 'seminary,' Uncle John," I said smiling.

"Cemetery or seminary . . . what's the difference?

216

You're just as good as dead once you get there." Jackie was his usual witty self.

"Kenny, Father Walshe wants you to serve at the ceremony of the blessing of the bells. They're installing them in the tower of the new church this afternoon," Mum said as she brought in the apple pie.

"It should be opened soon. I wonder if it will be ready before I go to the seminary?"

"It's supposed to be ready to open by the parish feast of Christ the King and that is the last Sunday in October. Do you think you will be in college before then?" Jackie asked, putting some hot custard sauce over his pie, then added, "You'll probably be in and out, by then. That will give you a few weeks to be accepted and a few weeks to be rejected." He lifted the heaping spoonful of pie to his mouth.

I took the spoon and rammed it in his mouth playfully.

"Are you boys fighting again?" Mum asked shaking her head.

"I know Mum, I'm too old for that now, I'll be thirty next month," I answered already anticipating her next remark.

The new church of "Christ the King" was ready on time, in fact it was opened early, on September 4th, 1960, with a televised Mass celebrated by the same bishop who interviewed me when I was a teen-ager. He was over eighty now, and very feeble, but he was still the bishop of the diocese. The large church was packed to the doors where as a crossbearer, I led the procession into the church. Mum and Uncle John were sitting near the front and she looked quite proud as she gazed toward the altar with a look that said, "Look what twenty years of bake sales and carnivals eventually built!" During the sermon, I looked toward Mum and Uncle John, they both had their eyes closed and

217

if I didn't know better, I would have said that Uncle John was praying too.

On my birthday, we all went to visit Roy, Claire and the baby. Roy's home was a modern bungalow in the country, but was very large with all the usual American utilities, including the telephone. It was situated on an acre and a half of beautiful landscaped gardens. Mum was in seventh heaven here, as she strolled around weeding and pruning. Uncle John reclined in a deck chair on the lawn with his cap shielding his eyes as he slept. Jackie was using the large lawn to practice shots with a football while Roy and I played with the baby.

"Come here, Chris. Come to uncle Ken," I held my arms out to the baby where he lay in Roy's lap.

"Do you want to eat outside?" Claire shouted through the French windows.

"Yes, dear, if you don't mind," answered Roy.

"Ken, have you heard from the college yet?" Roy asked as he tickled Christopher on the cheek.

"No, not yet, but I don't expect to hear for at least a month. He's away until the middle of October. He has a weird name for the head of a seminary, 'Monsignor Butcher' and the school doctor who gives the medical is 'Doctor Blood,' " I said smiling.

"Sounds spooky," he replied laughing too.

"Would you two strong men like to carry this table out onto the lawn?" called Claire from the kitchen.

I watched Roy as he gave her an affectionate squeeze with one arm, still holding Christopher with the other. The three of them played happily. Roy was the picture of contentment: there was so much love in this house and it showed.

"I think Christopher is ready to be put in his crib for a nap," Claire said.

"Let me take him," I said. I carried him into his room and laid him in his bed, next to it was the enormous teddy bear I brought him from New York. He'll have to be at least four years old, before he'll be able to play with it, I thought as I left the room.

At last the long awaited letter arrived from Monsignor Butcher. I was instructed to report to St. Edmund's that Saturday morning and bring enough clothes for the weekend; the rector wanted to interview me and I was to take my exams.

Friday morning, I left the house to go shopping for a few things for my trip. "I should be back around four. What time are we going to have dinner?" I asked Mum.

"I thought about five, but no later, son . . . . See that you get here, Kenny. I'm sure Roy is coming over to see you off."

"I'll be here, Mum. I promise."

It was 5:30 before I was able to make a mad dash to the bus-stop. A terrible rainstorm had started about four. I spent the time talking with some friends from the QE I had met in the department store.

This bus is hardly moving—We've been stuck here for half an hour——What a traffic jam—It's 6:15—I hope I don't miss Roy—Claire won't want to keep the baby out in this kind of weather—Mum will be furious. I promised her I wouldn't be late.

It was 6:30 when I finally walked into the house.

"Mum, I'm sorry I'm late. It was that storm and to make matters worse, there was a traffic jam on Bitterne Road. The bus barely crawled. Where's Roy?"

Mum didn't seem to be listening. Uncle John answered, "They left . . . they were afraid the storm might start blowing up again," he said as he turned

219

his attention back to the TV. The evening news was just finishing.

"Some poor mother's son has just been killed in a terrible accident on Bitterne Road. We saw it on the news. We all ought to say the rosary," she said.

"Mum, you look pale. I don't think you should work hard in that garden. What's for supper? I'm starved!"

"It's in the oven, son. Can you get it? I feel a little weak."

"See, I told you not to be cutting those hedges and lifting all those baskets of weeds," I scolded her.

She wasn't listening again: her eyes were closed and her lips were moving in time with her fingers on the beads of her rosary.

I fixed my plate and decided to take it in the parlor and watch TV. "What's on, Uncle John?" Just as he was about to answer, we heard a knock at the door. I was surprised to see Father Walshe accompanied by another gentleman. I suppose he has come to wish me good luck.

"Good evening Father. How nice of you to come, especially on a night like this."

"Is your mother in, Kenneth?"

What on earth is wrong with him? Why is he so formal?

Mum stood up to greet the priest. I sat down to finish eating.

"It's my son, isn't it, Father?"

What is she talking about?—And what's wrong with Father Walshe? My God, he's crying!

"Yes ma'am, I'm sorry to inform you of the accident, but how did you know?" asked the detective.

"I saw it on the news flash at 6:00." Mum began to console Father Walshe.

"Would someone tell me what's happening?" I shouted.

"It's your brother, Kenny. Roy is dead," she said with an obvious strain to control herself. "And Claire and little Christopher?" she asked imploringly.

"Claire is in serious condition, but they think she'll be alright, but the baby was killed also," said the policeman.

"Now I know how our Blessed Mother felt when she saw her Son crucified. I just watched the account of my son's death on television, and my little grandson . . . ."

By this time I realized the shock: I reacted in anger.

"Is this the way God treats those who love Him? To hell with the seminary!" I screamed hysterically.

Mum took me in her arms and begged me, "Don't do this, Kenny. You mustn't give up now. Don't you see, God is testing us, and we must be ready to make the sacrifice. He has taken Roy to make us realize the value of the priesthood. Perhaps I'm not worthy to have a son, a priest. Our Blessed Mother sacrificed her Son so that heaven would be open to us. Now I have been asked to give one son back to Him so that another could help people find it. . . ."

CHAPTER EIGHTEEN

"By this will all men know"
Jn 13:35

JANUARY 1, 1961

It was the first day of the new year, and the first day of my new life!

"Kenny I have something for you. I want you to wear it always as a sign of your new life with Christ," Mum said as she placed a gold chain and cross around my neck and tucked it inside my shirt. "You look so 'priestly' in your black suit and tie." She kissed me on the cheek then started to cry: she cried easily since Roy's death. "I'm sorry to be such a baby, son. I don't want to send you off like this. I just thought of the many times Roy was here to say good-bye whenever you started something new. I don't know why I'm crying: I know he's in heaven with our Blessed Lord, but poor Claire, how hard it will be for her when she comes out of the hospital. Now go, dear, your taxi's waiting." Mum wiped her eyes and tried to smile.

"Pray for me Mum, and take good care of Jackie and Uncle John." I hugged her and held her for a moment. "Uncle John, don't you and Jackie fight too much while I'm gone," I said trying to joke, hoping it would make this good-bye a little easier.

Uncle John looked sad as I shook his hand at the gate.

"I put your other bags in the trunk," he said wiping his eye with one hand and straightening his cap with the other. "Must have something in my eye," he said sniffling.

Mum didn't come to the gate, but she was looking out from the front room window. I waved to her as I got into the taxi. She was smiling, but she turned away. I knew she was crying again.

"Can I have your old silver chain and medal?" Uncle John asked as I rolled the window down.

"Sure, I want you to have it, Uncle John." I reached in my pocket and handed it to him. As the taxi pulled off, Uncle John was trying to fasten the clasp of the chain around his neck. I sat back and recalled all that happened in the past few weeks.

222

The day after Roy died, I went to St. Edmund's for the tests and interview because Mum insisted, and the funeral wasn't to be until Monday anyway, so she knew I would be home in time to serve the Mass. It was the first funeral from the new church.

Monsignor Butcher was a very compassionate man and he dispensed me from any written tests. His oral exam, the next day after Mass, was so pleasant, it seemed more like a friendly chat. He handed me a breviary. "How is your church Latin?" he asked. I can still see the pained smile as I struggled to translate the Breviary. After a two-hour interview, he informed me I would find it difficult trying to catch up with the freshman class without a good working knowledge of Latin. He thought it better that I go to the Jesuit College at Osterley: they had a different system there where the students were graded into groups, rather than strictly scholastic years. My heart stood still when he picked up the telephone to call. "Do you know of Osterley?" he asked.

"Yes," I replied sheepishly. How could I forget it: that was the first seminary that refused me—all I can hope for now is that Father Tigar isn't there any more—That's silly, even if he is there, the bishop has already accepted me—He'll have to accept me too—I imagine?—

"Father Tigar? (My God, he is still there, I thought). This is Monsignor Butcher at St. Edmund's—Fine, how are you?—Good (I wish he'd get on with it!)—I have a student for the Dallas diocese in Texas who has just passed the entrance exams here, but I thought he would profit more by coming to you first—You can?—Yes, that's good. (What's good?—I wonder what he's saying?) After Christmas then—Alright, fine—January 1st, he'll be there!"

The taxi pulled into the bus station where the driver helped me unload my baggage. From there I boarded the bus that would take me to Osterley: the ride was to take three hours. How familiar the road was: I must have travelled it over a hundred times during my five years with BOAC. Finally I heard "This is your stop, sir. Osterley College is across the road, the first turning on your right."

The driveway led to the entrance of the main building, Campion House. As I climbed the steps, I was met by two boys, whom I judged to be in their late teens. "May we take your bags?" They led me into the main hall where I was greeted by the other students. They all look so young—They certainly are friendly— "Welcome to Osterley," one said. "If there is anything you need, please let me know," said another. "May I help you?" still another inquired—They're all so eager to be of aid—Maybe they think I'm a teacher instead of a student!

"Leave your bags here, we'll be going to supper as soon as the bell rings," directed a young man. He held out his hand. "I'm Tony and this is Eddie," he motioned to the boy standing next to him. I can't believe Eddie is old enough to be in college; he looks to be about fifteen. I couldn't resist asking, "How old are you, Eddie?"

"Seventeen, I'm one of the youngest here," he smiled.

"I'm twenty-one, a late vocation," said Tony.

If he's a late vocation at twenty-one, what does that make me? I'm thirty!

"Most of the students here are in the nineteen or twenty year old group, but we have some all the way up to the late forties," Tony informed. That was a comforting thought—I guess they didn't think I was a new teacher after all—They're just that eager to please.

The bell rang and silence fell upon the entire community. Four priests descended the main staircase, passed through the students and led us to the refectory. Why did the bell have to ring now, just when I was about to get all the information on what to expect?

All of us were led to specified tables by fellow students. We stood in silence as Fr. Tigar intoned the Grace: he then picked up a little bell and at its command one hundred and eighty students took their place at table while a student proceeded to read to us from the pulpit. This is going to be hard to get used to: at home, most of our conversation was at meals— Even on BOAC we learned all the scoop at dinner—I wonder what I should do if I want some more bread? What if I would like some more water?—I guess you just have to do without—

My worries were in vain: every member of the table offered me everything before I had a chance to want more. I was amazed at the concern shown by each student for his neighbor: everyone was constantly watching for the other's need. Once again the little bell rang and we all stood for Grace again. Fr. Tigar led the procession of faculty followed by students to the House Chapel where we made thanksgiving prayers.

"Father Tigar wishes to see you," said a student. I followed him up the hallowed stairs to Father Tigar's quarters. "Someone's in there now, but you can see him next. Just take one of those chairs."

I sat down and picked up a magazine to read as I waited. No matter how I tried to concentrate on the material before me, all I could think about was "I wonder if he will remember me?" I began to get that feeling of anxiety in my stomach. A student came out and closed the door behind him. "Here goes," I thought as I stood and knocked on the door.

"Come in."

There he was sitting at his desk. He was just as I

225

had remembered him. He was a very ascetic, stern looking man: the most outstanding characteristic was his eyes. When he spoke, they seemed to search your very soul: one had the feeling he was reading your mind instead of listening to your words. Father Tigar was known for his eloquence too: he pronounced each word as if it were the most important in the whole sentence; his diction and pronunciation were perfect. And always, he spoke very slowly: he could make "Mary had a little lamb . . ." sound like a Shakespearean sonnet.

"Hello Father," I said nervously.

"Hello . . . Sit down," he answered while he studied my scholastic history and the results of my exams at St. Edmund's. "I see you are a linguist," he closed the file, turned to me and stared. "Why do you want to be a priest?"

There's those eyes again—It should be "Tiger" instead of "Tigar"—That's what those eyes remind me of—I don't know if he's going to growl or purr—I was so nervous, I didn't really hear what he was saying.

"I beg your pardon, Father. What did you say?"

"I said—Why do you—want to be—a priest?"

Oh no, not that again—I got this one wrong last time!

"Because I believe God wants it and I have come here to see whether I want it too. At the present time, I believe with all my heart, that I do," I answered meekly. I hope it's right this time—somehow I don't think my "Intelligence" training in interrogation would do any good with him—I have to say "how I really feel."

"Very good . . . very good," he said as he placed his hands together as if in prayer while touching the end of his nose with his finger tips, and at the same time, nodding his head up and down. "Now we want to see whether we want you." He paused, looked away for a moment, then "turned on his eyes" again. "You will not find this place easy, certainly not what you have become accustomed to . . . . Here we endeavor to break your worldly spirit. Great emphasis is placed on obedience and silence. You will have to be a real man to continue to live here, we sort out the men from the boys. I wish you luck and may God give you the strength to persevere." He nodded for me to leave.

I felt relieved. I walked toward the door when he spoke again, ever so slowly. "I have seen you before Roberts. When was it?"

Oh no, he does remember! I turned to face him. "It was over ten years ago, Father."

"What happened?" he asked intently.

"You told me I had no vocation." I swallowed hard.

"Did I?—Well—I must have been wrong—Welcome to Osterley!"

I opened the door eagerly. I better get out of here before he changes his mind!

I ran down the steps where Tony was waiting to show me to the dorm I shared with four other students. While we were talking, the house bell rang.

"That is for study hall assembly. Do you have any books yet?" Tony asked.

"No, I'll lend you one of mine. Once you get inside the study hall building there is strict silence. Whenever you are in any gathering and the bell rings, you must immediately obey the silence."

As soon as we had all settled in our seats, a student began with a prayer to the Holy Spirit and we all sat for an hour's study. That first night's study period seemed endless. I couldn't concentrate. Why is it just when I begin to become involved in conversation, a bell rings and it's time to be quiet again. No wonder everyone was talking to me when I came in, they were thankful for the opportunity to speak! Another bell rang. Now, what? Everyone stood for a prayer of thanksgiving and silently filed across the campus grounds to the college church: I just followed the crowd trying desperately not to look like a newcomer.

Everyone took their assigned places in the church to await the arrival of Fr. Tigar; this was the time set aside for him to give the nightly points for the next morning's half an hour meditation before Mass. He walked in his brisk manner up the aisle and stood in front of the altar. He was a very dynamic, dramatic speaker, who commanded great reverence as he spoke.

"For tomorrow's meditation, we will take the words, 'Our Father.' What does this 'Our' signify in our lives? What response does it call from us as 'brothers' of the same Christ?" He continued for the next fifteen minutes. The bell rang again and we all stood and recited the Lord's Prayer at the end of which we knelt for the blessing. Now, it was time for the "Magnum Silentium" (grand silence) and bed. It was 9 o'clock.

I lay in my bed trying to sleep. I'm really impressed with Osterley—There's a kind of spirit here I've never seen before—What is it?—Perhaps I should try to meditate on Fr. Tigar's words "brothers of the same Christ"—that's it—Everyone here acts as if they were really brothers: all sharing the same father, with Christ—And there's a sharing—It's love—Their love for Christ is shown in doing for each other—Please God, let me become one of them—A plane's hum could be heard—Boy, that's loud—Of course, we're not that far from the airport. That last reflection diverted my meditation and took me back to BOAC. I looked at my watch—10:30—I used to be just going out about this time—Wonder what some of the aircrews are doing right now?—Can't think about that—I must sleep—I wonder what tomorrow will be like?—All this silence and meditation—I better think of all the questions I want to ask so I don't forget them when it's time to talk—Those bells, too—Will I ever get used to them?—I must really concentrate on studies—and meditation—and prayer—and BELLS—Everybody else is sleeping—I can tell by their deep breathing—I began to laugh to myself—I wonder if it would be breaking the rules if you "talked" in your sleep?

The next morning, which began at 5:30, was a typical day of how I was to spend the next year and a half at Osterley. We were awakened by the ringing of a bell, of course, then proceeded to the washrooms for shaving and washing. We returned to our room to dress: from there, we went to the chapel for a half hour meditation followed by Mass. Another fifteen minutes of silent prayer, then the bell rang, breaking the Great Silence, and calling us to breakfast. After eating we returned to our rooms to make our beds and if time allowed, we could have a quick smoke, but only in the entrance hall. The times for smoking were specified: this was another sacrifice to me. There's nothing like a second cup of coffee and a cigarette after a meal. Classes began at 9 a.m. and continued till 11:45, time to grab another cigarette then assemble in chapel for fifteen minutes of silent prayer and examination of conscience and the Angelus. After lunch and more study or classes, we were assigned working places for two hours of manual work. I was assigned to "weeding" the long field. The first part of this work period, we were allowed to converse, but only in Latin. We didn't talk much! At four, we stopped for tea. In the next hour, the showers were available. 5:30 was the Angelus and supper, followed by another quick smoke, then study hall, meditation, the Grand Silence and bed.

It didn't take me long to learn the routine, but it did take some time to adjust to it, especially the bells which Father Tigar referred to as "the voice of God" that must be obeyed at all times. I'm quite certain that "brotherly" spirit prevailed among the students, not only because of their deep religious commitment, but because Fr. Tigar was really like a real father watching over his sons. His door was always crowded by students who sought counseling and even at meals, he took turns sitting with a different group. The feeling of love and joy was contagious within these walls and it took me no time at all until I too, became infected with it.

There were still many nights in that first semester when I would lie awake and be distracted from my task of trying to get to sleep by the noise of the planes flying overhead: taking me back to the glitter and excitement of earlier days, but with prayer and the discipline of "the bells," I soon learned to school myself to getting to sleep quickly. Conjugating dull Latin verbs always helped!

It was time for summer vacation: Father Tigar was to give us advice on how to conduct ourselves "out in the world." I wasn't prepared for the advice he gave however. His sermon on the last day was unforgettable:

"It is now time for summer vacation . . . and I suppose you are wondering just how you are to conduct yourselves as prospective priests. Perhaps I can help you. If, for instance, you feel you would like some female company, go right ahead. You have my permission. If you feel you would like to take a young lady on a date, go ahead. You have my permission.

(I don't believe it: I would never have thought he was that liberal.) And if you feel so inclined to even kiss her, go ahead. You have my permission! (I didn't know seminarians did all that.) You, my dear students, have my permission to do any of these things—But, if you do—DON'T COME BACK!"

I was glad to return home to see Mum and the family again. I took a job as a breadman for that first summer. Mum was very proud of me whenever we went to church. I think this was the only vanity she ever allowed herself. Although Mum would never admit it, she took special pride in "showing me off" to one particular lady in the parish who considered me too worldly for the priesthood and made no secret in spreading her opinion to others to Mother's dismay.

One Sunday, as Mum and I were walking out of church, this "professional Christian" lady met us at the door. "I see you are still in the seminary . . . . Do you think you'll make it?" she asked with a sarcastic grin. It was hard to anwer her question for I knew she would dissect my every word. If I showed doubt, what was I doing there? If I showed certainty, I had pride. I prayed for guidance and answered.

"I'm studying to be a priest, not a prophet!"

Mum smiled, then chastised herself for being so unkind as to laugh at the woman's indignation.

I was both happy and glad to return to Osterley. I hated to leave Mum again, but I was glad to return to the community life and the Christian brotherhood that I had come to love.

During my second year, Father Tigar appointed me to positions of responsibility and I continued to progress under his saintly guidance, both spiritually and academically. By the end of the year, I was a different

231

person: Osterley and Father Tigar had produced an entirely different Ken Roberts. Now, I was ready to go to St. Edmund's!

Final exams came with terrifying speed, and I was apprehensive about the results as I waited outside Father Tigar's office. When I entered, he was searching for my papers.

"Ah, here it is. You were going to St. Edmund's, weren't you?" He didn't look up.

"Were going!"—Perhaps I've failed. Does he mean I'm *not* going now?

"I am not going to St. Edmund's, Father?" I asked timidly. I could feel my thoughts racing: panic was beginning to set in.

"No, you are 'not' going to St. Edmund's—You are going to Rome, you and three others will be going to the English Beda College in Rome. Do you realize the honor? You will be near the Holy Father and you start the same day as the Vatican Council. You have done well here, Kenneth. You are very blessed, . . . but don't let Rome change you . . . . Always remember: 'they will know you are Osterley students by your love!' "

CHAPTER NINETEEN

"Beloved who are in Rome . . . ."
Rm 1:7

I crept up the steps quietly: I didn't want to wake Jackie and Uncle John. I knew Mum was still awake: there was a small shaft of light coming from under her bedroom door.

"Kenny, is that you?" she called softly.

"Yes, Mum. Don't get up. I'll come in," I said as I closed the door gently behind me. I sat on the bottom of her bed. She was sitting propped up with pillows, her rosary was still entwined around her fingers.

"You look so tired son. Do you have to work so hard, it's past 1 a.m. Kenny if it's money you want, I have a little in the bank . . ."

I was working as a short order cook in the Hasty Tasty restaurant, putting in almost fourteen hours a day. It was beginning to show. Already I was starting the second month of my summer vacation.

"I don't need your money, Mum. But I would like to work as much as I can now, then I can quit a couple of weeks before I go to Rome and take a short vacation. It will have to be a modest one though. I don't know what my living expenses will be once I start college again."

"You will be there Saturday, won't you? George and Marian are looking forward to you coming with us." She took a long sigh. "Isn't God good to me, son? All these years, I have been praying for George to come back to the faith and now even Marian and their son, Terry, are becoming Catholic."

"I'll be there, now get some sleep. We'll talk more in the morning," I said as I patted her cheek and started to leave.

"Kenny, I almost forgot . . . Marian called today and said the priest that has been giving her instructions, Father Robin Noel, will be there and she wants you to meet him. He used to be an Anglican priest, when he decided to become Catholic, he went to the Beda college for his studies, the same college where you will be going. Isn't that nice?"

"Yes Mum, I'm anxious to meet him. Now, go to sleep. God bless."

233

"God bless, son," she said as she switched off the light on her bedstand, only to switch it back on again.

"Kenny?"

"Yes."

"Are you happy?"

"I'm happy, Mum."

"That's all that counts. Good night, son."

The modest vacation I was looking forward to turned out to be quite an experience. Father Noel invited me to take my vacation with him to visit some relatives, but he didn't tell me until we pulled up in front of a castle, that his relatives were the Elweses, a family comparable to the Kennedys in the United States. Their estate was Warwick Hall: Father Noel had a cottage near the lake on the grounds. I ended up spending a very relaxing week in a very palatial setting. On the way back, we visited another one of his uncles, a duke. I was very impressed that this man who seemed so at ease in George's and Marian's simple home was the same man to whom the servants bowed and addressed as, "My Lord."

The vacation also granted me the opportunity of learning more about the Beda: my day of admission was drawing near.

"You're going to love it at the Beda, Ken. You'll meet many interesting people there since the Beda is designed for late vocations."

"Sounds interesting. I'm really looking forward to it."

"The most fascinating thing about the Beda to me was the students themselves, doctors, lawyers, engineers, business executives, many clergymen of different denominations and all sharing the same goal, to become priests. Life is never dull there with all the colorful personalities," said Father Noel, smiling. He was silent for a few moments. I imagined he was reminiscing about his own days at the Beda.

"I would think that it would be a great transition for these men to leave a professional life and all the comforts that went with it, to assume a rigid community life in the seminary. I suppose many of them find it extremely difficult to adjust," I said, thinking back to the first few months at Osterley.

"That's the beauty of the Beda: they gear their curriculum to these men. They are aware of the problems of adjustment. I think you're in for quite a surprise, Ken, with the contrast of the Beda to Osterley. What makes the Beda unique is its very origin. It was founded in Rome soon after the conversion of Cardinal Newman, the famous Anglican convert of the last century. After his conversion hundreds of Anglican priests converted to Rome and it looked like the entire Anglican church would return to the allegiance of the Pope, so the Vatican started a college where ex-clergymen who already had their theological studies completed, could study without the rigid discipline of a normal seminary. This great influx of convert clergymen was called by the Church, the 'Second Spring,' but it didn't last long and the number of clergy converts dwindled so the Beda opened its doors to degreed men of other professions."

"It must be very old, then," I said, picturing the building standing from the time of Cardinal John Henry Newman.

Father Noel laughed, "It's practically brand new, one of the most modern colleges in Rome. The old building, which was once the Beda, is no longer a part of the college: the Beda college as it stands today is

235

a very modern building outside the walls of Rome. You'll see it all for yourself very shortly."

When we arrived home, I invited Robin to visit with Mum.

"I always feel blessed to have a priest in my home," Mum said as he was leaving. She knelt and asked him for his blessing.

I walked to the gate with Robin and thanked him for the trip.

"Don't mention it. The pleasure was mine. Ken, don't worry about your mother while you're away. I'll visit her often. I think she's a saint!"

"I 'know' she is," I added. We shook hands and he got into his car.

"Good luck in Rome. I wish I were going back to the Beda with you," he said as he drove off.

I sat in the aircraft and it was a strange sensation as I watched the cabin crew walk up and down the aisles. This was the first time I had flown since that day I was sacked from BOAC. I thought back to the many stop-overs in Rome and the night life. Thank God, all that is behind me. The microphone switched on. "We are about to land at Rome airport. Will you please extinguish your cigarettes and fasten your seat belts. . . ." That sounds familiar—How many times have I made those same announcements?

"Good-bye, sir. We hope you enjoyed your flight," said the stewardess as I descended the steps. I am in Rome again. I walked across the tarmac to the airport buildings and passed through the immigration hall. It was swarming with bishops. They were all arriving for the Vatican Council which was to start the next morning. How symbolic, I should start my first days of study in Rome with representatives of all the countries of the world to which I had been. They were bishops:

their countries represented my old life; their job as apostles of Christ was symbolic of the new life on which I was embarking.

I walked through the customs barrier into the arrival hall where I was greeted by a young man in a cassock. "Are you for the Beda?" he asked looking at my black suit and tie.

"Yes, my name is Kenneth Roberts." We shook hands.

"I'm Austin Hunt. I'm in my second year here," he said leading me away to the chartered bus for the Beda students who were arriving by plane.

I climbed the steps of the bus and sat next to a very refined gray haired gentleman with a very articulate Oxford accent.

"Hello, my name is Stanley Luff. I see you are new, too," he said moving over to make room for me.

"I'm Ken Roberts . . . Glad to meet you," I said shaking his hand.

"What were you doing before you decided to become a priest?" he asked.

Before answering I turned to a student in a Roman collar behind us. "How long does it take to get to the Beda?"

"About an hour, this time of the day," he replied.

I turned and looked back at Stanley. "I don't have time to tell you. Tell me what you were doing, I have four years to tell you what I did!" We both laughed. I like him already: he has a sense of humor.

"I'm a writer. I write awfully boring books about archeology and Church History, nothing frightfully interesting, but sometimes I write for the 'Lady,'" he blushed and laughed boyishly.

"The 'Lady?'" I repeated.

"Yes, it's a ladies' magazine. I'm kind of a 'Dear Abby' . . .," he laughed again.

237

I learned later that Stanley was a well-known author and lecturer; just as I found out the list of Beda students was even more interesting than Father Noel had foretold. The youngest in my class was the twenty-nine-year-old Sebastian Dilke, a graduate of Winchester and Kings College, Cambridge who held a Master's degree in architecture. The eldest was the sixty-four-year-old George Fenech, a former chief electrical engineer of the Malta electricity department and lecturer of engineering and professor of mathematics at Malta's Royal University. The students of the Beda held more degrees between them than the faculty of most universities. One particular thing that appealed to me was that, unlike at Osterley, I was one of the younger group which we referred to as the "Beda Babes."

The Beda is truly a beautiful college. "It looks like the Hilton," joked Stanley as we entered through the glass doors.

Stan and I had rooms opposite each other on the third floor. When I opened the door, I couldn't believe it: the room was magnificent, my own bedroom and study; the window looked out onto the Benedictine Monastery and St. Paul's Basilica. The sun was beginning to set over the top of St. Paul's and the sky was a brilliant red. Is anything more beautiful than a sunset over the Eternal City? Rome, I'm back again! This is to be my room for the next four years.

The next hour, I spent answering the knocking at my door as one student after another entered to introduce himself. Some came with tea cups, cutlery, pots and pans, and a small stove for heating water; I was even handed a carpet. I found myself refusing items: I already had more than I could use. The bell rang for supper, I stopped abruptly in the middle of conversation; they all looked at me in anticipation. Why are they looking at me like that? "Go on," said one of the

students. "Yes, hurry, the bell rang for supper," said another. They're talking!

"Can we speak after the supper bell rings?" I asked puzzled.

"Of course, now finish your story."

I finished what I had to say, then they led me to the refectory, conversing the whole way there. I was instructed that that bell was just a call to meals. Once in the refectory, we were to be silent and listen to the readings: the only exception was a big feast or if guests were present. Quite a change from Osterley, I thought. They did warn me, however, that although the rule was lenient, the Rector was extremely strict about the *Magnum Silentium* which began at 9 p.m. and ended after morning Mass: we were free to talk during breakfast.

The refectory was a beautiful dining room with large picture windows that overlooked a delightful rose garden, in the middle of which was a fountain. Once again, I found myself opposite Stanley. Since this was the first day of the school year, we were allowed to talk during the meal, an excellent one with wine served by the college waiter.

After dinner, we proceeded to the recreation room: it resembled a gentlemen's country club. "They told me I was coming to the Beda as a late vocation. I think they made a mistake . . . . It's more like a late *vacation!*" Stanley said looking around in awe.

The next day in St. Peter's Square, Pope John XXIII would open the Vatican Council. A council of the world's bishops that will change the Catholic Faith for its 500,000,000 adherents and affect the attitudes of even the Protestants. The Catholic Church was letting in some fresh air: some people will think it a hurricane.

239

A million people packed St. Peter's Square and the nearby streets as four thousand of the world's bishops in cope and mitre stretched out in a long line across the Square and up the steps of St. Peter's. The bishops were followed by the almost one hundred cardinals, then, finally, carried aloft above the heads of the people, came the Beloved Pope John smiling and waving his blessing to the kneeling multitude. The Sistine choir and a fanfare of trumpets announced to the world, the twentieth century reformation of the two-thousand-year-old Catholic Church.

On that same day, our second at the Beda, we were assigned places in chapel for our first introductory talk. We awaited the entrance of our beloved Rector, Monsignor Jeremiah Curtin, whom we affectionately referred to as "Jerry," though never to his face. He was a tall, handsome white-haired man, very poised. His accent was cultured, high-pitched and pained. An eloquent speaker, a tremendous wit, and although he did not like us to think so, he was a very compassionate man: and a first class teacher. When he spoke, he sounded as if someone was extracting a tooth; he increased this impression by the pained look on his face, an effect which could be obtained by discreetly smelling a bad egg.

"Gentlemen, welcome to the Beda! Contrary to popular opinion, we do have rules at the Beda, and today I will outline them, tiresome as they may be . . . ."

I was amused by the talk and immediately knew I liked him. Unfortunately, his feelings for me were not mutual that first year, and his sense of humor didn't always consider me so amusing.

It was just before Christmas, and we were entertaining the students from the other English speaking colleges whom we invited to our rooms for cocktails

after the Christmas play. Strange as it may seem, I was no longer used to alcohol having abstained completely since Osterley. After two dry martinis in our rooms and the wine at supper which one student kept pouring into my glass, I became a little boisterous. It so happened that night, I was to lead the rosary. I was under the impression I did a pretty good job until Stanley came in after breakfast. "I think you had better apologize to the Rector. He was awfully angry with you last night. If he had seen you after chapel, I believe he would have expelled you on the spot." After that bit of information, I went directly to the Rector's room and knocked.

"Come in," the Rector called in his most suffering voice. I entered and stood directly in front of his desk. He wrinkled his nose and whined, "So you've come . . . I was going to send for you." He looked at me as if I was the "bad egg" he was constantly smelling. "What do you have to say for yourself?"

I knew that if anything even a hundred times less serious had happened at Osterley, I wouldn't be standing in front of Fr. Tigar explaining. It would be expulsion. "Well Monsignor—I am sorry about the rosary, I believe I was a little loud—"

"A *little loud!* It was a cross between a Shakespearean actor and a sergeant major on the parade ground. Not one decade correct . . . and you mixed up the Joyful with the Sorrowful mysteries. I want an explanation!"

"I'm sorry to say, Monsignor, I was a little high. It was an accident of course—You see,—I don't drink normally—"

"No, you don't drink normally, you drink ABNORMALLY! If I had found you after chapel last night, and your Osterley brothers had not spirited you away, I would have expelled you on the spot. You are lucky

241

that I have just said Mass and am feeling more compassionate. Get out of here, and let this be the last occasion I see you like that."

I bowed my way out, sufficiently humiliated.

The rules were really easy. Unlike Osterley where we never got out except on Sunday afternoon, at the Beda, that was the only time most of the students were in, taking a siesta. We were allowed to eat out at any meal as long as we signed the book. I know one student who had eaten only one meal in College in four years, his first day. He was the same student who asked the Rector's permission to go to his dentist.

"Don't ask me if you can go to your dentist. Of course, you can go to your dentist. You're a fully grown man . . . . Don't ask for such stupid permissions!"

The student was not seen for a couple of weeks. When he eventually returned, the Rector asked him where he had been.

"To the dentist," he replied innocently.

"To the dentist?" the Rector repeated bewildered. "Where is your dentist?"

"In New York!" replied the American student.

Although the students all seemed to enjoy themselves at the Beda, it was not all play. We had Philosophy, Dogmatic, Ascetical and Moral Theology, Old and New Testament, History, Canon Law, Psychology and homiletic studies and lectures, and unfortunately therefore, we also had two weeks of exams both written and oral to pass. Many students were burning the midnight oil a week before exams. I was one of them.

We had a short vacation after Christmas; we were free to leave the college, but not Italy. A group of us spent the five days in Naples and Capri. The new semester was full of new things to learn. As we were hashing away at our books, the Vatican Council was making progress and the liberal movement in the Council was firmly established. Changes were coming fast: the Mass was to be revised after 400 years and Latin was to be dropped after fifteen hundred years.

Pope John often visited small churches or even took walks in the streets dressed as a simple parish priest. The last time I was to see Pope John publicly was Ash Wednesday in the Dominican church. He was mobbed as he walked the streets to the church where he decided he would preach the sermon, as he did often without warning in the poorest of churches. He mounted the pulpit to preach, then turned to the parish priest and remarked, "You have a good crowd." He then directed his attention to the packed congregation. "Why did you come, to see the Pope? . . . or Jesus Christ?" He genuflected to the tabernacle. "See the Pope is like you. He has to kneel to Jesus Christ. My dear children, don't come to see the Pope, if you don't come to worship Christ. He is our King!"

By Easter, it was exams time again. It was rumored that the Pope was not well, but he appeared on the balcony to give his blessing to the world. Although the Vatican denied it, the rumors grew.

Pentecost approached: the Pope was on retreat, a retreat he was not to complete. Now the world knew he was dying. His agony was watched by the world from St. Peter's on television. "My bags are packed and ready to go," the Pope said. The agony lingered. Pentecost Monday, a Mass was to be celebrated by Cardinal Traglia, the Vicar General of Rome. The Mass would be celebrated on the steps of St. Peter's. Those who could not get to the Square, watched it on TV. The Cardinal and all the beloved in Rome and the world were united in prayer for his peaceful release. It was the old Mass: the Cardinal reached the words of the Last Gospel, "There was a man sent by God and his name was John . . . ." Pope John XXIII was no more. The simple Pope had left the world, but he left it a renewed Church.

Our final exams for the year came and passed. The results were out and those of us who were successful were jubilant, those that failed were sad; they wouldn't be coming back.

The Beda students had a special flight to take them home to England for the summer vacation. As I looked down at the Eternal City, as I had done so many, many times before, I felt a new sensation, I felt I belonged. Rome, it's just a short good-bye this time—I'll be back to you and all the "beloved who are in Rome."

CHAPTER TWENTY

"The foolish to shame the wise"
1 Cor 1:27

"Kenny, I didn't expect you back until tomorrow! Has something happened?" Mum said, running to the door to meet me.

"He's left the cemetery . . . I knew it," Uncle John murmured as he followed slowly behind her.

" 'Seminary,' Uncle John, not cemetery . . . and I haven't left it at all. We were allowed to return home a few days early because of the death of Pope John." I put down my bags and hugged Mum. "Mum, you look wonderful." I turned to Uncle John, "Aren't you going to ask me anything?"

"Ask you what?"

"If I brought you any cigarettes."

"Did you?" His face lit up.

I opened my small grip and handed him a carton. "I have something for you too, Mum," I said as I searched my bag for the relic of St. Pius X.

"Kenny, you shouldn't spend your money on such foolish things. You have too many expenses." When she opened the small box and realized the contents, she said, "Forgive me, son, I shall treasure it always. I'll keep it under my pillow . . . ." Here come the tears again!

I was grateful for the first week at home to give me some time to relax. I spent two days visiting Osterley. To be with my "Osterley brothers" once again, strengthened my personal commitment to serve God through others: and I felt quite certain that the early Fathers of the Church had these students in mind when they said, "And you will know they are Christians by their love." We all sat together in the college garden listening anxiously to the commentator's account of the scene at St. Peter's Square: several of us huddled round the radio until finally we could hear the loud voice of Cardinal Ottaviani: "Habemus Papam . . . Giovanni Battista Montini!" Pope Paul the Sixth was our new successor to the throne of St. Peter: we celebrated the occasion with "lemonade and tea cakes."

Jackie wasn't spending as much time at home these days as he was dating quite steadily: Mum suspected that he and Maureen were becoming serious due to the fact Jackie was talking more about her than soccer. Until this time, sports had always been his first love.

Claire visited us often. After Roy's and Christopher's deaths, she adopted a baby girl, Susie, whom Mum was falling in love with more and more. Mum looked forward to their visits: it gave her another opportunity to fuss over the baby and make certain Claire was well.

After the first week of vacation, I took a job as a road construction worker: the pay was good and it gave me a chance to reserve the last two weeks before returning to college, for another vacation with Robin Noel to Warwick Hall. I had never used a pick axe before and I found I wasn't too good at it. I felt every muscle in my back would rip as I lifted it clumsily into the air, coming down with all my might, only to disturb an inch of soil. Many times, I pictured myself saying my first Mass from a wheelchair!

Although I knew Mum was happy looking after Jackie and Uncle John and thrilled with her new grand-daughter, Susie, I especially hated to say goodbye this time. She was sad when I left. "I know I'm selfish, son, to cry like this, but I worry in case I die before you are all settled. Once you become a priest and Jackie gets married, I'll be ready," she said hugging me at the door.

"What about me?" asked Uncle John laughing.

"Yes, you too, John. I pray the Blessed Lord takes you before me . . . . All we have is each other, and if I go first, you'll have nobody."

"Come on, Mum, . . . no more of that morbid talk," I said. Then in an effort to divert her thoughts, I turned to Uncle John. "When I come back next vacation, I'm going to bring you a new cap. That one's getting pretty old. How would you like a brand new one?"

"Me cap's fine. Just bring the cigarettes." He adjusted it on his head.

All the good-byes I have said in my life, and each

246

one is harder. How I hate them. I got into the cab and drove off.

OCTOBER, 1963

A crowd of students gathered in the Beda discussing their vacations.

Most of them were telling of their fabulous trips to the Holy Land, Greece or other colorful places.

"Where did you get your tan, Ken . . . in the south of France?" asked one of the students.

"No, I was working as a construction laborer on a road gang," I laughed.

Monsignor Curtin was passing and overheard my comment. "I do hope you were good at it . . . you may need to go back to it, if you don't shape up," he said smiling. I remembered Moon Mullins—maybe Jerry likes me after all. "I want to see you in my office," he said beckoning me to follow him.

He took his seat behind the desk, interlocked his fingers and looked up at me with that "bad egg" expression. "As you know, the most important social event in the college year is the Christmas play. I want you to produce and direct it," he said lifting his nose higher and pursing his lips tighter. My hunch was right; he really does like me. I began to relax. Suddenly his expression changed to a definite frown. "You were acting in last year's show, and I must say . . . in front of all those English and American bishops that attended the performance, you made a complete ass of yourself!" He stopped talking and looked at me with an extra pained face imploringly. "Promise me . . . *You won't* be in it!"

For the next two months, I set aside every spare minute away from study working on the scripts, casting and directing. Another student, Jimmy Clarkson, one of the funniest men I have ever met, helped me with the dialogue. The two and a half hour show was an overwhelming success: it received a standing ovation from the students, bishops, and faculty. After the performance, they all gathered to congratulate me; Monsignor Curtin was one of them. "I wish to congratulate you on the funniest show I have ever seen. I certainly laughed, more than I have in a long time. I see you have hidden talent." I thanked the Rector and as he was walking away, he called back, "If you don't make the priesthood, perhaps Hollywood will take you!" I knew I was finally in.

During this time, I became friends with another student, John Hopgood, an Australian student in his fourth year. With the aid of John's car, I was able to get around a lot more. I had naturally made contact with Bricktop my first year at the Beda, but now my visits could be more frequent. Bricktop introduced us to an American Embassy secretary, Maggie Kamoroski; from then on we had a place to go for Sunday dinner, and for the next three years, Maggie was to be a big sister to me and many other Beda students.

Many of the Beda students visited the English Center: there we could go and have tea and conversation in the tearooms. Soon I became good friends with Father Smith, the pastor of the English church that adjoined the Center, and two elderly ladies who always tried to make us students feel at home.

In spite of the busy social calendar, exams still had to be taken, and that entailed study, quite a bit of it. My burning the midnight oil paid off and I managed to receive grades in the 90's. Besides the house exams, I had to take my first Rome Vicariate exams for tonsure and minor orders. When my class arrived at 8:30 that morning, the halls in the Vatican office were already filled with other students. I looked around: they were from every corner of the earth: America, Britain, France, Germany, Asia, Spain, and Africa. The hall was a babble of languages and the pigment of the skin was from the fairest white of the German and Scandinavians, with the yellow and browns of the Asians to the blackest black of the Africans. It was truly the "universal" Church. My legs were shaking and my heart was beating fast when my name was finally called and I took my seat before the examination board of theologians. Thirty minutes later, I returned to my anxious classmates. "I passed!" I shouted excitedly. Now I was well on my way to the first stages on the road to the priesthood. In October, I would receive the tonsure (an initiation rite which entitles one to use the term "Reverend") and in November and December, I would receive the first and second minor orders.

It won't be long, now—Mum must really be doubling up on her prayers.

OCTOBER, 1964

It was the feast of Christ the King, October 4th and today I was to receive the tonsure. As we proceeded into the great church amid all the pomp and solemnity, I couldn't help but smile to myself at the contrast. Just one month ago, I was earning money serving drinks behind a bar in a Southampton pub. I was amused remembering the Saturday nights and the many fights I had to break up as the seamen brawled in the bar. Mum was worried about my taking such a summer job, but it did afford me the opportunity to end up my vacation with a trip to Warwick Hall to visit the Elweses with Father Noel, quite a change of scene from the pub. I thought of Mum weeping as I said farewell, Jackie and Maureen planning a wedding, Claire and little Susie becoming closer with each day, and good Uncle John. He was so pleased with the new felt cap I brought home for him, but he still didn't part with the old one. "Me old one's still good for sweeping the leaves," he said placing the new cap on his head. He still wore my old medal and chain I gave him the day I first left for Osterley. Perhaps those were his two prize possessions, the medal and chain and his old beat-up cap. I wish they were all here now. After this ceremony, I will be "Reverend Kenneth J. Roberts"—me, a Reverend!—I can't believe it. Well, Lord, you've taken me this far, now let me do the title justice. My thoughts were interrupted as the Master of Ceremonies called my name in Latin, "Canicum Roberts!" I looked up quickly, cleared my throat, and replied in a nervous voice, "*Adsum.*" I left my place and joined the long line of students that were walking towards the Cardinal. At last it was my turn. I knelt at the prelate's feet as he took the silver scissors and cut a little of my hair from the crown of my head. If Mr. Mullins could see me now!

This third year was the hardest scholastically; besides the house exams, each semester we had to learn two tracts in Dogma for the Subdiaconate, three tracts for the Diaconate, and five tracts for the Priesthood exams, nine tracts in theology in all in order to prepare for the Roman Vicariate examination board of theologians. Many a night I was to spend in study almost to the point of frustration, but I needed only to look out my bedroom window at the dome of St. Paul's Basilica and be reminded that "it won't be long now."

I made a new friend this year, Carl Campanova, a classmate who arrived from Philadelphia to finish his last two years of study at the Beda. He was a serious and pious student with a Master's degree from Villanova University where he had been a psychology major. After working as a high school counselor he decided to become a priest. Although Carl was an American Italian, his knowledge of the language left much to be desired so he used me as his interpreter for his many Italian relatives. At Christmas, we decided to make a short trip to visit a group of his mother's relatives. John Hopgood (it was now Father John), Carl, and Ian, an English convert clergyman, and myself made up the party.

The four of us headed south towards the mountains. John, being an Australian, was not used to driving in the snow. The winding mountain road was slick with ice. All of us huddled in the Volkswagen bracing ourselves with each turn. Suddenly we began to slide as John slammed on the brakes. "Don't use your brakes on ice," I shouted nervously.

"How am I supposed to slow down then?" John shouted angrily.

"Use your gears," I answered sarcastically.

"Okay, wise guy, you know so much . . . you drive," he screamed as he stopped the car and got out grumbling.

I was amused at his display of temper, but I was glad to take the wheel. For the next ten miles, I negotiated the narrow hairpin bends very slowly. At last, we came to a long stretch of straight road. I increased the speed to 40 miles per hour. Then it happened: the car went into a skid. I turned into the skid and we swung around to the other side of the mountain highway, dangerously close to the fifty foot drop. Carl became excited, Ian stiffened himself against the back seat, never saying a word. I knew we weren't going to make it as slowly we rolled.

251

"This is it! Everybody hold on!" I said as I clutched the steering wheel tightly and braced myself for the fall. As I began a quick "act of contrition" and centered my thoughts on meeting St. Peter, a voice pierced my very soul. "MY BLOODY CAR!" John shouted.

We turned over and stopped upside down. I was surprised to see we were all still alive. By a chance in a million, a tree was growing out of the side of a precipice and we were wedged in it upside down. After some time, we were rescued and the car repaired. That was the last time anyone offered to drive with me again!

The year passed slowly as we third year students sweated over Theology, Scripture, Canon Law and Church History. Besides our regular lecturer, we listened to the best brains in the Church, people like: Cardinals Suenens of Belgium and Ottaviani of the Curia; theologians like Hans Kung, Rahner, Charles Davis, and Schillebeeckx; scripture scholars, the most interesting of whom was Abbot Butler of Downside. Our minds boggled as we argued with ourselves after each lecture. By the end of our third year, we had met the greatest names in the Church, conservative, liberal, and moderate. We were molded by this unique experience as the Vatican Council progressed and we struggled within ourselves to understand what was happening within the Church.

May was the big month: Stanley and I graduated Summa Cum Laude from the Pontifical Institute of Christian Archeology, but if I didn't have a diploma to prove it, I would find it hard to think of myself as a qualified teacher of Paleo Christian Archeology. In June, with the Subdiaconate exams successfully behind us, we returned to the Roman Vicariate for our exams for the Diaconate. This examination was very important as the Diaconate is the first order we would receive that is part of the sacrament of Holy Orders: the others were ritualistic stages to the sacrament. I was quite confident when I entered as my name was called. I really know the subjects of my thesis: this one's a snap!

Two hours later, I left the building: John and Stanley were waiting for me. "What took you so long?" Stan asked.

"We've been worried. It's been two hours!" John said looking at his watch. "Did you pass?"

"Yes, eventually. . . ."

"Eventually?" asked Stan puzzled.

"Well, I was so cocky with my elaborate thesis, but he wasn't interested in the new explanations and fancy terms of my thesis. He was really a conservative. He said he was more interested in knowing whether I knew the catechism. Do you know something? . . . I almost flunked the catechism. He told me I was a proud and foolish boy, but he gave me a passing grade."

"Well, you've made it. That's all that counts. Now, let's go eat," John said as we all piled in the car. John turned on the ignition and began laughing hysterically.

"What's so funny?" I asked.

"How did you make your First Communion if you didn't know the catechism?" he asked laughing even harder.

Stan sat back in his usual dry manner and grinned, "He chose something foolish to shame the wise," he said making a pun on the Scriptures.

John laughed still harder. "That's good . . . get it, Ken? 'chose something foolish to shame the wise'?" he repeated Stan's words almost convulsing.

"Yes, John. I get it. You needn't explain it to me," I said rather annoyed. But the thought that I had

253

passed in spite of everything, made me reluctantly admit to the humor of the whole incident.

Two days later, I received a phone call from Mother Agnes, a nun whom I had known since childhood from Redcote Convent. She had just arrived in Rome. Times like this, I appreciated John, for he was very generous in granting us the use of his car to show the nuns the sights of Rome. Mother Paul, another dear old friend, was to accompany her on the "grand tour" of the Eternal City. I asked Stanley to come along as a guide: he knew all the famous landmarks and even more important, the complete history surrounding them. I was certain the Sisters would be impressed. They must have been since after two days of sightseeing, they invited me to have dinner with them at the convent. It was to be a special dinner thanking us for being their guides. She instructed me to invite four other seminarians, also.

I invited John and two other seminarians to come along: naturally Stan would come and I depended on him to continue the "good impression" the Sisters would have regarding my fellow students. I wanted my "old" friends to be impressed with my "new" ones. With Stan along, I had nothing to worry about: he was one of the most cultured men I had ever met.

The meal was truly a banquet: the sisters had gone to much trouble to prepare a delicious cuisine complete with wine. Mother Paul and Mother Agnes plus two other English sisters sat at the table completely enraptured by Stanley's boundless knowledge. Stanley was not a drinker of any sort, and it became quite obvious that the wine was beginning to affect his speech. Being a slow, deliberate speaker normally, his words almost slowed to a stop as the conversation and meal progressed. We were all shocked when in a loud voice, hesitating between each word, he said, "I—think—I'll —have—a—wee wee—"

There was a deathly silence as we looked at Stanley in horror. What is he saying?

". . . drop of wine!" he continued as he reached for the wine bottle.

We all laughed heartily except for Mother Paul, who was French. She thought we were laughing at Stan's French accent. "Wee wee," she said and shrugged her shoulders.

That same week, I received a letter from Mum telling me of Jackie's and Maureen's plans to be married on June 6th. By the time I received the letter in the middle of June, they were already married. I knew Mum was going to be quite lost, but she still had Uncle John to look after and he was a lot of company to her.

June 20th, the Beda broke up for summer vacation. Before returning home, John, an Australian priest, Carl, and myself decided to take a few days and drive to Luxembourg. From there Carl would take a flight home, John and the Australian priest would fly to New York where they were doing parish work for the summer, and I would return home to England. The next morning the four of us squashed into John's Volkswagen, which looked top heavy from all the baggage piled on the roof of it. About 6 p.m. we arrived at Bologna, the See city of Cardinal Lercaro: we pulled up to the Cardinal's palace.

"Kenny Babes, you're going to put your charismatic gift to work. You are going to use your beautiful Italian to get us an interview with the Cardinal!" John said as he jumped out of the car and rang the door bell.

"John, you're nuts!" I called after him, but seeing

that he was already waving to us to enter with him when the servant motioned for him to come in, we got out of the car and followed.

I explained to the servant we were visiting clergymen from England, Australia and the United States. He then led us to an elegant audience hall decorated with hanging tapestries, oil paintings and elaborate chandeliers. We walked across the thick soft carpet and took a seat. The setting was truly regal. The door opened and the Cardinal swept into the room. We all knelt and kissed the bishop's ring on his proffered hand. Immediately, I launched into my best Italian and introduced the others and myself to him. He began to converse with me in Italian, while John kept making rude remarks in Australian slang on the side. I turned to John and said, "Shut up, what if someone understands English and overhears what you're saying?"

"Don't be stupid. Nobody here speaks anything but Italian." He then looked at the Cardinal and smiled cordially. The Cardinal was smiling cordially, too. "Why don't you get the old boy to invite us for supper? Never ate in a Cardinal's palace before . . . . He should be able to afford four more for dinner. Have you ever seen anything like this?" he said looking around the room.

"Nothing doing. I'm not about to ask him that. Now let's get going!"

I turned back to the Cardinal and thanked him for the audience, then knelt and kissed his ring. "Have you eaten yet?" he asked in Italian. I answered that we hadn't. "I would like you to have dinner with me," he said then instructed a servant to set four more places.

The banquet hall was full of poor young Italian students with whom the Cardinal shared his palace.

We were served from silver dishes an elaborate meal fit for a king. As the servants entered with the food, they knelt and kissed the Cardinal's ring. His own meal, however, consisted of a simple salad. John continued throughout the whole meal to make remarks about the way the servants kept bowing. "He's like an Eastern Potentate," John laughed. After the meal, the Cardinal again accompanied us to the audience hall and John continued his remarks to me as I was trying desperately to converse with the Cardinal and distract his attention away from John.

I was grateful when it was time to leave. We all knelt and kissed his ring once again. John said as we were walking to the door, "I must admit, the old boy surely lives well, but I was impressed with his humility and the way he took all those poor students into his home. I'm glad I got to meet him."

"I'm most happy to have met you, too, Father!" said the Cardinal *in English!* He smiled and walked away.

When we reached the car, I was still convulsing in laughter. John wasn't laughing, however, his mouth was still wide open and he looked as if he were going to be in shock at any second. Finally he brought himself to speak, "He understood every word I said!" This was all he managed to say: the shock was still too great for him. I remembered the day when I almost flunked the exams and John had a good laugh at my expense. I couldn't resist the temptation to "rub it in" even more.

"This time, John, the scripture text was reversed . . . 'The wise has shamed the foolish!' "

CHAPTER TWENTY-ONE

"Can you drink of this cup? . . . ."
Mt 20:22

"What kind of a welcome is this?" I said laughing as Mum continued to cling to me tightly sobbing the whole time. I thought she was crying because she was happy to see me. "Mum, if you cry like this when you're happy, what do you do when you're sad?" I teased. "Now quit crying, Mum. Wait till you see all the religious articles I brought home this time," I said reaching into my luggage: I pulled out a carton of cigarettes. "Where's Uncle John? He'll be more interested in these . . . ."

"Kenny, that's what I'm trying to tell you. Uncle John's gone," she said wiping her eyes.

"Gone? Where did he go?" I was confused.

"Kenny, he died just three weeks ago," she began to sob again.

"Oh no Mum . . . why didn't you contact me?" Now I understood those tears and I was fighting hard to hold back my own.

"There was nothing you could do, Kenny. And I knew you were busy with exams . . . I didn't want to give you anything else to worry about." She wiped her eyes and stiffened up as if she had allowed herself all the time she needed to get it out of her system.

"Now come in the kitchen, dear, I'll make us some tea then I'll tell you all about it."

The house seemed extremely lonely as I sat in the kitchen watching Mum prepare the tea. I looked in the dining room and in my imagination recalled the day when I came home from the QE after handing in my resignation. There was Mum, Claire, Jackie, Roy, Christopher and Uncle John. Now Claire was busy looking after Susie and teaching school, Jackie had a wife to think of and had his own home to worry about, Roy, Christopher and Uncle John were all gone. I looked back at Mum as she was pouring the tea, just two cups this time. I wanted to run to her and grab her and say, "You'll never have to cry again . . . I'll see to it!" I vowed this vacation at home, I would have one goal, to make Mum happy.

Three days later I landed a job as a waiter in the most fashionable night club in Southampton. I hesitated about taking the temporary job at first, but when I weighed all the advantages, I decided to take it. I knew this last year in Rome would incur a fantastic amount of expenses with the ordination festivities: another thing that appealed to me was the fact that I wouldn't have to start work till early evening thus giving me the whole day to spend with Mum. The pay was extremely good so I knew I again could leave a couple of weeks open before returning to the Beda, but this time, it would be spent showing Mum a good time. My biggest problem now was how to break the news to Mum that I had taken a job in a night club. I knew she wouldn't like it.

"Mum, sit down. I want to talk to you," I said firmly, but gently.

"What is it?" she said as she wiped her hands on her apron and took a chair opposite me.

"I start work tonight. You know I need the money for the tremendous expense this year, so I found a job where I could earn the most money."

"You're starting work tonight? What kind of a job is that . . . working at night?" I denoted a little apprehension in her voice.

When I finished explaining the respectability of the club and the good reputation it had, she seemed a little more at ease, but still not thoroughly convinced that it was the right thing to do. "If you think you must do this, I won't try to talk you out of it. But Kenny, the most important thing to me in this whole world is that you become a priest, not just a priest, a 'good' priest," she said with stern conviction.

"And what do you consider a good priest?" I asked smiling at the stern look still on her face.

Her face softened and those peaceful eyes seemed to become aglow. "Son, to me a good priest is one who loves, and because he loves, he serves. He must never become too busy to stop and comfort an old lady, or console a sick or troubled person. He should find time to listen to the problems of children no matter how slight he may think them in the world of an adult. He must be compassionate with the sinner and tolerant of the stubborn. He must lead gently and through his works bring people to Christ. Whether he is saying Mass, giving a sermon, visiting in a home, attending a carnival, he must be Christ to all he meets."

"That's quite a big order to fill, Mum."

"Not really, if you remember just one thing. Whenever you don't know just what to do, ask yourself 'What would Christ do?' and Kenny, He'll show you . . . I'm sure of it."

"Mum, I think I should take you back with me to the Beda. You would be the most fantastic spiritual director any seminary has ever had," I said smiling.

"I'm serious, Kenny. Don't joke with me when you speak of the priesthood." She was becoming stern once again. "If you are not a good priest, I'll come back and haunt you! The seed is sown, now you must bear fruit."

I had overslept one morning: when I came down the stairs to the kitchen, Mum was not there. I called to her in the garden and there was no response. I looked at my watch; it was 10 o'clock. She should be home from Mass by now, I thought. I went to the neighbor's because I thought perhaps she may be visiting there. "Your Mum went to 8 o'clock Mass. She said she had some special Mass for the Catholic Women's League or something like that." I thanked her for the information and went home to fix some breakfast. It got to be 1:00 and I was becoming very worried. I thought I had best walk up to church and look for her there. After leaving church and finding no trace of Mum, I went to Redcote Convent to inquire, still no luck. It was close to 2:30 when I returned home. Mum still wasn't in. I was beginning to panic. Where could she be? Finally at 4 o'clock, she walked in the door, breathless.

"Where on earth have you been? I've been half crazy worrying about you!" I said trying to control myself.

"Fix me a cup of tea, son, and I'll tell you all about it. I had the most wonderful day."

"I'm happy for you, but do you know what you put me through? Where have you been?" I half shouted.

"Well, after I left St. Joseph's church—You know that's where they had that special Mass today?" I nodded waiting for her to get on with the story. "Well, after I left there, I decided to take a short stroll through the park and here I found this poor man lying on the park bench. I stopped to talk with him . . . and son, do you know that the poor thing hadn't had a decent meal in months. Well, I didn't want to give him the money, I was afraid he would spend it on drink, so I took him to the steak house, that way, I was sure he would have a warm meal. And Kenny, it was such a pleasure to watch the poor soul. He must not have enjoyed anything like that in a long time." She paused and took off her shoes.

"Weren't you embarrassed walking in a restaurant like that with a bum?" I asked in amazement.

"Shame on you, Kenny. Remember what our Blessed Lord said, 'What you do for the least of these my brethren . . . !' "

"Yes, Mum. I know the scriptural quotation. But what I don't understand is how that could have taken you all that time?"

"Well dear, I got talking with this man and he was so nice. But Kenny, he didn't even have a bed to sleep in so I emptied my purse into his pocket. I wish you could have seen him, son. He had tears in his eyes. I gave him a medal of the Blessed Mother too. I can't tell you how good it felt to know you made someone happy." Again she paused, just sitting there smiling.

"But Mum, that still doesn't explain why you were so long in getting home," I said impatiently.

She started to laugh. "That's the funny part," she said.

"Thank God, there's a funny part. Would you care to tell me about it?" I was being sarcastic, but Mum didn't even notice.

"After he had gone, I realized I gave him all my money, including my bus fare so I had to walk home. I started puffing a little though, when I reached Lancer's Hill. But I made it! I just pretended it was Calvary and made a mental pilgrimage." She sat back in the chair still smiling, then took a deep sigh. "Isn't our Blessed Lord wonderful to give us so much joy and so many chances to show Him how much we love Him?"

If only I had her humility—She is so humble, she isn't even aware of it.

One afternoon, I visited the Sisters at Redcote. Mother Paul came in with a large cardboard box. "Look what I have here, Kenneth. It's for you," she said in her French accent. She opened the box and removed two sets of vestments, one red, the other, white. Before long, I was swamped with gifts from the Sisters, albs, amices, cinctures. The Sisters laughed and giggled as they crowded the parlor. "I hope I make it. I haven't passed the priesthood exams yet," I said.

"You'll make it, with so much prayer on your behalf, how can you fail? Sister Mary of the Immaculate Conception has been praying the rosary for you every day for years. And your mother, Kenneth, everything she does is a prayer for you to be a priest," said Sister Gertrude.

When I arrived home with the vestments, Mum was so excited, too excited to keep her news to herself any longer. "I have a surprise for you. I was going to surprise you in Rome, but I can't wait any longer. Guess what?"

"I can't guess, what?"

"You are going to have your very own chalice. What do you think of that?" She was beaming. "I put money aside in the bank for this for a long time."

"Mum, you can't. It's too expensive. You should

keep that money in the bank. It will give you security," I argued.

"I want security at the altar, not in the bank. I'm giving it to Christ. Don't begrudge your mother the honor of giving Christ a chalice for His Precious Blood. There is no argument. Take the money and order the chalice of your choice. Make sure it's gold. I'll see it when I come to Rome."

"Thank you, Mum." I stooped to kiss her cheek.

"I ask only one thing, Kenny."

"Anything. What is it?"

"When you choose the chalice you want, will you have an engraving put on it?" she asked very intently.

"Whatever you want me to have on it, that's what it will be," I assured her.

"Well son, just so you will never forget to pray for me every time you say Mass, I want it to read: PLEASE PRAY FOR ME, and sign it, MOTHER. Then you'll always remember that I'm asking for your prayers."

"It's a promise," I said watching her smile from ear to ear. She's happy!

The following Sunday, Mum and I went to Jackie's and Maureen's for supper. After we ate, Jackie and I settled down in the parlor: I was telling him about my plans after ordination. I told him all I knew about Texas. Mum came running in the room. "I wish you wouldn't remind me about that Texas again," she said looking a little troubled. "That worries me."

"Why should it worry you, Mum?" "You know I'm being ordained for that diocese and I would like to send for you as soon as I get settled there."

"It's all those cowboys and Indians that have me upset," she said nervously.

"Mum, there aren't any cowboys and Indians as you think of them," I said trying to assure her.

264

"Don't tell me, Kenny. Just last week, there was a movie about them and they said they were in 'Texas.' If you wanted to be a missionary, why didn't you plan on going to someplace that's safe . . . like Africa?"

I couldn't help laughing. "That was years ago when all that Indian stuff went on, Mum."

"I'm telling you . . . ," she was very insistent. "I saw it just last week on channel eleven!"

I spent my last two weeks at home taking Mum all over. I quit my job at the Silhouette club to devote this time just to Mum. She was laughing all the time and talking constantly about Rome. Every time we were near a shop, she would ask, "Do you think a dress like that would be suitable for the ordination?" Many times when she talked about her impending trip to Rome, she would say, "If only I get my nerve to fly."

I was amused one afternoon when I was taking her to visit some nun friends in Salisbury, she came in my room and asked, "Kenny, are you allowed to wear your Roman collar now?"

"Yes Mum, we wear it all the time in Rome, but here in England the seminarians don't wear it until after their Subdiaconate . . . why?"

"Well, I would be so proud to show you off to the dear Sisters in your collar. Do you think it would be alright?"

"Of course," I said. I went through my drawer and found it and began to put it on when she stopped me.

"Could I help you do that?" She sounded almost timid.

She reached up and fastened the back at the neck. "Now turn around," she said. She stood there looking at me and started to cry, but she was still smiling.

265

"Don't get angry with me, Kenny. These are happy ones," she said wiping a tear from her cheek.

A few days before I was to leave for Rome, Stanley arrived to spend the remainder of the vacation with Mum and me. Then John arrived with a carload of Australian priests. Mum loved all the excitement: she had people to cook for again and the house was jumping. It was her idea to have a farewell party the night before we left. We had a houseful of priests and students including the local Protestant minister whom Mum kept calling "Father" by mistake. "I hope you don't mind me calling you, 'Father,' " Mum joked as she served him at table. "I was ecumenical long before the Vatican Council!"

The day I left for Rome, Mum received a letter from Susie. "She's coming home, Kenny, and Molly's coming with her. They are both coming with me to your ordination! Poor Molly, I expect she's very lonely since Big Jack died. It's been three years now." Tears began to fill her eyes. "There I go again, being selfish, when I should count my blessings. Susie is coming home for the first time since she left as a young woman, Molly will be here with her, and soon I will be going to Rome to see my son become a priest! God is so good to me!"

Right before I was getting ready to leave, Mum called me into the kitchen. "Son, I wanted a few minutes alone with you before you left," she said. "I am so happy right now, as I know you are. Remember Kenny, I am praying for you constantly. There will be much excitement and celebration after your ordination ceremony, but the glamor of the priesthood is like a marriage . . . . First comes the honeymoon, then the vocation begins. Can you drink from the cup Christ will give you?"

This was one farewell Mum didn't cry. She was smiling and bubbling as I kissed her good-bye. In just six months, she would be joining me in Rome for my ordination, a day she looked forward to as much as I did. She stood at the gate waving. I looked back at her as the car pulled down the road: she was still smiling; she threw me a kiss, then waved again.

OCTOBER 30, 1965

A crowd of students gathered around the notice board in the hall. Stan was just leaving after having read it. "What is it, Stan?" I asked.

"Tomorrow, we receive the Subdiaconate at St. Marcello and we have to be there by 7:30 a.m. so we will have to be up early," he answered.

"Where is St. Marcello?"

"You know St. Marcello's . . . it's that big church in the Corso, not far from the Victor Emmanuel Memorial."

"Stan, there must be twenty big churches right there . . .," I laughed.

"It makes no difference. You'll be there . . . they have a bus chartered to get us there. All you have to do is get out of bed, get dressed and make sure you have all the necessary vestments . . . . Of course you may want to shave. It would be nice to make a good appearance on the day you make your vow of celibacy," he teased. "Come on, let's go for a walk. I'm nervous."

Later when I returned to my room to get ready for supper, I stood at the window gazing at the sunset over St. Paul's, a habit I had cultivated in my three years here. I looked down at the street: a man was strolling with two small boys, one of them was apparently just beginning to walk. The toddler quickened his awkward steps in an effort to keep up with the older boy, and fell. He began to cry pathetically. The man picked him up, brushed him off, and held him tightly for a few minutes comforting him until the little one stopped crying. The man, whom I presumed to be the father, decided to carry the little one and reached out to take the hand of the bigger boy. I felt a pang of something I couldn't identify: I didn't know if it was loneliness, envy, compassion or nostalgia from viewing this touching scene. The bell rang for supper.

I returned to my room: I wanted to be alone and think. I sat for a long time by my window imagining the scene over again. Tonight is my last night before I take the vow of celibacy. I couldn't sleep. What is wrong with me?—For years now I've been prepared to sacrifice my manhood to God in order to become a priest—God knows that's my one real desire, to serve Him—Perhaps that feeling I had this evening watching that man with those children was envy—I will never know what it is to look at another human being and say, "This is my son . . . this is a part of me"—There will be no woman to hold closely and share my burdens with—No one to offer me consolation when I am lonely or troubled—I'll never hold a child in my arms and look at his face to find my own features there— Many people will call me "Father," but no one will ever call me "Dad"—This is what Mum was talking about when she said, "Can you drink of this cup, son?" That's what the Subdiaconate is all about—It's just dawned on me—Tomorrow, I will be giving myself completely to God, my total manhood—I will be the sacrificial victim—But at ordination, God is giving Himself totally to me: He is the victim—A feeling of joy overwhelmed me—There truly is more joy in giving than in receiving—I'm making the choice, Lord.

You are my first choice, now help me share in Your Priesthood with my whole being.

The sanctuary was filled as we prostrated ourselves flat on the floor resting our foreheads on our folded arms. The choir was singing the litany of the saints. As I lay there, the enormity of the sacrifice I was about to make hit me again, this time even stronger. The bishop's words echoed in my mind—Nobody is forcing me to receive this order; nobody is forcing me to renounce marriage; I'm still free to leave—Can I drink of the cup? I prayed for strength. *"Sancta Maria, Ora pro Nobis."* The chant of the choir penetrated my brain. The words of Christ came vividly to mind as I searched to find God at that moment—"My grace is sufficient for thee . . . ." I will drink of the cup!

CHAPTER TWENTY-TWO

"Take up his cross"
Mt 10:38

I wanted desperately to study, but it wasn't easy with so many exciting things to do. My mind was full of other things, all the preparations that still had to be done for the great day of ordination. I closed the book on Sacramental Theology and looked out the window towards St. Paul's Basilica, the most prayerful and beautiful church in Rome. I visited St. Paul's tomb daily to pray and I was certain the Epistles of St. Paul would always hold a special meaning to me: after all, we had been neighbors, sharing the same street for four years now. My thoughts were interrupted by a knock at the door. "Come in," I shouted as I turned away from the window.

"Ken, the goldsmith is downstairs with his display of chalices," said Carl as he came rushing in the room. His excitement was contagious.

"Let's go," I replied as I dropped my book on the bed and left the room. "Where is he?" I tried to keep up with Carl who was leaping down the stairs two steps at a time, holding his cassock up almost to his waist.

"He's in the library."

We walked along the table looking at the large selection. "I like that one, but I prefer the base on this one and the node on this other one," I said as I picked them up to examine them more closely.

"That's no problem, sir," remarked the Austrian goldsmith. "We can alter it to any design you choose."

I spent the next two hours planning with him the final details of my chalice. "Yours will certainly be unique, it's a combination of four designs with your own variations thrown in," he said as he put the final draft into his briefcase.

"How soon will it be ready?" I asked.

He checked his schedule to see when he would be returning to Italy. "I'll be back here after Christmas vacation. I should have it by then . . . . Is there anything else?"

"Will you do the engraving too?"

"Certainly, what do you want it to read?"

"I want it to say, *Please pray for me,* then sign it, *Mother.*"

He wrote the message and assured me it would be just as I specified: Carl and I thanked him and left the room.

"You sure you got what you wanted? It took you long enough to decide," Carl said.

"I'm sure, but I had to make certain the inscription was put on correctly. I promised Mum. She said it would always remind me that she was asking for my prayers when I said Mass."

"Let's get a pizza!" Carl motioned me to the door.

On the way to the pizzeria, I asked Carl, "How come you didn't buy a chalice?"

"I want to look around a bit. It's so exciting planning and I want to make it last."

"Hey Ken, what do you think of these holy cards?" Carl asked as we browsed through the religious goods shop.

"I like them, but do they have any of these photo scenes in color?"

"You mean these, sir?" asked the attendant lifting a tray of cards.

"This one is beautiful, Carl." I picked one up to show him.

It was a late sunset over a predominantly blue sea and sky, with the reflection of the setting sun casting a pinky white hue over the water as twelve men were bringing in their nets on the shore. The caption was most appropriate, "Come follow me, and I will make you fishers of men, and at once they left their nets, and followed Him." Carl liked them too. "I'll have five thousand of those," I said and continued to browse for some others.

"How do you like these, sir? They are modern, but in good taste." He showed me some of a chalice with a host above it and hands outstretched to reach it.

"I like it, I'll have the same order of those." I chose ten other designs including a Russian icon of the Blessed Mother and a picture of a wood carving of

271

the face of Christ. "That should be enough," I said to Carl as I completed my order.

"You'll need a lot when you're ordained in Rome as you have to give one to each person you bless after the ordination . . . . Then there's the first Mass in Rome, and then your parish church back home and all the churches where you will be saying Mass the first months," Carl said placing an enormous order to the assistant.

Soon it was the end of November and we were back at St. Marcello's for the ordination to the Diaconate. Carl was bubbling after the ceremony.

"Ken, congratulations!" He threw his arms around me in the customary manner of the Italians. Carl was a very emotional Italian, although he was born and raised in Philadelphia. "Can you believe it, Ken. We're deacons!"

Maggie Kamoroski, our American Embassy friend, was waiting to take us to lunch: we met her outside the church with Father John. "Congratulations Kenneth . . . Carl." We both gave our Roman sister a friendly kiss: this isn't an Italian custom for clergy to kiss ladies, especially on the steps of a church, but today, we didn't care. We were too happy to worry about convention. John gave us both a hug, Italian style, and congratulated us too.

"Let's get moving, Beda Babes, I'm starved. Where are we going to eat, Maggie?" said John as he opened the door of the car to let her in.

"We're going somewhere special . . . . Have you boys ever eaten snails?"

Tuesday, 14 Dec. 1965

My dearest Son,
   Thank you for your letter and card. No doubt

you have been worried because you have not heard from me, but I didn't want you worried because of your exams. I wanted you to pass. Well, now I can tell you, I have been very ill with pneumonia and it was touch and go with me. I'm up today for the first time in two weeks and I am pleased to say I am much better. I have been praying for you day and night and I hope you have done well in your exams. Now don't worry about me.

Well, my dearest son, this is all. Give my love to my dear boys and ask them to pray for me as I will pray for you all. Soon I will see you in Rome.

> Lots of love and God bless,
> Mum

I must write to her immediately—Thank God, she is better now. That's just like Mum not to tell me so I shouldn't worry. I'll offer my Mass and Communion that she will return to good health and be back on her feet again.

JANUARY, 1966

"This is the year, Ken. This is the year the old Carl Campanova and Ken Roberts die . . . 'Father Ken' and 'Father Carl' are about to be born. Doesn't that give you a funny feeling?" said Carl.

The dreaded moment descended upon us. "Are you ready for the priesthood exams at the Vicariate?" asked Carl as Stanley and I sat in Stan's room questioning each other on our five tracts in Theology.

Paul Wilton, an American, and an ex-Navy lieutenant, came to the door. "Can I join you?" He took a chair and joined the conversation.

273

"Who's ready for the Vicariate exams?" he questioned.

"I don't know if I am or not," I said bewildered as I looked down at the many notes before me.

"It all depends now on whether we get a conservative or liberal theologian as examiner. You know that conservative theologian you had last time, Kenny? . . . Well, he failed ten deacons last week because they defended con-celebration. He said it denied the efficacy of the private individual Mass," said Carl with a worried look, but he really had no need to worry: he was far from liberal.

I remembered the third degree he gave me at the Diaconate exams and how he almost failed me because I didn't know the catechism by heart: I began to get a sick feeling of worry. I better get to work on the catechism, just in case.

Carl was in the examining room and Stan was talking at a rapid rate to one of the examiners. I sat with another student waiting for my turn to go in: I used these last few minutes to go over in my mind a few of the points that may be asked. The student next to me was hunched forward in his seat wringing his hands. Neither of us spoke. I imagined he was using these precious minutes to do the same thing, pray!

"Do you have a cigarette, Ken?"

"Sure, but I didn't know you smoked."

"I don't," he said as he lit the cigarette, took a deep drag and coughed.

Two students stood to leave one of the examining tables. Oh no, one of the examiners is the conservative. The student in front of me was ushered to his table: I breathed a sigh of relief.

The hours ticked by as slowly the Dutch theologian grilled me. I felt like I was before the Spanish Inquisition, or perhaps a firing squad. My mouth was dry and my hands were cold and wet. I glanced over at the conservative's table: he had passed ten men since I sat down. Guess they knew their catechism . . . I wish I had been one of them.

"Tell me, how could you prove the real presence in the Eucharist and please don't talk about substance and accidents."

"From Scripture," I replied and quoted the institution narrative, "This is my Body."

He shook his head in disgust. (What did I say wrong?) He took a picture of Paul the Sixth from his desk. "This is Pope Paul. Is it really he or his image?" I got the message. "Don't use the Scripture like the Pharisees," he said in anger.

I searched for the right answer. "Well, there are many scriptures which if you read them all in context you . . . ." I began to quote St. Paul to the Corinthians.

"Enough, enough," he interrupted. (Now what did I say wrong?) "The important words you have said, 'If you use them in context.'" He looked pleased: I felt relieved. "That is why there is Christian disunity and hatred and bigotry because each denomination has its pet quotes from the Bible like poison darts, for then, we revert to the kind of Church that Christ condemned, legalists who see the 'way more important than the persons.' God and you . . . Good-bye, you have passed!"

"What took you so long?" asked John as he paced up and down. "Where's Carl?" He looked at his watch.

"Carl hasn't come back yet? He went in before me, he should be out by now." I was worried. I ran back in the building and up the stairs to the examining halls. I peeped through the door. There was Carl wiping the perspiration from his brow and still answering questions.

275

"Are you next?" asked my old conservative friend.

"No Father, I have just passed," I answered with relief.

He smiled; he seemed a little relieved too.

Finally, Carl left the examining room. "Did you pass?" I asked anxiously.

"Yes, but only 'just.' He was Dutch, I think," said Carl.

Both of us vowed we would always avoid both extremes of the Church.

"What shall we call ourselves, Carl?" I asked as we walked briskly to the staircase.

"How about 'conservative liberals'?" Carl joked.

"No, I am an 'orthodox progressive'!" I answered laughing.

Stanley came walking up behind us. "Why don't you ask me what I'm going to be?" We both did. "A Christian!" he said and we all laughed, hysterical with relief, running down the steps like children.

"You look like a bunch of giggling school girls. I take it you've all passed," shouted John as we came down the steps of the Vicariate still laughing uncontrollably. "God help you if any of you are ever made a bishop, you will have to be put in restraints. Let's get going."

We piled in the Volkswagen and headed for the Polesi Brothers. I had met them in my first year. Vincenzo, the elder of the two had been an air steward for Alitalia and Biagio had served in the British Merchant Navy, and for a long time was a waiter on the *Andes*. I had a lot in common with both of them. Now, they owned a restaurant at the Piazza Sforza Caesarini, right off the Corso Emmanuele. This was our favorite eating place and we frequented it often.

"Hello, how are you? Did all of you pass your exams okay?" asked Vincenzo as we took a table.

"Yes thank God! Vincenzo, I want to fix up a booking on March 26th for my ordination banquet. I'll probably need the whole restaurant," I said.

"Leave it all to me. I'll take good care of you."

Monday, Jan 24, 1966

My dearest son,

Just a line to let you know I'm better and to tell you to carry on with all your plans. I shall be able to come at last. I hope you are getting on fine and keep up your prayers. I'm saying my rosary every day that our Blessed Lord will give you the grace to be a good priest and bring souls to Him.

Molly and Susie wrote to say they would be sailing and will reach Southampton on March 17. We'll all be together in Rome soon. Give my love to the dear boys and ask them to pray for your old mother. I hope I get the nerve to fly.

Lots of love and God bless,
Mum

Fantastic! This is the letter I've been waiting for—She's had the okay from the doctor. Now, it's settled. This day of ordination will be as great for Mum as it is for me. Thank you, Lord.

"The goldsmith is here with your chalice," Paul said as he met us in the hall on our way back from lunch. "It looks terrific, one of the third year students took a picture of it so he can copy it next year."

I picked up the chalice. It was truly beautiful. Mum will love it.

"Come on Ken. Let's pick up our official announcements today," said Carl.

"I hope they don't get them mixed up. We both had the same design," I replied as we walked toward the door.

"Ken, that was a smart idea of yours to have the cross enlarged from a funeral card, by changing it from black to gold. It symbolizes the cross of glory." Carl was always interested in symbols.

"Is that why you hold a Master's degree at Villanova, because you're an expert on symbols?" We always teased Carl about his MA in psychology. "You are as much a psychologist as I am an archeologist . . . all we have are pieces of paper to prove it, right?" We both laughed and left to phone John.

February 25, 1966

My dearest son,

It won't be long now, just one month away. I'm feeling very well, but a bit weak on my legs. Dearest son, keep up the prayers and ask the boys to pray that our Blessed Lord will give me good health so that I will see you in Rome. Molly and Susie will be here very soon. Tell me what I am to do. I know I must have a photograph taken and get a passport. Would the bank do these things for me? I'm sure we all have a lot to be thankful to our Blessed Lord. I know I have. Well, my dearest son, remember me to all the dear boys and don't forget to tell them I keep them in my prayers. So with my love and prayers to all you dear sons who are giving up your lives to our Blessed Lord, may He bestow on you special grace.

Lots of love and God bless,
Mum

P.S. I love those fancy cards for your ordination you sent me. That picture of your chalice is beautiful. I'm so glad you remembered to have it engraved. Now you will never forget to pray for me each time you say Mass.

I'm so pleased Mum likes the announcement cards and the chalice. I was anxious to hear her reaction.

I was in a panic. Here we were just over a week to go and I still hadn't addressed all my announcements. Ian, Carl and Stan came in to help me. Carl typed the envelopes while the other two put in the announcements.

"Thank goodness, you sent off all the announcements to England and the United States or they would not have received them in time," Stan said sealing the local ones.

"Look at this name, . . . is this the Greek Orthodox friend?" asked Stan. I nodded affirmatively. "Lord, look at this invitation list. You have Protestants, the Greek Orthodox . . . I haven't seen any Jews . . . "

"Christ will be there," I said teasing. "But if you know of any others give me their names and I'll invite them."

"You certainly are ecumenical," Stan laughed. "I'm telling you, I don't believe this list," Stan continued. "There are night club stars, a secretary to the American Embassy, British aristocracy, janitors, maids, the head of Boy's Town in Italy, Monsignor Carroll Abing . . . . Oh Ken, you have forgotten the Queen!" he joked.

"Yes, but my friend, the first secretary to the British Legation to the Vatican is coming . . . . He can represent her," I said mockingly.

"No wonder all the faculty is going to your first

Mass, they don't want to miss the procession. I tried to invite one of the professors to my first Mass, and was informed they were all going to yours, now I can see why," Carl laughed, looking up from the typewriter.

"Don't worry, Carl. You'll have your hands full with your five hundred relatives," I teased.

"What is this here?" asked Carl.

"Cablegrams," I said as I typed another address.

"Aren't you going to open them?" Carl was looking at the places of origin.

"No, they are only congratulatory cables. I'm going to keep them until ordination day."

"How can you stand the suspense?" Carl was amazed at my lack of enthusiasm. "Let me open them for you and if there is anything more than a congratulations note, I'll tell you, okay?"

"If it makes you feel any better, go ahead, but I can wait," I said amused at his thrill for such simple things.

Stan and Ian continued to tease me about my guest list. All of us were so busy joking with each other that we didn't notice Carl sitting motionless at the typewriter. I reached for a stack of envelopes next to Carl's typewriter when I realized his silence. "What's up with you?"

Carl gripped my hand firmly. "Kenny, be prepared for a shock."

"My Lord, the Queen of England *is coming!*" Stan joked.

I looked at Carl's face and realized there was no humor in the air any longer. I grabbed the cable from him. I had that awful feeling in the pit of my stomach again. I looked at the brief message.

I stood motionless staring at the piece of paper. I banged my fists down on the typewriter and cried, screaming at the top of my voice, "No! It can't be! . . . Why God? Why? Couldn't you wait just a few more days. My God, why?"

I looked down at the cablegram once again that read:

MUM PASSED AWAY TODAY

Brother George.

CHAPTER TWENTY-THREE

"Be it done unto me"
Lk 1:38

Sister Claire and Sister Euphrasia met me at the airport. I was still numb with shock. We drove home to Southampton in silence. The Sisters tried bravely to help me converse, but what could they say?

"Mother Paul said you may stay in the guest cottage at the convent," said Sister Claire.

"Thank you," I answered. I was grateful for the invitation; I certainly didn't want to go back to Pound Street. What a shock for Susie and Molly when they leave the ship tomorrow. Poor Susie, so many years she had to wait to return home to see Mum and she missed seeing her by a mere three days. Tomorrow is St. Patrick's Day too. Mum always said that was a special day for Susie because she was born in Ireland.

In the peaceful atmosphere of the convent, I was a little more composed and began to talk with the Sisters more easily. Mother Agnes and Mother Paul proceeded to tell me about Mum's last few months.

"She had been very ill since Christmas, Kenneth. It was only will power that had kept her going," said Mother Agnes.

"Two of our Sisters found her only last week: she was trying to get into the parish church and she collapsed on the steps," Mother Paul interrupted.

"Yes, she was so determined to go to Rome. She told Sister Gertrude that she left the house to get a few last minute things for her trip. Sister Gertrude was sure she would be there, even if it cost her her life. She kept insisting the most important thing to her was to see you become a priest. When Sister Gertrude tried to reason with her by telling her that she could ruin your ordination by becoming very ill while in Rome, she seemed for a time to reconsider. She said that God would show her the answer," Mother Agnes continued.

"Yes, and she wouldn't let anyone write you to let you know how ill she really was. She made everyone promise. She knew you had exams to worry about," said Mother Paul.

Later that night, George came to see me at the convent and gave me more information. "The Saturday before Mother died, she was looking better than she had looked for years. She got all dressed up and came out to my house in the country. Marian and I wanted her to stay the night, but you know how stubborn and independent Mum could be. She insisted I take her home. When I got her home, she made me a cup of tea and told me to be still while she said her rosary. Mum looked extra peaceful when she finished praying. She asked me to fetch her bag. That's when she gave me her will and money. I thought she

282

wanted me to mind it for her, but when I left, she said, 'There is more than enough there to bury me.' That was the last time I saw her alive."

It was her nurse who found her Sunday morning unconscious, kneeling at her bedside still fully dressed with her hands joined in prayer, clutching her rosary. She recovered consciousness in the hospital: just after midnight, she asked the nurse to bring her a priest. It was Father Robin Noel who tracked down the priest who spoke to me on the phone. "I'm not long in Southampton and I didn't have the privilege of knowing your mother. She was so happy, yet she knew she was dying. She told me to tell you that she will be with you on March 26th, but according to God's plan, not man's. Then she died."

The next morning was St. Patrick's Day: the Sisters were wearing the shamrock as they came to greet me after Mass. Father Hendry, the assistant in the parish, was sitting eating breakfast with me in the convent parlor as they entered.

"I know how much your mother wanted to be the first one to receive your priestly blessing, wouldn't it be wonderful if you could give us your first priestly blessing on the feast of St. Patrick?" said one of the Irish nuns.

"I'm afraid I can't arrange that, Sister. I'm only a deacon and deacons can't bless . . . ."

"Unless they are carrying the Blessed Sacrament to the sick and a priest is not available. That's the only time a deacon is allowed to give a priestly blessing," Father Hendry interrupted.

"Is that so, Father? Well then, we will have to pray to Mrs. Seagrave to help us," said the old Sister as she left the room.

About fifteen minutes later, she came running back

283

in the room. "Prayer certainly works!" she said with a smile. "Sister Mary of the Immaculate Conception has regained consciousness and she wants the sacraments."

"That is the Sister who has been praying all those rosaries for me. Is she ill?" I asked surprised.

"Yes, Kenneth. She has been dying now for several weeks; she has been semiconscious for two weeks."

"I still can't give the sacraments to her, Sister. There is a priest here," I said.

"Excuse me, I have an urgent appointment, Ken. You take care of it," Father Hendry said with a wink and grabbed his pipe and left.

Soon I was vested and a group of Sisters carrying lighted candles led me to the sickroom. I had to break the host into a tiny piece so that the old Sister could swallow it. The convent bell was ringing to assemble the entire community into the chapel. When I arrived back with the Blessed Sacrament, they were all kneeling, waiting for my blessing. I glanced toward the back of the chapel to the vacant chair where Mum used to kneel. I felt she was there too, receiving my first priestly blessing.

Molly and Susie joined me later that afternoon for lunch at the convent. The meal was very quiet: they were both still shocked. They had just arrived that morning and weren't prepared for this kind of homecoming. They didn't learn of Mum's death until they arrived in Southampton. Molly finally broke the silence, "Did you see Mother yet, Ken?"

"How could I have seen her? She was already dead when I arrived home," I answered a little puzzled.

"In America, the body is laid in state for the friends and relatives to view," she explained.

"I don't know if the morticians allow that in England. Besides, I prefer to remember Mum as I saw

284

her last when I left after my summer vacation. She was standing by her flowers smiling and waving good-bye. I'll go to the mortician's with you if you like, but I don't want to see her."

Susie was quite shaken as we left the mortuary; she was distressed because they had done no cosmetic work. I had intended not to see her, but when I arrived there, I changed my mind. I thought she was beautiful in her natural state. She lay there with a soft smile on her face and her hands clutching her rosary.

On the evening of the 18th, Father Walshe permitted me to receive the body into Christ the King Church in a closed casket. Here, Mum would lie in state before the High Altar where friends and relatives could visit throughout the night to pray. The following morning, on the feast of St. Joseph, patron of a happy death, the church was packed for the funeral. Father Walshe was the celebrant and I was the deacon: Father Anthony Carroll served as the sub-deacon. The sanctuary was packed with clergy and there were three choirs. Brother Gregory led the Brothers' choir from St. Mary's. The Sisters' choir and the parish choir also sang. It was quite a tribute. I led the coffin out of the church and down the steps to the hearse, behind me were all Mum's priests, brothers, and nuns. I was sad, but I felt proud. It seemed that everybody was acknowledging her life as I looked at the crowded sidewalks. "The seed has been sown, Mum, now help me bear fruit!"

I returned to Rome immediately: my class was making the necessary week's retreat before ordination. I had already missed the first day. On the plane, I was able to think a little more clearly than when I had made that trip a few days before. Then I was too bitter to think of anything, but why God had to take her now. The shock had worn off and gradually, I was beginning to understand why this all had to be. It was like Mum said, "according to God's plans, not man's." I needed this retreat, it would give me more time to think.

The retreat master told me not to try to keep the silence during the retreat, but to speak any time I wished. He suggested I spend the time deciding on a priestly motto, but by the end of the week, I had thought of nothing. I was too distracted, and the ultra modern abstract picture on the wall didn't help. What was it meant to be?

As I entered the chapel on the last day of the retreat, I was surprised to see flowers on the altar and the white vestments. Why isn't the priest wearing purple during Lent? Suddenly, I realized it was March 25th, the feast of the Annunciation. It clicked! That abstract painting was Mary and the angel. I understood it when I read the Latin inscription: *Fiat Mihi Secundum Verbum Tuum* (Be it done unto me according to thy word). I thanked the Blessed Mother for the motto.

MARCH 26, 1966

"Are you up, Ken?" Stan asked from outside my door.

"Yes, come in, Stan," I shouted back.

Stanley came rushing in the room. "I'm so nervous, I feel like a bride," he said joking in an attempt to make me laugh.

"You aren't as pretty, though," I joked back.

Stanley looked at my new cassock. "That's beautiful material. Did you have that made at the Propaganda College?"

"Yes, I had this suit made up too," I said as I took it out of the closet.

Stan became serious. "How do you feel, Ken? You are bearing up wonderfully and we all admire you for it."

"Can I come in?" said another voice.

"Of course, come in, Carl."

Carl was so excited, but he looked a little sad as he asked, "How are you, Kenny?" They are all so kind, I thought, as I reassured them.

"I believe Father Noel brought some Mass vestments from your parish in England," said Stanley.

"Yes, Miss White, you met her when you were in Southampton, she made me a purple set for the ordination."

Paul Wilton came to the door. "Let's go. It's seven o'clock. We have to be vested and ready for the Cardinal."

We were being ordained in St. Paul's Basilica across the street from the college. "The Mass doesn't start until 8 o'clock. What is the rush?" asked Stan.

"Let's go anyway. It's so exciting watching the crowd fill the Basilica," said Carl ushering us to the door.

As we walked into the gardens in front of the Basilica, I became excited too. People were streaming into the great church and already the car park was almost full with tourist buses. We passed the statue of St. Paul and climbed the steps: we went through the porch and into the massive edifice. It was cool inside. The altar looked so far away. People were still streaming in from all the different entrances while the choir was practicing their final notes.

"Isn't it exciting?" said Carl squeezing my arm. "Do you realize, Ken, when you go out that door, you will be a priest forever?"

His words hit home, "a priest forever"—Can it be true—Am I really going to be a priest?

It took some time to walk the length of the church. We arrived at the high altar under which was the tomb of the apostle, Paul: we all knelt in silent prayer. Stan was looking very moved and Carl was bubbling. "We're joining the greatest brotherhood in the whole world, Apostles of Jesus Christ, Ken."

Paul Wilton left the line to talk to his parents. He hadn't seen them in four years. "His parents are Lutheran. Paul is a convert," said Stan as we walked into the sacristy. "How many of your family will be here, Ken?" Stan asked.

"I know Susie and Molly will be here, but I doubt if Jackie can make it. A lot of my friends from my old jobs said they were coming."

"These are your vestments here, Ken," said Ian who had laid them out for me. I put on the amice, alb and cincture. As I put the stole over my shoulder, I realized it would be the last time I would ever wear it this way. In a short while, the Cardinal Secretary of State of the Holy See will place it over both shoulders in the manner of a priest. I trembled.

"How are you, Ken? I was sorry to hear your bad news," said Father Joe Schumacher, chancellor of the Dallas diocese. He was going to assist me during the concelebration of the Mass after the ordination. We shook hands. Father Joe tried to put me at ease, "Hey relax, you're all tensed up." He made me take a seat.

Soon the sacristy was full of officials, dignitaries and newspaper reporters. Cameras were flashing. "You are celebrities," joked Father Joe. The Beda ordinations always brought out the press because the ordinands

288

always have such unusual backgrounds. Joe Lowry, the ex-vice president of Pepsi-Cola was being photographed now. The bulbs continued to flash as student after student was interviewed. Cardinal Cicognani, the ordaining prelate, as Secretary of State is accorded all the military honor of a head of state. He must be arriving—we could hear the honor guards clicking to attention.

We took our places in line, all ten of us: the remainder of our class was being ordained in their own parish churches. All the students and faculty of the Beda, vested in white surplices, took their positions in front of us: in front of them were the hundreds of visiting clergy. We each carried a lighted candle, and on our left arm, the priest's vestments. The clock struck eight: we were told to move off in procession. As we entered the Basilica, I was moved by the fanfare of trumpets that announced our arrival. The choir, in dulcet tones, raised their voices to heaven in four part harmony: it was like a great opera. The Beda choir was singing in English instead of Latin, as we had received permission from the Holy See for an English Mass, the first ever in St. Paul's.

We continued the long walk across the transept of the church to the apse, where we were to take our places in the sanctuary pews. The whole Beda College was assembled in the pews behind us. Once again, we answered to our names and took our places in front of the Cardinal. As I walked to take up my position, I glanced at the congregation to see whether Susie and Molly had arrived. Jackie and Maureen waved discreetly: they had come too! Thank you, God. Thank you for Jackie today. As we knelt in front of the Cardinal, each of us gave our candle to one of the masters of ceremony.

At last, came the big moment! We took our places

on the carpeted floor and lay flat on our stomachs. I had time to think—It will take the choir fifteen minutes, at least, to sing the litany—I felt like a drowning man as my life came back before my eyes—"No, Kenneth, your right hand, not your left!"—"Let me be a priest too, so I can give children their first communion"—"Kenny, have you been down to the track again?"—"Apologize, not because you are all wrong, but because you're a Christian"—"Here come the 'three Musketeers!' "—"Get your hair cut, Pretty Boy."—"Blessed Mother, I do worry about that boy"—"If you can drink and walk a straight line, you're a man, son!"—"Left, left, left right left"—"Come down to earth and live"—"We also have high moral standards on BOAC, Mr. Roberts"—"Yes, but do you require the vow of chastity?"—"The Holy Spirit has His hooks on you"—"I'll pray for you, son"—"Did you know that man was the head of a gold smuggling ring?"—"Son, I love you"—"You will know they are Osterley students by their love"—"What I need is to settle down and get married"—"You're meant to be a priest. I'll bet my life on it"—"Got any cigarettes?"— "I'm not worthy to have a son, a priest"—"The Blessed Mother gave her son to us so He could open heaven. Now, I must give up one of my sons so another can help people find it"—"Pray for me, son . . ."— Was this my life? It WAS, but I am lying down here to die in that life. When I stand, it will be a new me, a new life.

I knelt in front of the Cardinal. His hands are on my head. I stood.

I AM A PRIEST FOREVER!

After the ordination, we returned to the altar rail for the first priestly blessings. Jackie was kneeling be-

fore me. "May the blessing of Almighty God . . . ."
I made the sign of the cross and he kissed my newly
anointed hands. Hundreds of people came and knelt
as I blessed each one singly. No, it can't be—
Father Wilson! "I haven't seen you since the *Queen
Elizabeth*." He knelt and then his mother.

"Monsignor Carroll-Abing, how good of you to
come"—"Brother John, I am so glad to see you here.
It's been a long time since you taught me geography"—
"Father Mike Bowen, thank you so much for coming."
And so the procession of friends continued. The
strangest feeling was when my fellow students and
professors knelt before me. "Congratulations, Father."

FATHER! That's me! I am a priest!

"Father, we have something for you." I turned to
look. It was the two elderly ladies from the English
tea room. "'We thought you might like this little
gift." I opened it. It was a picture of the Annunciation. "Be it done unto me according to thy word!"

On the way back to the Beda, people were
kneeling in the street. "May I have your blessing
please, Father?" I was still numb as I climbed the
stairs to my room. The third year students had
decorated the room in my absence. For the next
hour, it was crowded with people who came to
congratulate me and seek my blessing. Soon it was
time to leave for the luncheon at the Polesi Brothers'.

"So it's Father Ken, now," said Jackie as we got
into John's car. He looked at me as if he were in a
dream too. "I can't believe it. My brother, a priest!"

The next morning we all met at the Motherhouse
of the Cenacle Nuns where I was to celebrate my first
Mass. Once again the chapel was filled with friends.
Father Noel and Father Joe helped me to vest as

Father John looked on as we waited to start the eleven o'clock Mass. The procession formed and we entered to the singing of Cardinal Newman's hymn, *Lead, Kindly Light*. I still couldn't believe it was I who was saying Mass. "In the Name of the Father, and of the . . . ," I bowed low for the prayers at the foot of the altar. Ian read the Epistle as I sat pondering what had happened and what was about to happen. Tomorrow, I say Mass at St. Peter's. I contrasted the splendor of St. Peter's with the simplicity of St. Patrick's. I thought back to that procession of children in the little tiny church. The Epistle was finished. Father John knelt at my feet with the book of Gospels and asked a blessing: he walked to the pulpit to start the reading. The day after tomorrow, I am going to say Mass at St. Mary Major's, then St. Paul's; the day after that, we are going to Assisi to say Mass at the tomb of St. Francis: then the following day, we will celebrate the Eucharist in the catacombs. John was reading the Gospel.

Father Joe Schumacher began to preach. I looked down at Jackie and Maureen: they were sitting next to Susie and Molly, they all looked happy. Maggie seems quite enthralled too. I glanced over the congregation. My theology professor, Father Mike Bowen, was sitting next to the vice-Rector, Monsignor Buxton.

At the offertory, Jackie brought up the chalice; Mum would have done it if she were still alive. I must remember to pray for her.

Now, the moment arrived! I will never forget it. I took the bread into my hands. My hands don't seem to be mine any more. Why do I feel so weak? "This is my Body!" I raised the Host. The bell was ringing and so was my head. I gazed at the Host. This is the Body of Christ! My hands seem to be detached from my body. I took the cup. "This is the cup . . . ," I lifted the cup. Now, I feel like I have never felt before—I feel as if God is lifting me. Now, I know what it is to be a priest.

It was the next afternoon and we sat waiting in the Vatican Palace. The Holy Father was about to enter for our private audience. We all stood as His Holiness entered the room. He made a short speech to apologize for keeping us waiting, but he had been giving an audience to the King and Queen of Belgium in the next room. He whispered something to an aide and then to my astonishment, he came walking towards me. "Dear Brother in Christ." He put his arms out to me. "I am sorry to hear of your dear mother's death. Christ surely must have a special task for you to give you such a cross to bear so early. I'll pray for your mother at Mass, tomorrow." The Pope is going to pray for Mother! God's way is certainly greater than mine. On the wall of the audience room, was a tapestry of the Annunciation. "Be it done unto me according to thy word," was the inscription.

The following morning at St. Mary Major's, the fourth century Basilica dedicated to the Blessed Mother, I said Mass again. I took the cup—THIS IS THE CUP OF MY BLOOD—I lifted it and said the words, "Do this in memory of me!" Above my head was a mosaic of Christ crowning His mother. I looked at the Chalice in adoration. My eyes caught the engraving—Why hadn't I noticed it before?—The engraver forgot to punctuate!—Now, I was petitioning her!—PRAY FOR ME MOTHER.

EPILOGUE TO THE PAPERBACK EDITION

The reader will no doubt be wondering what has happened to me since my ordination and if I have found fulfillment in my vocation as a priest. I assure you, I have.

After a week's festivities and celebrating in Rome, I returned to Southampton for my first Solemn High Mass in my parish church. Father Walshe, the pastor of Christ the King, preached the sermon in which he paid tribute to my late mother. He also drew attention to the Scripture quotations I had chosen for my holy cards, "Whose sins you shall forgive . . ." He noted that it was in the Gospel reading for that Sunday, a coincidence he hoped was propitious.

I spent the next two weeks celebrating Masses at churches around England for my many friends, including at Arundel Cathedral and Warwick Hall. But the most emotional experiences were returning to St. Patrick's to celebrate Mass for the children of the parochial school, and St. Mary's College where Brother Gregory addressed me now as "Father September Fourteenth!"

I returned to Rome for the completion of my studies, and during this period I worked with Father John as a chaplain to Boy's Town. After graduation from the Beda College, I returned to England that summer for a brief visit and farewell to Southampton and England.

I arrived in Texas on the vigil of the Assumption, August 14, 1966, and immediately took up duties as

Catholic Chaplain to the Texas Christian University and Assistant Pastor of St. Andrew's in Fort Worth, where I profitted greatly under the guidance of the pastor, Rev. Msgr. C. MacTamney. While at T.C.U., I was very much involved in ecumenism. There I was elected chairman of the Campus Ministers. I learned a great deal from my association with these wonderful Christian men and I was proud to be the first Catholic priest ever to serve on the board of the Religious Activities Committee for that university. I wish to take this opportunity to thank Dr. Floyd Leggett and the Reverend James Farrar for the wonderful cooperation and inspiration I received during my year with them.

In the fall of 1967, I was transferred to serve in Garland as Assistant Pastor of Good Shepherd Catholic Church. During my year there, I became more deeply involved in ecumenical and youth work. I was elected chairman of this ecumenical group. As chairman of the Garland Ministerial Alliance, I preached frequently in the many Protestant churches of Garland. I wish to thank all the many good and holy Christian men and women I met in this work. Two outstanding men I was proud to know as friends at this time were a Presbyterian, Reverend Ed Gerhardt, and a Baptist, Reverend Clyde Herring.

In the summer of 1968, I came to work in St. Louis, Missouri, where I am at the time of this writing. In my first year in this wonderful city, I served as a relief priest at St. Ann's in Normandy, Presentation in Overland; and St. Norbert's in Florissant. I wish to thank all the clergy and hundreds of people with whom I worked during this period.

For almost three years, I was Assistant Pastor at Transfiguration Parish in Florissant, where I was also moderator of the youth activities and taught in the parochial school. In this parish, I grew in maturity under the patient guidance of the pastor, Father Clarence Good. It was during my stay at Transfiguration that I wrote *Playboy to Priest*.

Once again my life was to take a major change in direction. On Aug. 15, 1971 (the Assumption), I was to offer my first Mass as Chaplain to Marygrove School for girls, a school run by the Sisters of the Good Shepherd. These Sisters wore the identical habit of Mother's Sisters at Redcote in England and both orders shared their origins with St. John Eudes. The reader will remember St. Theresa's hostel when I was a boy and the work there with problem girls . . . a coincidence? I have been their chaplain for the past three years. At the same time, I became a Retreat Master for the Cenacle Sisters in St. Louis, but within months, this became a national apostolate as I began to travel from city to city on the Cenacle circuit. Through these good Sisters and their retreat houses, I have made hundreds of friends in Christ—in St. Louis, Chicago, New Orleans, Milwaukee, Minneapolis, and Memphis. Was it a coincidence that I said my first Mass at their Motherhouse in Rome? I like to think that maybe God planned it that way.

My life in the priesthood has been most rewarding . . . and even more exciting than I had ever dreamed. My apostolate has taken on new dimensions through the writing of this book and a second book, *The Rest of The Week*. I have been privileged to appear on radio and TV in almost every major city in the country to testify that men are still finding fulfillment in working for Christ and His Church, in some way to counteract the unhappy image that a few ex-clerics have projected.

I owe gratitude to so many who have helped me in my apostolate. To the Bishop of Dallas, Bishop Thomas Tschoepe, who has kindly allowed me time off to write this book and to work in the Archdiocese of St. Louis, and John Joseph Cardinal Carberry, Archbishop of St. Louis, for allowing me to work in his Archdiocese. To the Sisters of the Good Shepherd, too numerous to mention by name (although, I must mention Sister Mary Columba because she is very special . . . and from Ireland!), and all the Sisters of the Cross who pray so hard for me in their cloistered chapels as I give retreats. To the Cenacle Sisters, especially Sister Roberts, who is now United States Provincial. She was at my ordination and first Mass in Rome. To the many Bishops and hundreds of Priests, Sisters and lay people who have in any way helped me in my work for the Lord . . . thank you.

Last, but not least, I wish to thank God for the most wonderful friends I have ever had, Jim and Ann Dickens, a couple who has become a brother and sister to me, and their five children, Jimmy, Johnny, Timmy, Terri, and Carrie. Without their help and encouragement, I doubt whether this book would have ever been written.

I hope the reader will see the priesthood in a new light after reading this book. I hope that the young may be inspired to find love and peace in the same Christ that died for all men. I would like to think this book will encourage all who read it—priest or layman, Catholic or non-Catholic, believer or nonbeliever, liberal, moderate, or conservative—to think about the purpose of life. I would like to believe it will aid them in their search for true happiness; to learn the brotherhood of man, to realize that we are all sinners, but that Christ can bring them peace if they finally accept His words of peace, "He breathed on His apostles and said, receive ye the Holy Spirit, whose sins you shall forgive, they are forgiven. . . ."

April, 1974